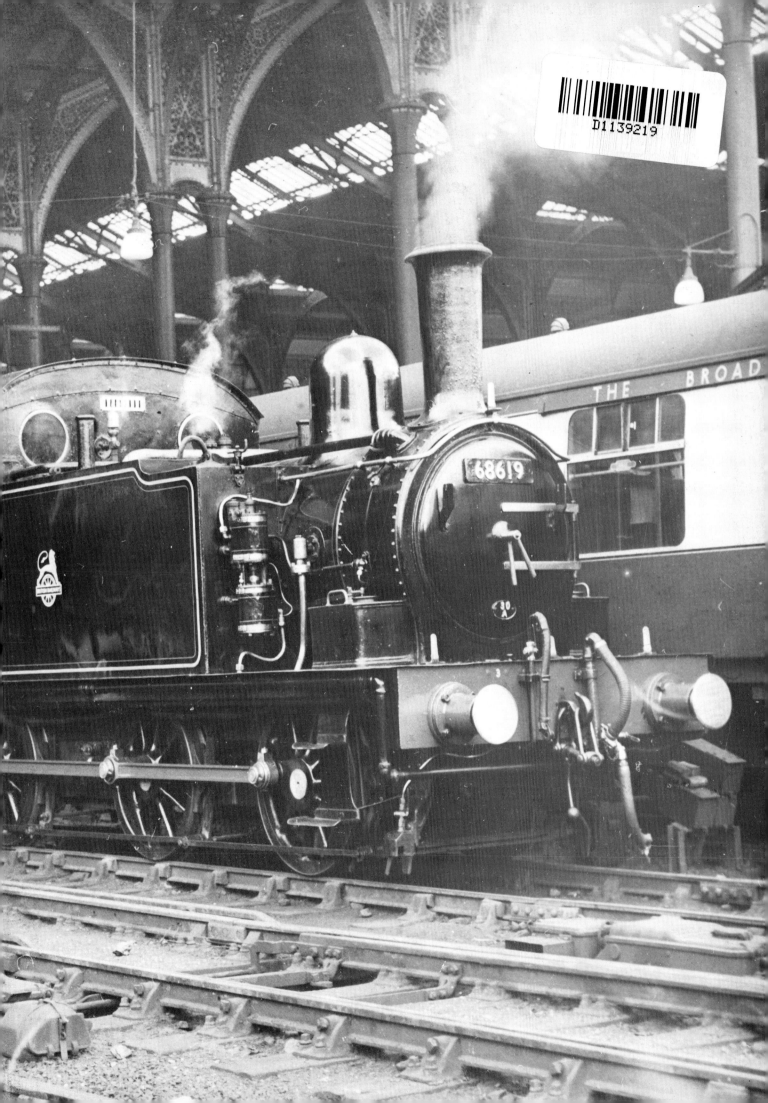

Design for Steam
1830-1960

Front endpaper: The station pilots at
Liverpool Street in May 1957, resplendent in
BR lined black livery and displaying a rare
degree of cleanliness; reminiscent of
pre-Grouping days.

Rear endpaper: Nine Elms shed in the final
years of steam.

Half-title page: A bridge in the Blisworth
embankment, L&BR, with a Bury engine and
passenger train.

Title page: Fowler 'Patriot' class 4-6-0
No 45501 *St Dunstan* storms past Handforth
Sidings, Cheshire, with a Manchester-Cardiff/
Plymouth train in March 1953.

Design for Steam

1830~1960

Brian Haresnape

LONDON
IAN ALLAN LTD

For Claire and Paul Haresnape

First published 1968
This edition 1981

ISBN 0 7110 1081 1

Published by Ian Allan Ltd, Shepperton, Surrey;
and printed by Ian Allan Printing Ltd at their works
at Coombelands in Runnymede, England

This page: Bulleid lightweight 'West Country'
class Pacific No 21C101 *Exeter* heads the
Pullman 'Devon Belle' train in 1947.

Contents

THE
DEVON BELLE

Preface

The main narrative of this book was first published in two volumes entitled *Railway Design Since 1830* some 12 years ago. Such have been the dramatic changes in the railway scene since then, that I have recently written a comprehensive sequel entitled *British Rail 1948-78, A Journey by Design*. This included, as an introductory scene-setting, a précis of the preceding 120 years, based upon the earlier two volumes. It then became clear that a more substantial treatment of this earlier period would form a useful companion work, and as a result I have produced this present book, *Design for Steam*, which is an amended and combined version of the original chapters covering the period. Many new illustrations have been added, but the basic text remains the same. The later chapters in the original book have been deliberately omitted, as they were concerned with events after the decision to abandon steam on British Railways.

The British steam railway might well be described as our greatest gift to the world. It changed the whole face of nations and made immeasurable change in social conditions. The steam locomotive, which made the whole thing possible, has now been replaced by the diesel and the electric, although we are fortunate that a large number have been preserved in full working order. In the period covered in this volume the steam locomotive was developed from a crude invention of uncertain future to a magnificent and highly sophisticated machine, and then in due course to one which had the emphasis placed upon utilitarian functionalism, set against a background of declining standards of maintenance. Steam has gone, but the railway it created is still very alive and well.

This is a book about the more abstract qualities, of aesthetics and amenity; about design in the *artistic* sense of the term rather than the technical. It is not intended to be a history in the true sense, although for convenience sake it follows a reasonable chronological order. There are countless books already on technical and historical development of our railways

Above: **Contrast in chimney styles. Stirling's Single and Gresley's A4 Pacific.**

(enough to fill a small library, in fact). Authors more able than I, have delved deeply into the mechanical operation, into the day-to-day performance, and into the management of the railways of Britain. In passing some have dwelt upon the subject of the appearance of the locomotives, trains and stations. None, to my knowledge, has gone very deeply into the subject (with the notable exception of C. Hamilton Ellis).

This then is a book about the *visual* aspect of railways — or rather I should say, *appeal* of railways. Whether we realise it or not, it is the outward appearance of trains and stations which go to create the individual character. What made the GWR so different from the LBSCR? — Practically every visible item, which was 'stamped' with the character of the company. As we shall see, this was to a large extent due to the influence of the superb engineers, who paid close attention to the appearance of everything they were associated with.

Locomotives alone do not make the character of a railway, although they are undeniably the 'figurehead', so to speak. The carriages, stations, liveries, uniforms, signs and notices all contribute towards the general scene.

In dealing with this subject I have deliberately omitted some aspects of our railways. No mention will be found of track or signal design, or of associated railway enterprises such as steamships. I have not discussed goods wagon design (such as it was!), but rather have I deliberately concentrated upon the passenger side of railways. It is this aspect that we all experience, and because it is bound up so much with our environment as human beings it is of the greatest importance in our assessment of the character of railways.

By the last years of Queen Victoria's long reign, the British railway companies had established themselves as a virtually monopolistic land transport concern, and they had achieved tremendous progress in the design of locomotives and carriages. What I hope will become apparent to the reader, is that these trains were works of art of a very high order indeed. The locomotives of men like Stroudley,

Johnson, Robinson, Wainwright, Dean, and many others, were probably the finest examples of industrial design produced during their period *anywhere in the world*.

Without doubt the later years of Victorian and Edwardian rule should be described as the proud years for the railways, when they ruled supreme in the realm of domestic transportation. Their locomotives, rolling stock and architecture had achieved notable elegance, although it must be admitted that on occasion their standards of amenity fell short of those which we would now consider essential. A magnificent sense of pride was reflected in the immaculate standards of maintenance and cleanliness bestowed upon their steam locomotives, to which one can find no parallel in today's utilitarian modes of transport. Even the consciously glossy shell of the latest automobile cannot inspire the beholder with the same sense of awe that the noble, animated steam engine commanded from laymen and enthusiast alike. Nor can the sophisticated jet age efficiency of a great international airport compare with the sense of excitement which the arrival of a steam train could arouse at a station.

Two world wars impeded railway design and development during the present century, but the period 1920-1939

Below: Victorian elegance and wartime austerity, an unusual contrast in locomotive designs, taken at Brighton in 1947, with Stroudley 'Terrier' No 82 *Boxhill* (restored to original condition) and Riddles' 'Austerity' 2-8-0 No 77181 just out of the works after repair.

witnessed the classic big engines of such engineers as C. B. Collett, R. E. L. Maunsell, Sir Nigel Gresley and Sir William Stanier, and after World War II, there were some impressive designs by O. V. S. Bulleid, H. G. Ivatt, R. A. Riddles, etc — albeit of a more functional nature except in Bulleid's case.

The story of the development of railway carriage design is taken as far as the earlier standard BR Mark 1 type, and it is perhaps worthwhile recalling that many of these are still in everyday service on British Rail. Some readers will be surprised to find no interiors of Royal carriages discussed or illustrated. Again, the omission is deliberate. These magnificent carriages have been so widely illustrated and described that further repetition seems unnecessary. Some wonderful examples have been preserved and anyone can inspect these at will at the National Railway Museum, York. I have preferred to concentrate upon the day-to-day passenger carriage for my examples of design. Nevertheless it is essential to recognise the fact that the 'Royals' were invariably the most superb examples of coachbuilding, and ahead of their times in terms of amenities.

Because this book is concerned with Britain's railways in the age of steam it cannot show the recent achievements of BR in cleaning and restoring many old stations, and in building excellent new ones. Thus the latter part of the book reflects the dismal state of affairs which existed some 30 years ago. Similarly, the posters and printed ephemera, the liveries

and lettering that have now transformed British Rail's image cannot be included. These have been well illustrated in *British Rail 1948-78, A Journey by Design*.

It must be emphasised that if the later chapters of the narrative would seem to show a decline in railway design in the latter years of steam, this is surely true and largely the result of events beyond the control of those involved. Changing social habits, the growth of motoring and many other factors led to the decline and fall of steam. Many people still maintain that this was not inevitable. I would prefer to reserve judgement; with hindsight! Who knows what the next 30 years might bring?

Many of the illustrations included in the early part of the volume are taken from originals dating back over the last 130 years. Without the masterly draughtsmanship of the topographical artist J. C. Bourne, our record of the early days of the L&BR and the GWR would be far less complete. Later, the development of reliable portable cameras allowed photographic records of the railway scene to be made. Railway photography has never been an easy proposition; in Victorian days it must have been formidable, with cumbersome equipment and fragile glass negatives. Despite this some superb photographs were obtained, and to all those intrepid enthusiasts of the Victorian era, my sincere thanks for making this volume possible.

Brian Haresnape FRSA NDD
Dorking, Surrey

January 1980.

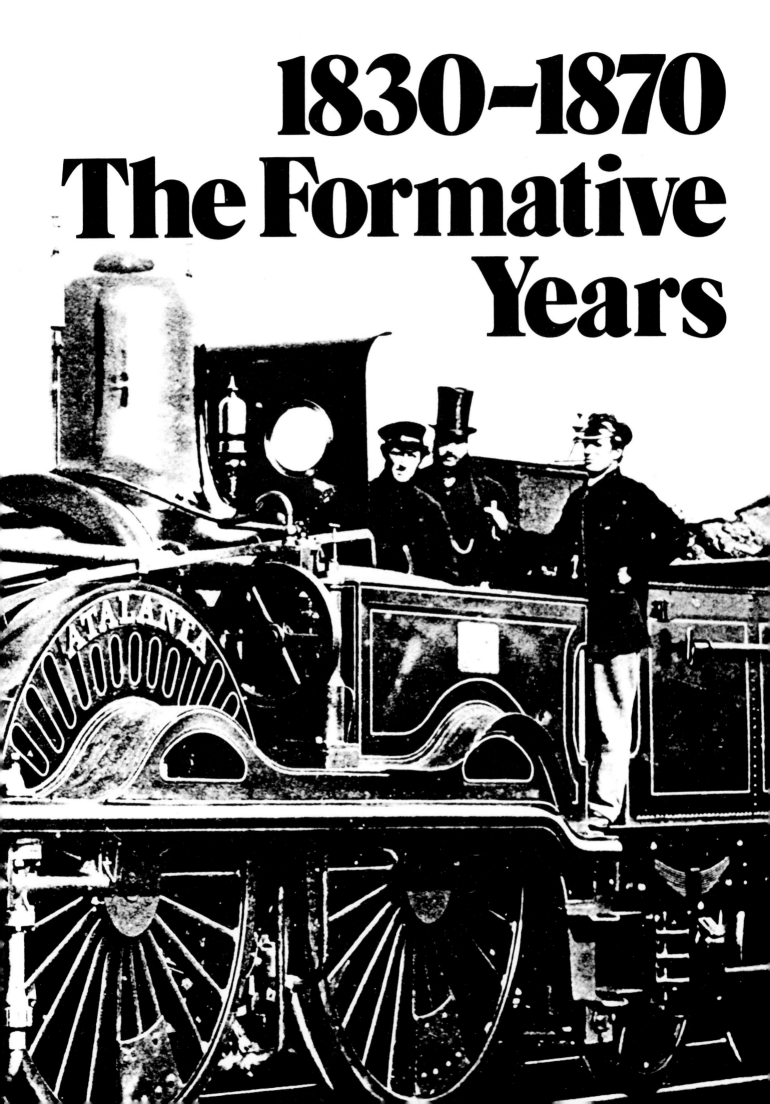

1830-1870
The Formative Years

1 Steam Locomotion Takes Shape

Once introduced the employment of steam power as a practical alternative to the horse for transporting people and goods, remained to be proven. If the various early solutions looked crude it was because that was quite honestly what they were. A great deal of improvisation was to be expected, for both raw materials and machinery were scarcely of the finest quality, and they all too often dictated the limits of inventiveness. As an inevitable result, the earliest locomotives suffered from many failures and shortcomings, with consequent effects upon their reputation. Thus it is hardly surprising to learn that for some considerable time people's faith in the future of steam locomotion was at a very low ebb indeed.

In his scholarly *Centennial History of the Liverpool and Manchester Railway* Dendy Marshall lists only 18 locomotives doing useful work in England in 1825, out of a total of 30 built at various times, and he points out the significant fact that no one except George Stephenson had continued to build steam locomotives after 1814. A contributory factor to the poor reputation the steam locomotive had gained was the inadequate track, which was far too weak to carry the locomotive's weight and constantly broke under the strain. Fortunately there were others who shared Stephenson's faith in the future of steam railways, but for some time the opposition was sufficiently strong for the whole issue to be very much in the balance. One alternative proposition, with some powerful supporters, envisaged cable haulage driven by stationary winding engines. This system was proposed at one stage in the planning of the L&MR, but in the event George Stephenson and his supporters won the day. However, cable haulage was used on the steeply inclined sections (with stationary steam engines supplied by Robert Stephenson), as the ability of the existing types of steam locomotives to haul trains up quite severe gradients was still to be proven.

To the public eye the early locomotives must have looked both ridiculously clumsy and terrifyingly strong. They were likened to horses — but then how else could they

be judged? The horse, well trusted and well used (and abused) was an integral part of the everyday environment, in much the same way that the soulless motor car has become part of ours today. So when the new-fangled steam locomotive made an appearance, before eyes as yet unaccustomed to mechanical invention, and began to perform duties previously entrusted to the horse, the inevitable comparison was drawn. It possessed a crude but strangely lifelike personality. It breathed steam and sighed deeply, or panted. It devoured water and coals with voracious appetite. Soon the inevitable title 'iron horse' was bestowed upon the brute creation, but only a few visionaries looked to the day when it would replace the horse as the fastest means of travel available to man on earth.

It is interesting to learn that, by 1828, Robert Stephenson was feeling concern over the *appearance* of his locomotives. In a letter to Michael Longridge, one of his partners in the firm, dated 1 January 1828, he stated that he had spoken to his father about 'endeavouring to reduce the size and ugliness of our travelling engines'. This he proposed to do by placing the cylinders either on the sides of the boiler or else below it entirely. Timothy Hackworth had in all probability inspired this by the improvements he had demonstrated in his *Royal George* for the S&DR, which had proved to be a considerable advance over the two original Stephenson engines built for the line. Robert Stephenson commenced his endeavours with the *Lancashire Witch* of 1829; placing the cylinders in an inclined position on the side of the boiler at the rear end, but as yet there were little or no signs of any other improvements in appearance.

Considerably more refined, in proportion and detailing, was the *Rocket* of 1829, a locomotive destined to achieve unparalleled fame. The *Rocket* displayed many signs of Stephenson's efforts to improve the appearance of his designs. The standard of workmanship was certainly higher than previously achieved. The colour scheme of bright yellow and black, with a white chimney and polished

brass mountings, was Stephenson's own choice. The tender, although very primitive to our eyes, was much better than had existed until then. A well-known coachbuilder, Nathaniel Worsdell, was employed on this. The use of a barrel was very much a functional means of carrying the water in a tender constructed mainly of wood.

The story of the Rainhill Trials has been repeated often and well, and does not require further repetition. It will suffice to say that it established renewed public interest in the L&MR 'iron horse', and demonstrated the suitability beyond question of steam locomotion for the new L&MR. More important still, to our story, it began to show that railways had a certain appeal, as yet latent, of their own. By emerging the winner of the trials Stephenson's *Rocket* helped to set the seal for the future lines of steam locomotive design development in this country. The simple, but rugged and reliable Stephenson conception was to remain the hallmark of British steam locomotives throughout the ensuing century or more.

The *Rocket*, as built, had no smokebox, an external firebox, and steeply inclined cylinders. It was soon rebuilt with a more dignified chimney mounted upon a proper smokebox. In place of the original tender, a new design with flared raves, minus the barrel was attached. The final form had the cylinders lowered to a nearly horizontal position to improve the steadiness of the locomotive when running at speed.

After only a few improved 'Rocket' (or Northumbrian) type locomotives had been constructed, Robert Stephenson introduced his 'Planet' type, in which (as foreshadowed in his letter to Longridge, already mentioned) he placed the cylinders *inside* and at the front end, and he developed the sandwich frame, of wood between two iron plates — an arrangement which was to be used for more than 50 years, on countless hundreds of locomotives.

Public enthusiasm for the L&MR exceeded expectations to a degree which caused some astonishment to the directors, who had envisaged the line as chiefly transporting merchandise. One wonders to what degree the elegant little steam engines of Robert Stephenson had helped to convert popular opinion. Certainly by the time he introduced his 'Planet' in 1830, he had transformed the 'iron horse' from a clumsy foot-sore carthorse, to a flighty little thoroughbred which displayed a nice turn of speed. The personality bestowed to each by the choice of names, such as *Rocket, Planet, Arrow, Meteor, Dart, Phoenix, Majestic, Mercury, Samson, Goliath* and *Venus,* leaves us in little doubt of the spirit of the times.

Somewhat naturally, the encouraging results of steam locomotives on the L&MR turned other people's minds towards the lucrative possibilities of locomotive building. Some weird and wonderful creations were offered to the directors for trials against Stephenson's engines, but the latter remained supreme in their time and fitness for purpose and general performance. Two other engineers, Hackworth and Bury, were producing locomotives of a more or less successful nature, but in Hackworth's case they continued to feature what was, by then, a very old-fashioned appearance with cylinders steeply inclined, or vertical. In his 0-4-0 engine *Liverpool* of 1830, Edward Bury produced a compact and neat little design with inside cylinders, bar frames, and a 'haystack' firebox (a design which was to be associated with his name for the next quarter of a century). His *Liverpool* was attractive to the eye, and had a most ornate chimney top featuring a design motif of 'liver' birds.

Robert Stephenson & Co steadily developed the inside cylinder single driver locomotive, and in their 'Patentee' of 1834, we see the precursor of the characteristic British 2-2-2 express passenger locomotive, with sandwich frames. The 'Patentee' was basically a lengthened 'Planet' with a rear pair of carrying wheels added in an attempt to improve the far from satisfactory riding qualities that were a feature of existing engines. Judged from the aesthetic viewpoint the 'Patentee' was a remarkable advance upon the *Rocket*, in the short space of five years, and displayed in embryonic form the hallmarks of classic Victorian steam locomotive design. Engine and tender seem to 'belong' and the general sense of balance in the proportions was spoilt only by the rather clumsy chimney, which gave a heavy appearance to the leading end. The driver and fireman were completely exposed to the elements, but at last they had a sensible platform (or footplate) to stand upon, protected at the sides by railings.

Although many strange inventions were still to be vied against the Stephenson conception from time to time, other locomotive builders were quietly beginning to follow his example. As in all trades, men exchanged jobs in search of promotion and better living conditions, and inevitably they took with them a good deal of 'know how' from previous firms; in such a manner invention is cross-fertilised. Locomotive development proceeded apace, matched by a virtual bonanza of railway building and speculation, and the machinery and manufacturing techniques were also improving steadily. A steady flow of orders for new locomotives encouraged both engineers and builders to yet further improvements in design.

One man who pursued a lone course in locomotive design, persistently remaining faithful to his own ideals, was Edward Bury. He continued to introduce locomotives of his small bar-framed design for service on the L&BR until 1846, by which time they were hopelessly outclassed and undersized, causing considerable embarrassment to their users.

By the mid-1830s attention had begun to shift from the industrial north of England where railways were flourishing, to the west, where Brunel's GWR was to be constructed to a 7ft broad gauge. Stephenson had, until now, settled upon a gauge of 4ft 8½in as suitable for railways, although there were isolated examples which did not conform to this. But 7ft was really courageous and, it seems, quite typical of Brunel's vision. Many historians have lamented the 'battle of the gauges' which followed in due course, the outcome of which remains with us in the restricted loading gauge of our present railway system. Had Brunel's ideas won the day, what a different course railway history might have followed. But in 1838 no one could foresee the trouble Brunel's conception would cause him in the way of opposition, and perhaps this was of scant concern to him, even as a possibility.

For the opening, in 1838, Brunel ordered 20 locomotives, from various manufacturers. Regrettably they proved, when delivered, to be (to quote Ahrons) 'the most extraordinary collection of freaks'. Only two, built by Stephenson, and originally intended for an American 5ft 6in gauge railway, and then converted to the 7ft gauge, proved successful. These were the *North Star* and *Morning Star*, and followed Stephenson's typical layout, with sandwich frames and inside cylinders; being of course somewhat larger than most of his designs.

At the time of ordering the 20 locomotives Brunel specified that they should be not only big and fast, but as handsome as could be made — because, as he put it, 'a plain young lady, however amiable, is apt to be neglected'. Evidently Stephenson's attempts to produce good-looking locomotives were enthusiastically received by Brunel, for when awaiting delivery of the two locomotives, he wrote to Stephenson stating 'I look forward to having such an engine as never before'. When he actually received *North Star* he became so excited by it that he wrote to a friend 'We have a splendid engine of Stephenson's, it would have been a beautiful ornament in the most elegant drawing room'.

We might pause here, on this enthusiastic note, and briefly consider the stylistic trends of the British steam locomotive, as they were evolving in the years 1838-1840. The typical passenger engine was of Stephenson inspiration, with inside cylinders, sandwich frames and neat clean lines. Boilers generally had a clothing of wooden (mahogany) lagging strips, which were tenoned and grooved; finished by staining and varnishing, or perhaps paint and varnish. As a rule, boiler bands of polished brass, or painted metal were bound around the wooden clothing. The exterior of the firebox had been left bare until now, with rivet heads showing, but it was becoming the practice to lag these with wood, at least partially. The actual shape of the firebox ranged from the slightly raised round-topped variety, to the distinctive 'haystacks' of Edward Bury which were D-shaped and made first in iron and later copper, and to the equally distinctive 'Gothic' firebox, so called because it had a somewhat pointed pyramidal shape to the top of the casing. Chimney design had changed considerably over the 10 years since *Rocket* had sported its spike-topped affair and Bury's *Liverpool* had had 'liver' birds grouped around the rim. The typical chimney was now a cylindrical iron casing of considerable height, with parallel sides built-up in two or three sections. The top was flared like a bellmouth, often of polished metal. Boiler mountings were beginning to display a certain elegance of their own, with polished brass or copper finish. No protection was given to the enginemen apart from handrails each side, and no doubt they welcomed the high 'haystack' or 'Gothic' fireboxes for the added shelter they afforded!

By now, other builders were establishing their own typical style just as Stephenson had done, and the next 10 years were to see considerable invention in applied ornament for locomotives, with the products of different makers being readily identifiable by their boiler mountings and other details.

As already mentioned, apart from *North Star* and her sister engine, the remaining 18 locomotives ordered by Brunel for the

GWR did not come up to expectations. Faced with the problem of building a stud of reliable new engines to operate the line, Daniel Gooch, the young man appointed in charge of the Locomotive Department (in his early 20s), took Stephenson's design as the basis for his own 'Firefly' class 2-2-2s, of which 62 were built to a standard specification by various firms between 1840-42. At the time these were without equal in terms of power and speed. No doubt his knowledge of the disastrous experience of the initial batch of 20 locomotives that Brunel had ordered helped Gooch to establish a case for standardisation, and he issued full specifications and templates to each builder to ensure this!

By one of those curious twists of fate, Robert Stephenson, having established the successful basis of the 19th century steam locomotive, then proceeded to lose sight of it for a while by trying to establish the 'long boiler' design. He was anxious to obtain a lower centre of gravity, and also to increase boiler efficiency. He set out to do this by designing a long, low boiler. But the turntables in current use restricted him to a short wheelbase, with the result that the wheels were all crammed into the space between the back of the smokebox and the front of the firebox, with a considerable overhang each end. Except for freight duties, they were not a great success, proving unsteady at speed. Nevertheless large numbers of 'long boiler' engines were produced up to 1847. Particularly on the Continent where they proved more successful.

Another attempt to lower the centre of gravity was made by T. R. Crampton, who conceived the idea of putting the single driving wheels right behind the boiler and firebox. This meant that only small diameter carrying wheels need be placed below the boiler, which could therefore be pitched lower than was possible when allowance had to be made for the driving axle. Crampton's engines had a very mixed reception in this country, with more than their share of troubles, but the basic idea was a brilliant one, and, like Stephenson's 'long boilers', they were far more successful on the Continent for some obscure reason. Anyhow a 'Crampton' was a most distinguished locomotive to gaze upon, with the huge driving wheel set right back and with the enginemen placed on a footplate within two commodious splashers. Particularly noteworthy was the use of external valve gear to the driving wheel at a time when most designers were following Stephenson's example and hiding this discreetly from view. Perhaps the 'Cramptons' were too foreign to the English eye to be readily accepted; certainly they possessed a totally different aesthetic quality from that of most of their contemporaries.

Whilst Stephenson and Crampton had been involved in the experiments just described, other locomotive builders were steadily producing their own progressively improved variants of Stephenson's 'Patentee'. Notable were the 'Sharpies' of Sharp, Roberts & Company, built as their standard railway engine for many different companies, and perhaps most famous of all, the 'Jenny Lind' design by David Joy for E. B. Wilson. This has traditionally been held up as the finest example of the designs of the period, in aesthetic terms, and study of the drawing tends to confirm this widely held opinion. There is an undeniable grace about the whole design, whilst the handling of the details is nowhere clumsy. The fluted dome and safety valve columns lend a distinctly classical air to these dominant features, whilst the chimney has more slender and dainty proportions than hitherto. The inside bearings used for the driving axle, together with the slotted treatment of the splasher give the big wheel an elegant appearance. Points of interest are the square bases to both dome and safety valve and the metal sidesheets enclosing the handrails on the footplate sides, extending round to meet the side of the firebox.

The use of distinctive detail design, for example the fluted treatment of dome and safety valve, with hemispherical cover to the dome, mounted upon a square base (shown on 'Jenny Lind'), became (as remarked earlier) a form of trademark adopted by builders to distinguish their products. Some chose very simple but shapely treatments, others went in for elaborate and imposing affairs, more suited to architecture than engineering. Perhaps the choicest of all was that adopted by R. & W. Hawthorn. This was of plain flared iron, but beautifully matched for chimney, dome and safety valve casings. The drawing of *Plews* (photo 11) shows how well this scheme fitted the overall appearance.

This contemporary marriage of aesthetics and engineering was partly instinctive but, as we have seen, partly deliberate. A developing sense of fitness for purpose is evident in such lovely designs as the 'Jenny Lind'; just as the most beautiful sailing ships evolved from crude beginnings, so the steam locomotive progressed — but in a very short time indeed. No longer did crudity of manufacture make itself apparent in the finished product, and the outward aspect was one of great attention to detail. This is one of the most fascinating aspects of locomotive design during the period 1830-1851; namely that it stood almost alone as an example of true machine produced design, developing naturally out of constant search for improvement and refinement, and assuming shape through this process.

One final locomotive type produced prior to 1851 which remains to be mentioned, is Alexander Allan's 'Crewe Type'. This was clearly distinguished by having outside cylinders, slightly inclined, supported on double frames with a flowing curve linking the smokebox wrapper and cylinders, and continuing under the cylinders to meet the outside frame. The leading and trailing wheels were supported on outside bearings and the driving wheel on inside bearings. The side rods were between the frames which had a slot cut into them to permit access to the crosshead, slidebars and piston assembly. Alexander Allan had worked for George Forrester at the Vauxhall Foundry, and he developed his design from some early locomotives built there for the L&MR, Dublin & Kingstown and London & Greenwich Railways. He in due course made it the 'hallmark' of locomotives produced at Crewe Works, the first of these being *Columbine* built in February, 1845. Prior to this some engines of his type had been built in France under licence from him. Numerous versions of the basic 'Crewe Type' were destined to appear, and it was still being developed on certain railways 30 years later as we shall see later.

The 'Crewe Type' were characterised by very neat little boiler mountings, in particular the single Salter valves, and in general they followed Stephenson's conception of simple straightforward finish, whilst possessing a distinctive character all their own.

Thus by the year 1851, just over 20 years since the opening of the L&MR, the steam locomotive had been transformed from an unknown quantity, gamely trying to prove its worth, to an accepted and honoured new influence upon everyday life in Britain. In the aesthetic sense it was rapidly becoming a classic of engineering skill and artistry combined, although the superb heights of 20 years hence nowadays tend to cloud our appreciation of this fact.

1   Steam locomotion had taken crude shape by 1813. This end view of William Hedley's *Puffing Billy* clearly shows the rough manufacture of early locomotives.

2   A broadside view of *Puffing Billy* built in 1813 for Wylam Colliery. Seen here in a later, somewhat modified, condition, as running in circa 1860.

3   S&DR No 9 *Middlesbro*, a Timothy Hackworth type locomotive. Note the steeply inclined cylinders and makeshift design of tender.

1

2

3

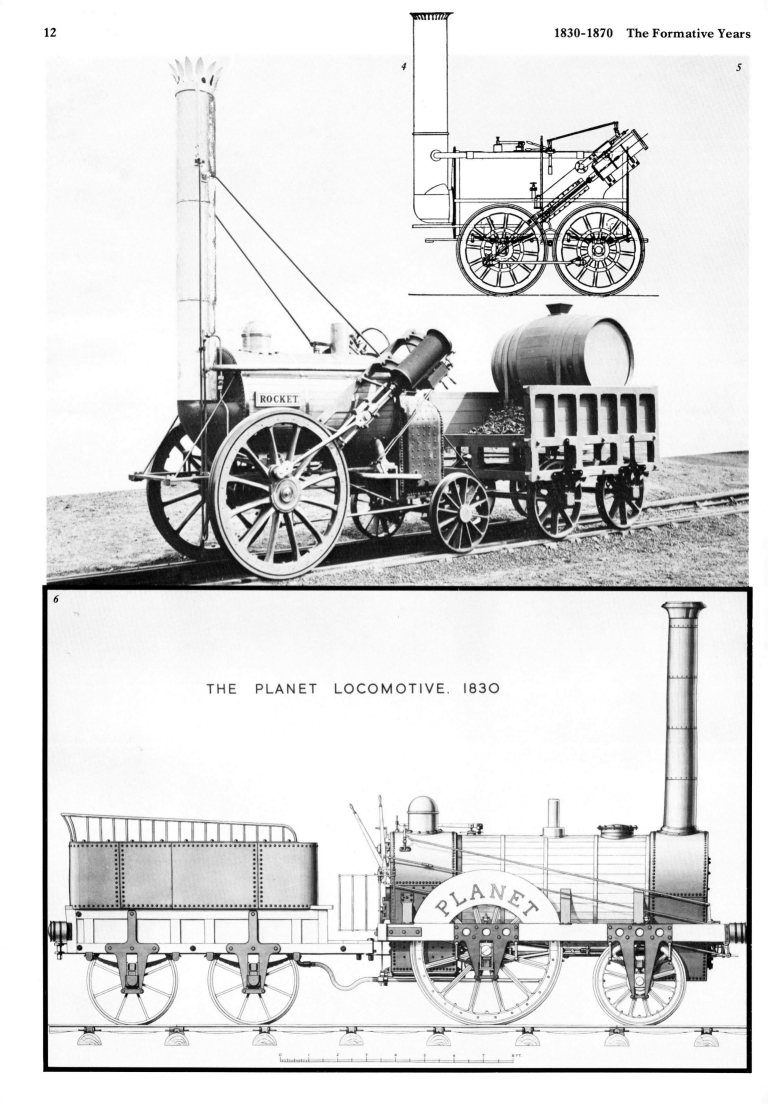

THE PLANET LOCOMOTIVE, 1830

4 Lancashire Witch. Stephenson's first attempt to 'reduce the ugliness of our travelling engines', showed some Hackworth influence.

5 Stephenson's celebrated *Rocket* was a considerable advance in terms of detail design and finish. Illustrated is the replica made for Henry Ford showing the original 1829 condition.

6 Stephenson's 'Planet' class of 1830 for the L&MR. The cylinders were placed between the sandwich frames. The overall design had a neat simplicity which was to become characteristic of Stephenson's engines.

7 The elegant little *Novelty* was destined to remain exactly what its name implied. Nevertheless it was a favourite amongst the spectators at the Rainhill Trials.

8 A typical Edward Bury locomotive of the L&BR, with 'haystack' firebox, inside cylinders and bar frames. No 32, a 2-2-0, is shown leaving the Camden Town engine house in this detail from a lithograph by J. C. Bourne.

9 Stephenson's inside cylinder 2-2-2 standard passenger engine of 1838, a later example of the 'Patentee' of 1834.

10

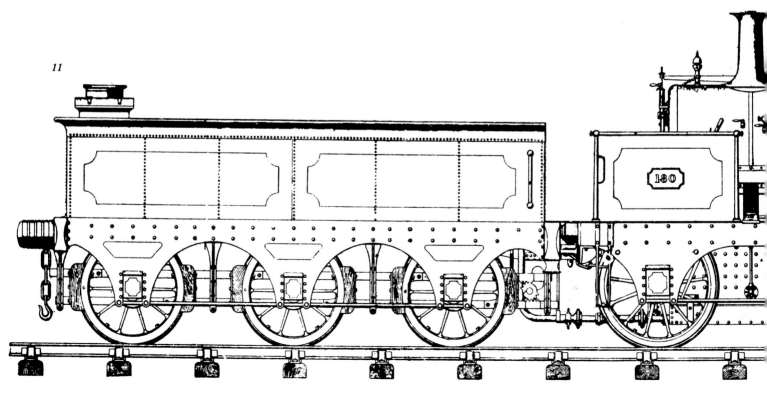

11

Steam Locomotion Takes Shape

12

13

14

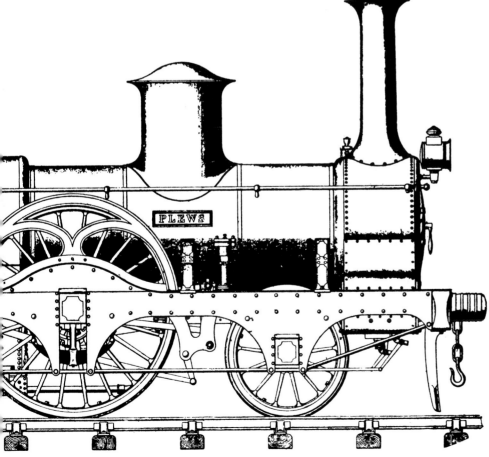

10 Stephenson's engine *North Star*. This locomotive and the similar *Morning Star* were delivered to the 7ft gauge GWR. Brunel was most enthusiastic about them, and alone of the initial 20 locomotives ordered for the line they were to prove successful in service.

11 The splendid *Plews* of the York, Newcastle & Berwick Railway, built by Hawthorn in 1848. A most distinctive design of the period. Engine and tender are well matched, and the sweeping curves of the cutaway driving wheel splasher are noteworthy.

12 Frequently cited as the most beautiful design of the period was David Joy's *Jenny Lind*, designed for E. B. Wilson of Leeds. This type saw service on a number of British railways; the example illustrated was built for the MR in 1852. The classical treatment of dome and safety valve column was a hallmark of E. B. Wilson's products.

13 A rare early photograph showing Crampton's *Kinnaird*, of the Dundee, Perth & Aberdeen Junction Railway, one of seven built by Tulk & Ley between 1846-1854. A Crampton engine possessed a totally different kind of aesthetic appeal, with the long wheelbase, and huge driving wheel set behind the firebox.

14 Ex-LNWR 'Crewe Goods' engine on Manchester Milford Railway (which never became more than a local line from Aberystwyth at Llanybyther) complete with station staff.

2 Travelling on the Railway

The coming of railways spelt slow but certain death to the mail and stagecoaches which plied the roads of Britain. At the same time it opened up new opportunities for travel to all classes of society, including the poorest who had previously either travelled just as far as their own two feet could take them; or else perhaps had travelled on one of the slow, lumbering stage wagons. For the wealthy, already accustomed to more frequent travelling, and possessing their own chaise or coach, the railway was an acceptable equivalent provided one travelled first class. Nevertheless, for some time many preferred the privacy of their own horse-drawn vehicle, and for rail journeys they remained in it whilst it was hauled along the line mounted upon a flat carriage truck.

For those who had previously endured long road journeys seated 'outside', the railway alternative of an open carriage with seats, was quite feasible. For the really poor, an open carriage *without* seats would bear comparison to the discomforts of a stage wagon — and the journey was far quicker!

Such then were the conditions of rail travel considered suitable by the directors of the earliest passenger railways, and one must acknowledge the period of social upheaval that Britain was going through at that time, with its very positive strata of society, to appreciate the fact that to begin with at least no one saw anything very strange or wrong in the vastly different travelling conditions offered on the railway, to different classes.

As mentioned in Chapter 1, the promoters of the L&MR had the conveyance of goods between those two cities as the uppermost thought in their minds. Much to their surprise when the line opened, the volume of passenger traffic soon exceeded the volume and value of goods consignments, and they were pressed to order more passenger rolling stock to meet the demand.

The earliest carriages built for the line had included some weird and wonderful experiments (for who could say *exactly* what a railway carriage should be?), but

the demand for additional stock enabled the lessons to be quickly learned, and by 1834 a clearer solution to the requirements was emerging.

A contemporary account of two of the original 1830 designs, from *An Accurate Description*, etc, by J. S. Walker, is worth quoting:

'The most costly and elegant contain three apartments, and resemble the body of a coach (in the middle) and two chaises, one at each end — the whole joined together. Another resembles an oblong square of church pews, panelled at each end, and the rail which supports the back so contrived that it may be turned over, so that the passengers may face either way, and the machine does not require to be turned.'

The first passenger carriages for the L&MR line were on wagon style underframes with four wheels and cantilever springs as on road coaches. It was not at first considered necesssary to provide any form of lighting or heating, or to make any sanitary provision. A slight acknowledgement to the unpredictable nature of English weather was made in the open carriages by the provision of numerous holes in the floor to allow rain water to drain away — and of course allow draughts up the legs of travellers therein! The riding qualities of these short-wheelbase, loose-coupled carriages, with their padded leather buffers to take the shocks of starting and stopping, can be only too readily imagined.

The resemblance of the covered first class carriage (with three six-seater compartments containing well padded seat cushions, arm rests and padded back, and with droplights in the doors, with quarter-lights each side) to an enlarged road coach, has often been remarked upon. This was quite logical, and certainly must have helped to promote the idea of travel on the railway in the minds of the wealthier classes, by presenting a familiar aspect to a new mode of travel. Moreover it must be remembered that coach building was an art in itself, requiring skilled craftsmen, and one can appreciate the readiness of

railway engineers such as the Stephensons to hand this department over to those best equipped, while they tackled the problems of locomotive development and other aspects of railway engineering. The employment of the coach-builder Nathaniel Worsdell to construct a tender for Stephenson's *Rocket*, has already been remarked upon — what more fitting choice could be made when the problem of providing suitable passenger carriages arose? Besides which, the coachbuilders must have welcomed the new source of work the railway offered, for the road coaches were threatened by railway competition.

Externally the coachbuilder's traditions were carried most completely on to the first class railway carriages, with the characteristic panelling and curved quarterlights retained to each compartment. The nearly flat roof had railings enclosing a luggage space and there was often a seat on the roof for the guard to travel on, as in the days of road coaches. The second and third class railway carriages were derived more from the road wagon, rather than coachbuilding, practice. When, after some years, second class passengers were provided with coachstyle carriages these lacked the quarterlights, but many had open sides above the waists with a canopy above and curtains that could be drawn across for protection.

In the compartment layout of the first class carriage of the mid-1830s, which was only some 6ft high inside and not much more than 5ft wide, we nevertheless have the progenitor of the typical British non-corridor compartment carriage, of which countless thousands have been produced over a period of 120 years. Mention has been made already of the provision of a box seat on the roof for a guard. One of the guard's duties was to act as a brakesman and he was one of several stationed along the length of the train, which at first possessed no continuous brakes. From their elevated position they could observe signals from the lineside or the locomotive, meanwhile receiving more than their fair share of cinders and smuts in common with the poor unfortunates in the open carriages.

Improvements in the buffers and couplings between carriages, were soon made, and the stock of 1834, was equipped with spring buffering and drawgear with screw couplings. This must have considerably lessened the amount of jolting and jarring. There was also a certain new elegance in their design, one point removed from road coach practice, which has a familiar aspect to our eyes — emphasised by the repetitive, evenly spaced rectangular window arrangement.

When the L&BR opened to passenger business during 1837-38, the company chose to remain faithful to the conventions of the L&MR for passenger carriage design. At the time of the opening of the first section, from Euston to Boxmoor, on 20 July 1837, the company provided the following amenities (to quote their advertisement):

'First class coaches carry six passengers inside, and each seat is numbered.

'Second class coaches carry eight passengers inside, and are covered, but without lining, cushions or divisions, and the seats are not numbered.

'Third class coaches carry four passengers on each seat, and are without covering.'

(It should be pointed out that the numbers of passengers of first and second class referred to in that extract, as 'inside', are those *per compartment*.)

C. Hamilton Ellis, in his splendid book *Railway Carriages in the British Isles from 1830 to 1914*, reminds us that the punning nickname of 'Stanhopes' was bestowed upon the 'stand-up' third class opens.

An early, and very amusing description of railway travel is entitled *The Railway Monitor* and says:

'*To Travellers.*
The existing railway arrangements render it imperative that you should provide yourself with a large stock of philosophy, to enable you to put up with certain inconveniences, which you will be sure, to a greater or less extent, to encounter on most lines, and whereof a classification is hereby appended for your benefit.

'*First Class*
The chief inconvenience peculiar to this class is that your fare will be about twice as much as you ought in fairness to pay. You run, perhaps, rather less risk in this class than in the others, of having your neck broken; but you must not be unprepared for such a contingency.

'*Second Class*
In travelling by the second class, you will do well to wear a respirator, unless you wish to be choked with dust and ashes from the engine close in front of you. Also, if you are going far, you are recommended to put on a diving-dress . . . because, if it should rain much during the journey, the sides of the carriage being open you will have to ride in a pool of water. Your dignity must not be hurt, should you have for next neighbour a ragamuffin in handcuffs, with a policeman next him. The hardness of your seat is a mere trifle; that is the least of the annoyances to which you are judiciously subjected, with the view of driving you into the first class train.

'*Third Class*
Make up your mind for unmitigated hail, rain, sleet, snow, thunder and lightning. Look out for a double allowance of smoke, dust, dirt, and everything that is disagreeable. Be content to run a twofold risk of loss of life and limbs. Do not expect the luxury of a seat. As an individual and a traveller you are one of the lower classes; a poor, beggarly, contemptible person, and your comfort and convenience are not to be attended to.'

Carriages on the 7ft gauge GWR were, from the start, of definitely superior vein to their smaller contemporaries — at least for the first class passengers in which it was predominantly interested. For second class it provided some closed and some open carriages, whilst for a class described as 'persons in lower stations of life' travel was in uncovered trucks in the goods trains. Brunel had recommended the use of six-wheeled carriages and these were subsequently ordered for the first class. Although in common with the earlier railways' first class stock, the first class compartments were only 6ft high, they were no less than 9ft 6in wide, and there were four compartments each seating eight passengers. Upholstery was in Morocco leather, and a noteworthy feature was the provision of ventilation louvres above the windows. Some compartments had a central longitudinal partition with a glazed door, which gave a greater degree of privacy to the two sets of four seats. A special type of carriage, introduced by the GWR in its early days was the 'Posting Carriage', notable for the saloon layout (a sort of room on rails) and clerestory type of roof. Hamilton Ellis states that they were intended as a sort of extra first class, with an internal arrangement of two U-shaped leather sofas, surrounding card tables, and a central porch with door, each side. Public response to this layout was poor, probably due in part to the fact that

they were badly ventilated and rough riding (they were four-wheelers whereas the ordinary firsts were six-wheeled), and they were soon demoted to less frequent use as party or family saloons. Perhaps the most interesting feature of these 'Posting Carriages' was the clerestory roof, which gave increased headroom and better natural lighting. This seems to have been the first railway essay in this architectural form, which was to be used to great effect in the later years of the nineteenth century; but for the time being the idea did not catch on.

In August, 1844, Gladstone's Railway Regulation Act received the Royal Assent. This obliged the railway companies to provide weatherproof travelling accommodation for third class passengers, once a day. Many companies literally obeyed the word of the law and provided one such train a day, but at night or else in the early hours of the morning — thereby doing their best to discourage third class travel. These unearthly timed trains became known as the 'Parliamentary trains' and their slow and weary progress through the countryside was matched only by the cramped, unlit, and poorly ventilated carriages used. This well intentioned Act of Parliament did not abolish the old open 'Stanhopes'; on the contrary, they were utilised for passengers foolish enough to choose third class travel on trains other than the one 'Parliamentary' a day! They were also used for excursion traffic; presumably a trip to the seaside could be a reasonably jolly affair in one of these open carriages — weather permitting.

However, the Act did force the companies to improve their second class accommodation, and low partitions divided these into semi-compartments, with covered bodies, but poor ventilation and illumination remained their lot.

To begin with, first class passengers desirous of lighting facilities brought these with them, in the form of an individual candle in a holder which could be hooked to a suitable spot on the compartment wall close to their heads. But by the early 1840s lamps burning rape oil were used in some carriages. Placed in position through a hole in the roof, the lamps could be removed as necessary for refilling. The waterproofing of these potholes was not very effective, and sorry was the plight of passengers should the lamp not have been replaced properly on a wet and stormy night! Some companies decided that one lamp might well be shared by two compartments if it were placed in a position cut-out of the wall between the two. The housings for these rape oil lamps were a prominent feature on the roofs of carriages so equipped. On some of the enclosed third class carriages introduced

15

THE UNION

as a result
of Gladstone's
Act, one lamp sufficed to
illuminate the whole carriage,
which was of open layout crammed with
bench seats. Another innovation was the
provision of heating in cold weather, by
means of hot water footwarmers.

Smoking by passengers were generally
discouraged by the early railway
companies on their trains and stations, but
by 1846 attitudes were evidently
changing, because the Eastern Counties
Railway introduced a special smoking
saloon in that year, and later on special
compartments were set aside for
smokers, by the various companies.

By the time of the 1851 Great
Exhibition, development of railway
passenger carriages lagged far behind the
impressive progress in locomotive design,
railway engineering and architecture. The
reasons for this are not easily defined with
certainty, but it seems that a good deal of
the initial romance of travelling by train
had been lost, and complaints of travelling
conditions were voiced with increasing
vigour. Sad to relate, there was not much
improvement in carriage design over the
next 10 years or so, and just to prove
otherwise to all who imagined the
railways had achieved the nadir with their
third class, there were actually fourth class
carriages in use of certain lines for
excursions and cheap trips!

The construction of carriage bodies
advanced slowly, with some increase in
length (adding extra compartments) but
this was limited by the rigid wheelbase
used. The lighting was still rape oil, which
offered dismal illumination at the best.

Some improvement in the welfare of
second class passengers was achieved with
such luxuries as stiff cushions to sit upon
and quarterlight windows flanking the
door. The first class remained stodgily
comfortable, with panels and mouldings
picked out rather crudely in gold;
probably a mirror; ponderous buttoned-in
upholstery; curtains, and a carpet. The
inside of the door would usually be padded
with a thick buttoned leather squab. The
exterior was beginning to lose its road
coach ancestry and panelling was more
rectangular with possibly a curved
treatment remaining at each end of the
carriage side. Slotted 'venetian' ventilators
were inserted above the windows.

Some increase in the width and height
of carriages began to be noticeable in the
1860s, but there can have been little
incentive to make any great improvements
in this respect whilst lighting and heating
remained so poor. Nevertheless
six-wheeled carriages with larger bodies
began to replace the four-wheelers
(although as we have seen, the GWR used
six-wheelers from the outset). Although a
Mr Joseph Wright had patented bogie
carriage designs as early as 1844, British
companies did not take up the idea for
many years.

Sanitary facilities were unknown to
ordinary passengers of any class, and at
this time sleeping on a train was by means
of an improvised arrangement of seat
cushions across the compartment, with

bed linen hired
from the guard.
Not many people availed
themselves of this amenity,
however, and for the majority of stalwarts
who had perforce to journey overnight,
rugs about the person were advisable.

A development of the late 1860s was the
use of the family saloon carriages (which
met with greater success than the GWR
'Posting Carriage' design mentioned
earlier). Victorian families tended to be
large, and the saloon layout catered well
for these when travelling complete with
servants. There was also the very
desirable provision of toilet facilities — no
doubt a large family blessed this! But for
the present such sanitary provisions were
the exception rather than the rule.

Enclosed carriages in early years
followed road coach practice for their
external liveries, as well as construction.
The upper panels were usually black; the
lower, yellow, green or red. Names were
carried as in road coach days, and the
general intention seems to have been to
bestow as much familiarity as possible
upon their outward aspect, in order to
reassure passengers embarking upon their
first rail journeys. Open carriages of third
and second class would be a different
colour (blue seems to have been a
favourite) and the complete train would
present quite a colourful assembly.

As time went on, a more uniform livery
was selected by the individual companies,
and the practice of naming carriages was
dropped. Instead they were identified by
numbers, and usually carried a monogram
of the initials of the company, or possibly
a coat of arms. Panelling was emphasised

by 'lining-out' and painting the relief mouldings. It seems that quite early on it was realised that a more logical way of painting railway carriages (as opposed to road coaches) was to use a dark colour for panels below the waist and perhaps a light one for those above — or else a single dark colour overall. Traditional coach-building finishes were still followed, with great care taken over 'lining-out', which was often in gold leaf edged each side by a fine vermilion stripe. Varnishing completed the whole ensemble and this was applied by skilled hands to achieve an almost mirrorlike surface.

By 1870 rail travel was the fastest available means of transport in man's history; it was virtually without competitors — but it was by no means a pleasurable experience.

16

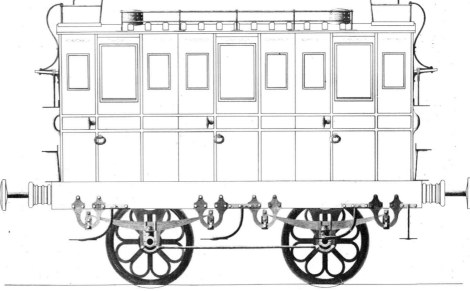

17

18

19

15 The first passenger carriage, built 1825 for the opening of the S&DR was a purely functional affair rather like a garden shed upon wheels. Passenger services were at first operated by a horse-drawn coach mounted upon flanged wheels.

16 A later (1846) S&DR carriage, clearly showing road coach influence.

17 The interior of the first class compartment is fairly typical of the period. Note the hole in the ceiling for a pot-oil lamp, and the silk cords to hang top-hats by the brim. These compartments were the progenitors of the typical British compartment carriage design.

18 Birmingham & Derby Junction Railway carriage. The bodywork has a more rectangular character than was typical, but otherwise this drawing illustrates clearly the general arrangement.

19 The interior of a first class compartment of the 1840s-1850s. Note the headrests between seats, together with padded armrests. Also the buttoned upholstery. An excellent contemporary painting, by Abraham Solomons, entitled *The Return*, exhibited at the 1854 Royal Academy.

THE EXCURSION TRAIN GALOP

BY

FRANK MUSGRAVE.

LONDON. BREWER & Cº 23 BISHOPSGATE ST WITHIN.

21

22

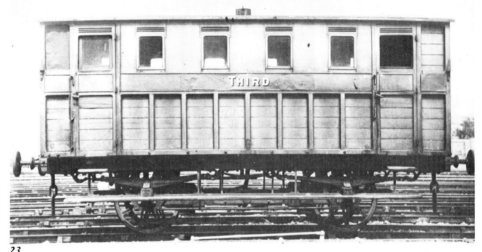

23

20   All the delights of a seaside-bound excursion train, SER 1844. Fortunately the sun is shining! This charming drawing appeared on the cover of a popular piece of music of the day.

21   An iron bodied third class carriage of the mid-1840s, for the Vale of Neath Railway, which later went to the GWR. The nearly flat iron roof afforded some degree of protection against the elements. A true horror of a

carriage, it nevertheless survived long enough to be converted to a milk van in 1870, lasting as such until 1887.

22   Interior of the special smoking saloon introduced in 1846 by the Eastern Counties Railway.

23   A former fourth class carriage of the Brighton Railway, circa 1860. Originally it would have had open sides above the waist. As

depicted here it was probably used on 'Parliamentary' trains, as third class. A solitary oil lamp illuminated the interior.

24   By the late 1860s carriages were longer, but still low roofed. This LMR example (photographed in 1874) was probably originally built as a composite first and second class, and later altered to first and 'improved' third. Note the end luggage compartment.

24

3 Improving the Art

The Great Exhibition of 1851 was Britain's showplace for her new industrial skills. Amidst the appalling clutter of machine-made furniture and domestic items — all vainly imitating hand craftsmanship (like over-decorated birthday cakes in their tasteless richness of applied frills) — two shining examples stood out, pointing the way to true industrial design attitudes. One of these examples was the very building housing the exhibition, the Crystal Palace, with its honest use of iron and glass; the other example was there (for those willing to comprehend it) in the locomotives displayed to the crowds. Unfortunately the strange mood of the times — with its mixture of industrial vigour, associated squalor and wealth, together with an almost poetic, unreal, seeking of the picturesque — clouded the vision of most onlookers. Machinery, science and taste were things to be treated seriously, but in isolation; locomotives could be admired as feats of engineering; but surely *not* as things of beauty?

By 1851, locomotives were being constructed to increasingly large dimensions, with a view to obtaining greater power and improved performance. This was partly due to the results of the comparative trials arranged in 1846 by the Gauge Commission between locomotives of the broad gauge and standard gauge. The larger GWR locomotives had demonstrated their superiority over their standard gauge brethren in no uncertain manner, and locomotive builders were striving to obtain better results for the now standardised 4ft 8½in gauge.

One of the locomotives exhibited at the Great Exhibition in Hyde Park was a GWR broad gauge 4-2-2, the *Lord of the Isles*, an example of the 8ft single 'Iron Duke' class designed by Daniel Gooch. This type was destined to remain in service, through successive batches and renewals, until the end of the broad gauge in 1892; in itself a remarkable tribute to the sound principles of design Gooch had developed at Swindon. The 'Iron Duke' class was developed from a locomotive built by Gooch in 1846, at a time when the 'battle of the gauges' was attracting considerable attention, and he intended it to demonstrate the superiority of the broad gauge. This 'one-off' locomotive was apparently scratch-built, without proper working drawings, and was the first locomotive entirely constructed at Swindon. With the appropriate name *Great Western*, it was a 2-2-2 with sandwich frames and a large Gothic firebox. Although it came up to expectations and performed well, it proved heavy at the leading end, and the front axle eventually broke, causing a derailment while the locomotive was hauling a train. As a result the front end framing was extended and an additional carrying axle was placed underneath; the wheelbase was rigid. The 'Iron Duke' class adopted this 4-2-2 wheel arrangement, and had a domeless boiler, raised round-topped firebox with polished brass valve casing, and a huge chimney with a very handsome polished cap which set the whole design off to perfection. Strong influence of the original Stephenson *North Star* (and its 'Patentee' origin) and the subsequent Gooch 'Firefly' class, can be seen in these massive locomotives, with their restrained but satisfying aspect, with beautiful bright metalwork detailing. One feature of interest was the provision of a hooded seat in a raised position at the rear of the low sided tender, to accommodate and shelter the 'porter' who acted as guard to the train.

The important point to remember is that these broad gauge engines were truly massive, nearly twice the size of the standard gauge types. No wonder Brunel and Gooch were confident in the superiority of their locomotives — they were world beaters!

An interesting attempt to produce a standard gauge equivalent to the 'Iron Duke' class is seen in Archibald Sturrock's 7ft 6in 4-2-2 No 215, built by R. & W. Hawthorn in 1853. Sturrock had gone to the GNR from the GWR, and a good deal of Swindon influence can be seen in the general lines of No 215, plus a few characteristic Hawthorn touches. She was before her time, and too heavy and large for the requirements of the day on the GNR, destined to remain the sole example of her class; but a most impressive machine to gaze upon.

From 1850 onwards the various experiments of the 1840s gave way to a more stable period of design. Many railways favoured the double framed outside bearing, inside cylinder type; also the *Jenny Lind* variety, with inside bearings on the driving axle. Although some builders continued to feature elaborate ornamental flourishes — such as E. B. Wilson and Hawthorn's — the trend was towards a more restrained approach with the emphasis on clean lines and flowing curves, with details handled in an unobtrusive manner.

Two notable exceptions to the general trend of design were the McConnell 'Bloomers' of the LNWR (Southern Division), and the outside cylinder locomotives of the 'Crewe Type'. There were also outside cylinder locomotives of new designs on the LSWR during the period, but in general little progress was made with this type for some years.

The McConnell 'Bloomers' broke away completely from the low centre of gravity theories of the 1840s, and in many ways they were advanced machines for their day. They had a bold, tall outline with a high running plate, inside frames and bearings and inside cylinders. The nickname 'Bloomer' derived from the fact that they were considered to show rather a lot of leg (or rather wheel!) at a time when a certain Mrs Amelia Bloomer was seeking reform in women's dress. There were extra large, large and small varieties of 'Bloomers' — the locomotive, not the garment — and they must have presented a truly brave spectacle to mid-Victorian eyes, for not only did they have singularly elegant polished brass boiler mountings, but they were painted a brilliant vermilion red. A notable advance in design was the tender for these engines, which was six-wheeled, and outside plate frames with slots cut out between the axleboxes, and springs placed below the platform or footplate level. Some featured india-rubber springs.

As already stated, double frames were a common feature of the period, producing an appearance which can aptly be described as the 'solid base' type. For four-coupled and six-coupled locomotives, inside cylinders, double frames and outside cranks were the usual features; exceptions were those of McConnell on the LNWR. The MR Kirtley Goods locomotives of 1852 had outside plain plate frames instead of the sandwich variety introduced by Stephenson. The 2-4-0 wheel arrangement was coming into more general use, a particularly interesting example being the outside-cylinder variety introduced by Beattie for goods work on the LSWR in 1855.

Some scant consideration was now shown to the engine crew, with provision of a frontal weatherboard with two porthole windows. These must have been welcomed despite the meagre shelter they afforded, because trains were now travelling quite fast and the consequent slipstream must have fairly whistled past the footplate. Enginemen at this time were a hardy lot who seemed positively to enjoy the spartan existence they led, but this weatherboard, or spectacle plate, seems to have been accepted quite readily by them, although they were to scorn the roomy cabs, complete with roof, of later years (see ante). The weatherboard was of minimal proportions, and the cab sides remained completely open above the waist-level side sheets. Another change in detail design during the mid-1850s was the smokebox door, which had usually been of double folding type (see photo 30), these began to give way to single doors of circular dished type (actually used on some Stephenson locomotives of the late 1840s, and probably invented by that firm); some railways continued to use doors of semi-circular Gooch type; which opened upwards about a horizontal hinge. The LNWR persisted with this type until the 1880s; an example is clearly seen in the illustration of a DX Goods (photo 32). Other design changes included the use of metal boiler casings in place of wooden lagging strips, and spring instead of dumb buffers.

The locomotive of 1855 still owed much to Stephenson's 'Patentee' of 20 years previously, but it had the benefits of refinements in manufacture, and considerably increased dimensions and capabilities. For express passenger work the single driver wheel arrangement remained a favourite for the time being.

Between 1855-59 the principle changes were the introduction of *express* engines with four-coupled wheels (as opposed to previous goods designs), and increased use of bogies. The leading bogie had existed in a primitive form by 1849, on some 4-4-0 tank engines of the GWR and South Devon Railways, to a design by Gooch which was perpetuated on the GWR for many years afterwards. Further attempts to use bogies were now made but the short wheelbase and frame, and lack of flexibility they had, hindered progress. In 1859 the LSWR made a significant move by abandoning single-wheelers in favour of four-coupled locomotives for express duties, and produced a 2-4-0 design built at Nine Elms with coupled wheels no less than 7ft in diameter.

Prior to this, 1854 must be noted as a significant year in the aesthetic development of the British steam locomotive, with the founding of the locomotive builders, Beyer Peacock & Co. From the outset this firm produced designs of remarkable beauty, and the standards set were destined to have far-reaching influences on locomotive design at home and abroad. In terms of detail finish a Beyer product was a definitely superior item, and one of the most notable features was the superb chimney, which had a distinct taper, being narrower at the top than the bottom, with a lovely polished cap. At the time of their introduction most builders were still using parallel chimneys, but Stephenson's and Sharp's had a similar taper, but not somehow of quite the same distinctive quality.

By the late-1850s there were already signs of a move away from the 'solid base' type of locomotive, although examples were to continue to appear for a good many years to come, particularly on the GWR which long favoured the iron and wood sandwich frame for the better ride it produced on its tracks. The reliable 0-6-0 goods engine, a truly British creation, attained about this period the final characteristics it was to continue to hold for almost a further century of steam locomotive design and construction. This remarkable 'maid of all work', as it has often been described, became the dependable standby of most of our railway companies, performing all manner of work ranging from local freight duties to emergency use as an express passenger engine. Countless hundreds were built to a basically simple rugged design, with inside cylinders and solid inside slab frames, with gradual increase in size and efficiency through the years. A striking portent of its usefulness was the mass production of no less than 857 standardised examples of Ramsbottom's DX goods 0-6-0 for the LNWR between 1858-1872; with a further 86 produced for the LYR. This early case of mass production to a standardised design was an important contribution by Ramsbottom, who had succeeded Allan at Crewe. Not only were locomotives of the same class standard, but many parts were interchangeable between classes. Policy at Crewe was one of small engines, cheaply built but robust and simple to maintain and operate. Not for Crewe the elaborate brass domes and valve casings of McConnell at Wolverton; a plain, severe outline was the order of the day, but nevertheless quite pleasing.

By way of contrast to the standard simplicity of Crewe, the LSWR had some remarkable gadgetry attached to its locomotives around this time, due to the apparent love of their designer, Joseph Beattie, for experiments with patent devices to improve his basically straightforward machines. Some ran with a sort of extra chimney, or even two extra, of slender proportions erected in front of the chimney proper and there were all manner of pipes, wheels and handles festooned about the boiler and firebox. For all this apparent inventiveness the locomotives were basically very good looking machines.

Between 1860 and 1865 the existing locomotive types were enlarged and improved, with only a few innovations. In Scotland, Benjamin Connor produced some 8ft singles, with outside cylinders, for the Caledonian Railway (1859-1865) which had definite affinities with the Allan 'Crewe Type' (of which numerous examples existed in Scotland), but with the cylinders placed horizontally, not inclined. Crewe's own contemporaries to these Scottish relatives were the 'Problem' or 'Lady of the Lake' class, of which 60 were constructed. These had more advanced features, with inside frames, inside bearings and outside cylinders. In common with other locomotives of similar wheel arrangement, the big single driving wheel was housed in a 'paddlebox' splasher, with a pattern of cutaway slots.

A further derivative of the 'Crewe Type' appeared on the GER in 1862 to a design by Robert Sinclair. Although these showed many Allan features they are noteworthy for two details incorporated. One was the plain stovepipe chimney, a hallmark of Sinclair, which was copied by Connor and Brittain on the CR. The other feature was the provision of quite a generous cab design, which after some initial distrust won the men's acceptance. Other railways to produce 'Singles' at this time included the MR, the GNR and the SER. Further types of 2-4-0 appeared, but perhaps the most interesting types of the period were the passenger engines with leading bogies, most designed by Stephenson & Co, of which six for the S&DR are particularly noteworthy.

The initial two, with bogie wheels of 3ft 6in diameter and 6ft coupled wheels, were built in anticipation of the opening of the line from Barnard Castle to Tebay, over the exposed Pennine Hills, and were named *Brougham* and *Lowther*, after the residences of Lord Brougham and Lord Lonsdale. They had outside cylinders and inside frames, with a long bogie frame, and in many ways they were advanced locomotives for their time, foreshadowing the designs of late Victorian years. Most remarkable of all was the provision of a large spacious cab, complete with side windows (discussed later), but it seems these were not favourably received by the stalwart drivers, as the following four engines of the class reverted to open footplates with merely the front weatherboards for protection.

Another 4-4-0 type was introduced in 1864-65, by Edward Fletcher for the NER, to work on the severely curved Whitby-Malton route. These 'Whitby bogies' seem to have been a successful design for the job, and they lasted some 25 years on it, but aesthetically they were very weak, with the small-wheeled short-framed bogie cramped beneath the front end. Only the flowing lines of the big dome casing, with its Salter valves, catches our eye, and this was a fairly typical style of the times, although Fletcher's version seemed even more curvacious than most. But these 4-4-0 ventures were exceptions and another 10 years was to pass before the bogie passenger engine really came into its own. However, by the end of 1866 most of the leading railways had discontinued new construction of Singles — except the GNR and GWR — although of course many hundreds of examples were in everyday use. As we shall see in a later chapter there was to be a Single revival, when steam sanding was introduced. The four-coupled express engine was gaining favour, but not as yet with a leading bogie.

As mentioned above, the GNR was an exception to the trend, due to the arrival on the scene of Patrick Stirling, who took charge of the Locomotive Department in 1866. Previously he had been with the GSWR, at Kilmarnock, and there he had developed his own Single designs, and he arrived at his new post determined to adhere to the Single. Back in 1857 he had produced a 2-2-2 at Kilmarnock with outside cylinders, a domed boiler and inside frames. This little engine bore a remarkable resemblance to the later 'Lady of the Lake' design of Ramsbottom's at Crewe. A later series of 2-2-2 engines built for the GSWR, between 1860-1868 had outside cylinders, domeless boilers and some of the class had the first examples of the round-topped cab that Stirling made a feature of his designs. In these locomotives we see the progenitors of the famous 8ft outside cylinder 4-2-2 of 1870 (see Chapter 6). For his first designs on the GNR, Stirling reverted to inside cylinders with domeless boilers and

round-topped cabs producing first 2-4-0s and then Singles . The plain outline, relieved only by a shapely safety valve casing, of the domeless boiler and flush firebox; the simple but effective cab design and the general lack of fuss in detailing of these locomotives of the late 1860s serve admirably to show how locomotive design was becoming more and more a true piece of industrial art — a marriage of function and appearance. Patrick Stirling was one of several locomotive engineers who were becoming increasingly aware that a locomotive could be handsome in itself, and did not require elaborate ornamentation to render it appealing to the eye.

Mention has been made above of several attempts to offer improved cabs to enginemen, in particular the spacious examples on the first two S&DR 4-4-0s built by Stephenson's. It seems strange that the men themselves should oppose such amenities, but this was in fact the case. The driver of 1860 was a fiercely proud individual, with dignified bearing, a deeply bronzed weatherbeaten face and in all probability a large beard. This appendage served him well on cold winter nights, and many are the tales of drivers arriving at their destination with large particles of ice in their beards, practically frozen stiff on the footplate! Such men would not take kindly at first to any suggestions of softening-up their conditions. But other factors played their part in the quite heated debate on the pros and cons of cabs. One of these was a suspicion voiced by some locomotive superintendents that if the drivers were too comfortable some would be prone to fall asleep on duty! Another factor was vandalism — which unfortunately plagued the railways in the 1860s just as it does in the 1980s. Ahrons, in his book *The British Steam Locomotive from 1825 to 1925*, states the following:

'On the Midland Railway in 1863 some boys threw bricks down from an overbridge at Loughborough, severely injuring the driver, after which Kirtley gave better protection by bending the top of the weatherboard completely over the footplate, supporting it at the back by means of two columns. This form of weatherboard rattled when the engine was running, and the 20 engines or so fitted with it were known as the "drummers". The drivers objected strongly to it, and asked for its removal. A compromise was reached whereby the weatherboard was bent over only part of the footplate and was not supported by pillars. This arrangement was standard until 1872 on the Midland'.

The important point is that gradual

acceptance of better shelter on the part of the enginemen was being won, and the designs of Patrick Stirling and Benjamin Connor pointed the way to future development, with a sensible protection overhead as well as to the front and sides, although the time had not yet come when men would accept the 'modern' fully enclosed footplate that Stephenson's had used on the S&DR engines of 1860!

By the end of the period reviewed in this chapter, the British steam locomotive had assumed definite characteristics, which may be described as a subtle combination of neatness, simplicity, harmonious lines and fitness for purpose. It was on the whole already an attractive machine, but some even more encouraging portents for the future could be seen in the shape of some early 2-4-0 locomotives by Samuel Johnson on the GER, in the Stirlings of the GNR and in some rebuildings of early Allan engines by a certain Mr William Stroudley on the far-off Highland Railway. Nor should we overlook the important contribution to locomotive aesthetics that Beyer Peacock & Co were already making.

Finally a word on locomotive liveries during the formative years. To begin with these were a matter for the fancy of the individual locomotive engineers. At the time of the Rainhill Trials Stephenson's *Rocket* was painted bright yellow with a white chimney, a colour scheme which one suspects was most carefully chosen to make his little engine more appealing to eyes as yet unaccustomed to steam locomotives. The chief competitor to *Rocket* in the popularity stakes was the dainty little *Novelty* which had an elegance all its own, and this was painted with blue frames and wheels, set-off by a polished copper boiler casing. The other two contestants — the aptly named *Perseverance* and Hackworth's elephantine *Sans Pareil* — both displayed little concern for appearance.

Locomotive builders soon adopted their own individual liveries, helping to distinguish their products which were seen thus on various railways. But by the late 1840s railways had become sufficiently numerous and closely grouped to make some form of distinctive *company* livery desirable. Locomotives began to appear in uniform colours, but not as yet bearing much else to show who they belonged to, except the running number and perhaps some initials.

Conventions soon arose, with certain colours definitely preferred for certain parts of the locomotive. Black was invariably used for smokebox and chimney casing, frames were most often in a deep brown, red or similar shade. Boilers, sidesheets and tender sides were in brighter shades with green a great favourite. But deep blues, purple-browns and Indian reds were also popular. A few railways chose really striking colours, most notably the vermilion red of the LNWR, Southern Division. Some special engines appeared in 'fancy' livery, such as the 'Royal Crampton' of the NBR finished in Tartan overall!

The basic colours were invariably relieved by 'lining-out', often in black and white, gilt, orange or red, or a combination of three or more of these. Yellow and pale green were also favourites for lining purposes. The practice of emphasising panelling by the painting was entirely logical, it drew the eye away from rows of rivet heads, metal bands and other constructional details. The outer surrounds of the panels would be in a dark colour separated by lining from the lighter colour within. A favourite style of 'lining-out' in mid-Victorian times had the corners cut off by reversed quarter circles. Buffer beams were usually vermilion, although this was sometimes confined to a central panel surrounded by the darker colour used for the frames.

Great care was taken with the finished appearance of locomotives, all metal working surfaces were finished bright and kept polished and oiled, and copper and brass fittings were highly polished. Varnishing was an elaborate process, very necessary to protect the pigments beneath. All these aspects are dealt with in greater detail in Chapter 9.

25

26

25 Engines of Daniel Gooch's 'Firefly' class, broad gauge 2-2-2s with huge polished brass 'Gothic' firebox casing, in the engine house at Swindon. Lithographed by J. C. Bourne.

26 'Iron Duke' class 4-2-2 *Hirondelle* of the GWR broad gauge. The hooded shelter on the rear of the tender was for the 'porter'.

27 Archibald Sturrock's solitary No 215 for the GNR, built by R. & W. Hawthorn, 1853. Considerable Swindon influence is apparent in the overall design, with some characteristic Hawthorn touches added (particularly the driving wheel splasher).

27

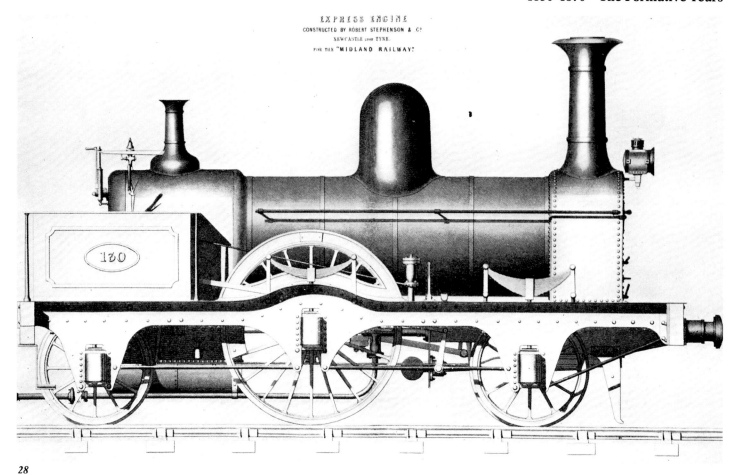

EXPRESS ENGINE
CONSTRUCTED BY ROBERT STEPHENSON & C°
NEWCASTLE upon TYNE.
FOR THE "MIDLAND RAILWAY."

28

29
30

28 A typical 2-2-2 express engine of the
1850s, built by Robert Stephenson & Co for the
MR. Compared with the 'Jenny Lind' type
(photo 12) the outline is more restrained, with
very simple treatment for dome cover and
safety valve casing.

29 McConnell's celebrated 'Bloomers' of the
LNWR (Southern Division), broke completely
away from the low centre of gravity theories
of the 1840s. These singularly handsome
locomotives were painted vermilion red with
highly polished brass fittings. Their high
running plate and exposed wheels earned
them their curious nickname. This example is
'Small Bloomer' No 103, built Wolverton 1857.
(See photo 66 for a detail showing the men's
uniforms.)

31

32

30   A characteristic Hawthorn product.
Engine No 69 of the Great North of England
Railway, at Richmond (Yorks) station. Note
the shapely weatherboard, also the old style of
double-folding smokebox doors.

31   Locomotive *Fitzwilliam* of the South
Yorkshire Railway, circa 1855. An
inside-cylinder mixed traffic 0-4-2.

32   LNWR Ramsbottom DX Goods No 1080,
in original condition. Photographed at old
Manchester station in 1868, by G. T. Rhodes.
Note the Ramsbottom ornamental chimney
cap, and the Gooch-type smokebox door with
hinge uppermost.

33   Some of Beattie's patent gadgetry on his
2-4-0 *Atlanta*, of the 'Undine' class. 1859/60.

34   Somewhat remarkable was the
perpetuation of Edward Bury's small
bar-framed designs until 1861, on the FR.
No 16 was built by W. Fairbairn & Sons.

33

34

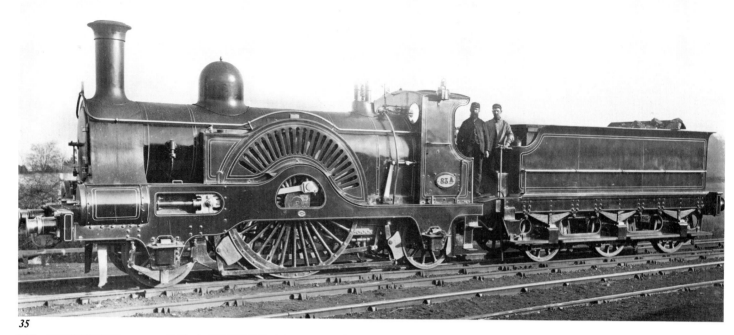

35

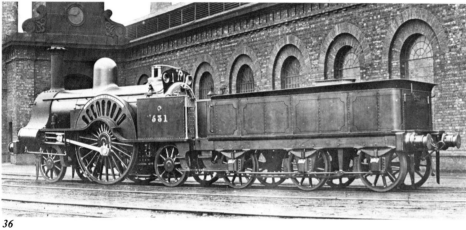

36

37

35   A 'Crewe Type' derivative. Benjamin
Connor's 8ft Single for the CR, the first of
which was constructed at St Rollox in 1859.
No 83A is shown here in later days, with
alterations including a Drummond chimney.
The driving wheel splasher had no less than
22 slots cut into it.

36   J. Ramsbottom's 'Problem' class No 531,
Lady of the Lake. Photographed outside
Crewe Works where she was built in May
1862.

37   A pioneer bogie 4-4-0. Edward Fletcher's
'Whitby Bogie' of 1864/65, for the NER's
severely curved line between Whitby and
Malton. A clumsy design with lack of balance
to the overall proportions.

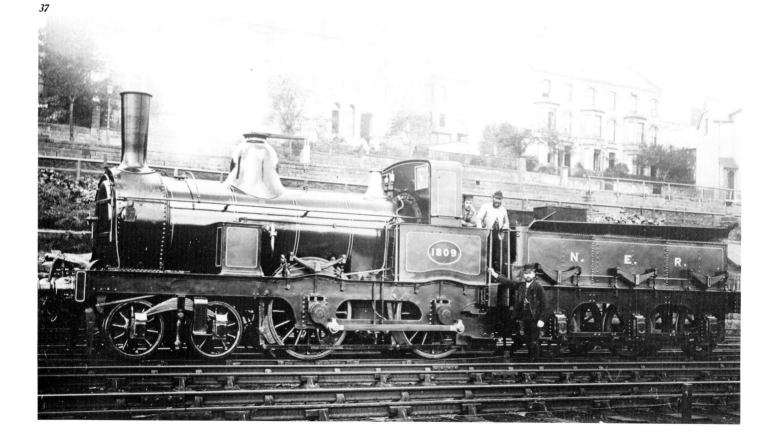

4 Early Railway Architecture

The development of railway architecture probably tells us more about the character of the men who pioneered Britain's railways than any other aspect. Indeed, the whole architecture of the Industrial Revolution is most revealing of the raw, vital, spirit of the times. In 1830 (as we have seen in Chapter 1) the steam locomotive remained very much an unknown quantity which was to undergo a long period of mechanical development, from which a gradual sense of style emerged. Carriage design, we have also seen, was largely borrowed from the road coach-builder and placed upon rails, following which there was very little real advance in amenity for over a quarter of a century. But when we come to architecture we are dealing with one of the most ancient and highly developed arts of civilised man, and the way in which it was adapted to the requirements of the new railways was one of the most interesting aspects of Victorian life. It is in fact almost impossible to overstate the importance of this period, both for the many examples of exceptional quality it produced, and for the sense of stability, dignity and purpose architecture bestowed upon the new method of travel by rail.

Today we are still surrounded by the buildings of Victorian England, a legacy in bricks and mortar; in crowded industrial streets, factories, civic buildings and our canal and railway networks. To our eyes it seems often dowdy, grime encrusted and outdated, particularly when in close juxtaposition to new concrete-and-glass structures, although in recent years a good many Victorian buildings have benefited from stone cleaning and a general 'face-lift'.

Victorian railway architecture is exciting because it is full of contasts; contrasts of style and treatment, of masterly handling of classic forms and of daring innovations in new media.

From the start there seems to have been a sense of adventure and of social occasion in railway architecture, and every opportunity was seized to build on an impressive scale when suitable occasions arose. Thus we have a number of large station buildings handled in the classical manner, with great dignity; for example Birmingham (Curzon Street), Brighton and Huddersfield. To these can be added such forthright statements of grandeur as the Moorish Arch of the Liverpool & Manchester Railway at Edge Hill, and the magnificent Doric portico at Euston — both symbols of a revolution, no less; built not for functional reasons but rather as gestures, just as Napoleon built his triumphal arches in France.

But behind these bold façades, handled with such superb confidence, there were totally new problems to be solved, and these were approached with admirable courage. Early solutions were tentative, but soon a positive conception was evolved. In this, I think particularly of the problem of railway station design. This fell into two distinct halves; the 'office block' (containing ticket office, waiting rooms etc) and the 'train shed' which accommodated the railway lines and allowed the passengers to board and alight.

The office block could be easily handled, being only one step removed from the conventions of civic and domestic architecture. But the train shed — as it became known — was a new problem, with its layout of railway lines and the need to control the people within. This division of office block and train shed, separated by a 'barrier' was to become a feature of our stations.

An awareness of social responsibility also seems to have ranked high in the minds of railway architects from the earliest days. Everything possible was done to make the new buildings, bridges, tunnels and viaducts belong to their surroundings, and to prevent the new railways offending the eye. Sometimes this resulted in the exterior of a relatively small and unimportant station or bridge being disproportionately grand, but research usually unearths a very good reason in such cases. We must remember that in many instances considerable opposition and resentment was experienced from powerful landlords when new railways were proposed and no doubt some tactful architectural solutions helped to win the day for the railways. Thus, stations and ancillary buildings were often designed to fit into, and enhance, the landscape; in fact many did this extremely well by adoption of existing vernacular styles.

Tunnel mouths, bridges and viaducts were given grand architectural treatment and many examples were singularly beautiful in proportion and details. Unfortunately the true beauty of the majority of these tunnel mouths is today hidden beneath the accumulated soot of a century and a quarter of steam locomotion, and our express trains speed into them so fast that we scarcely catch a glimpse. But picture to yourself the adventure of entering one of these long tunnels in the early days of steam, at a calm 30-35mph, and *no lights* in the carriages. How reassuring it must have been to have gazed upon the impressive portals of the tunnel entrance — a solid testimony of faith in these terrific engineering works.

Right from the start railway building was a fascinating blend of traditional styles and exciting new experiments. One reason was the need, already observed, to solve new problems unique to the layout of a railway. But another reason was the improvement in the manufacture of iron. We have seen how the steam locomotive progressed parallel to improved manufacturing methods, and better use of raw materials. The railway builders were quick to make use of this improved iron for structural solutions to such problems as the need to provide overhead verandahs, or roofs to the train sheds, at stations. There were large spaces to be covered over, and these had to be as free as possible from supports which could hinder the layout of lines below. Iron and glass were to become the basis of some magnificent solutions to this problem.

Wood had been considered a suitable material for the construction of some of the earliest train sheds, and the examples at Bath and Bristol by Brunel represent the finest handling of the material. The roof at Bristol (Temple Meads) survives to this day; a great aisled nave with a mock hammerbeam timber roof resting upon Tudor style arches. But trains no longer stand beneath it — the area under this masterpiece has become a car park!

For the smaller stations the verandah style roof was quickly adopted, sometimes supported on columns on the platform (at first on the outer edge, later set back), and sometimes cantilevered out from the side of the station buildings. Iron was soon used extensively for the supports, and some very decorative treatments were produced which blended the verandah and station building together very well (see Chapter 8).

By the mid-1840s railways were sufficiently large and widespread to create a need for much larger stations in major cities. From this need, and the greatly improved techniques of iron manufacture, arose the great series of iron roofs; beginning with Dobson's pioneer classic of Newcastle Central (1845) and quickly followed by Paddington (1854); Birmingham, New Street (1854); and Cannon Street (1866). In these great roofs we see a combination of architecture and engineering on a scale which marks it down as one of the greatest achievements of Victorian design. Paxton's Crystal Palace may have had the romance of the Great Exhibition to enhance its popularity, but Dobson's earlier Newcastle Central station (which was probably a source of inspiration to Paxton) remains with us today, as impressive to the eye as it was the day it was completed, and still serving a useful purpose.

Paddington, produced by Mathew Digby Wyatt and Brunel, is another superb example which possesses a great sense of spaciousness and unity. To appreciate these great roofs at their finest, we would have to turn the clock back and replace the diesel locomotives of today with their steam predecessors. The true vision must be one of columns of steam cascading high into the ironwork above, with slanting rays of sunlight breaking through, and all about us the echoes of a busy railway station. Today Paddington is impressive still — but cold. An architectural monument to the steam age which seems altogether too grand for the austere demands of internal combustion!

Two other London termini constructed during the period, and still with us today, must surely rank among the great classics of Victorian architecture. By strange chance they stand in close juxtaposition on the Euston Road. I refer of course to Kings Cross and St Pancras, a most interesting contrast of styles.

The earlier of the two, Kings Cross (1852) by Lewis Cubitt is a straightforward design with considerable emphasis upon its function as a train shed.

The two great arches — arrival and departure — project right through the facade to become a major feature of the design. All the offices are situated to the sides and treated in simple but effective manner. Many Victorians disliked it.

St Pancras is by way of contrast an example of the strict division of 'office block' and 'train shed'. It is without doubt a masterpiece of mid-Victorian architecture, showing the great diversity of styles, or ideals, then in vogue. For we have the great iron roof, spanning all the tracks without supports, by W. H. Barlow, a wonderful piece of engineering design of functional nature, and in front of this (and butted right against it) is Gilbert Scott's magnificent hotel and station building. The building is the very epitome of the Gothic revival, but one searches in vain for any visual expression of its function as a railway station! Nevertheless it is a magnificent building, with a tremendous skyline and wonderful handling of variegated materials. Quite understandably it was a tremendous attraction when new. Today a massive cleaning operation is slowly returning the building to its original freshness. What an impressive sight it must have been when the Euston Road was still the province of horses and pedestrians.

Besides the great stations, there were the viaducts — in stone, brick, timber and cast iron — carrying the passengers high over valleys, or the chimneys of industrial towns; the bridges, many with beautiful

architectural furnishings and of daring new dimensions (such as Brunel's graceful shallow spans across the river at Maidenhead); the tunnel entrances, and numerous specialised buildings *en route*. In this short essay there is hardly room to do justice to so vast a field. What it is important to stress is that, unlike the trains it served, railway architecture reached probably its finest heights of taste and achievement in the period 1830-1870.

38 A sense of the great social importance of the new railways was imparted by the architecture of early large stations, most often by a classical treatment, with porticos, colonnades, etc. Illustrated is Curzon Street, Birmingham, by Philip Hardwicke, 1838.

39 Less impressive, but very functional was the actual trainshed at Curzon Street, as seen in this contemporary engraving.

40 On a much grander scale was the London terminus at Euston, which possessed great dignity, with the Doric arch flanked by lodges. Here again the actual station area (visible between the two right hand lodges) was on a more modest scale, similar to Birmingham Curzon Street, which it preceded.

39

40

38

41

42

45

46

43

44

41   Monkswearmouth station (up side) frontage, Sunderland.

42   David Mocatta's Brighton station, 1841. An early example of the Italian manner which was to be widely used for the following decade.

43   An early wayside station; Parkside on the L&MR. Etching by Bury.

44   The new station at Tithebarn Street, Liverpool, opened in 1850. From a contemporary wood engraving.

45   Pangbourne, GWR. By the time the broad gauge main line was constructed, a much clearer concept of country station design had evolved. The elegant shelter roofs are remarkably modern in appearance. Lithograph by J. C. Bourne.

46   An early view, from a contemporary lithograph, of Tunbridge Wells station.

47   Brocklesby station, 1849, showing the arrival of Prince Albert for the laying of the foundation stone of Great Grimsby Docks. A charming exercise in Gable design, typical of many built in the Eastern counties about this time.

47

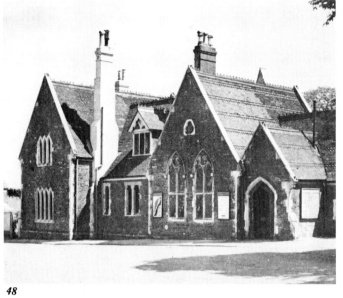

48

49

50

51

52

53

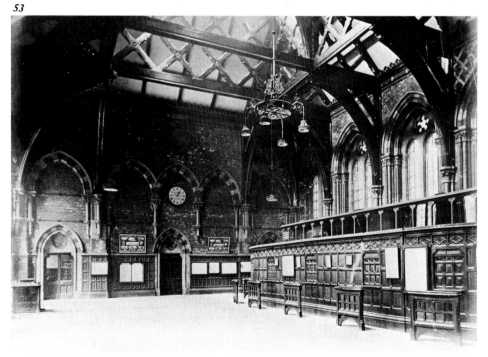

48   A perfect Gothic style station. Battle (Sussex), by William Tress, 1852.

49   Interior of Paddington, by Brunel and Digby Wyatt, 1854. Superb use of iron and glass, to create a spacious, well illuminated covered area. The slender columns supporting the roof are spaced out delicately along the platforms; altogether a most elegant concept.

50   The interior of Kings Cross, showing the iron and glass roof which replaced an earlier wooden structure of similar dimensions.

51   Lewis Cubitt's Kings Cross; one of the most powerful visual treatments ever produced for a major terminus. Although it possesses some of the same simple grandeur associated with the great railway viaducts, it was not greatly admired in Victorian times.

52   A masterpiece of the Gothic revival. St Pancras station, MR. This exterior view was taken at 6.45am on a sunny morning, in 1876.

53   The interior of the booking hall at St Pancras clearly shows the tremendous care in detailing and workmanship. It has more the atmosphere of religion than of workaday transportation.

54

55

56

57

58
59

54 Brunel's famous Box Tunnel, on the GWR main line. When built, it was the longest and straightest tunnel in the world. Lithograph by J. C. Bourne.

55 A remarkably bold and simple treatment for a tunnel mouth, at Milford on the North Midland Railway. Lithograph by Russell.

56 When occasion arose, bridges were designed in keeping with their surroundings, sometimes at the request of local landowners. This is a bridge at Rugby, L&BR. Lithograph by J. C. Bourne.

57 Carmichael's engraving of the Wetherall Viaduct. A harmonious blend of architecture and landscape.

58 Brunel's final masterpiece, the bridge over the River Tamar, at Saltash. This fine view was taken in 1960, with one of the piers of the new suspension road bridge visible whilst under construction, on the far side.

59 The impressive viaduct at Brighton, carrying the line to Lewes over the London Road. The arches in the left foreground were destroyed by enemy bombs during World War II, but were carefully rebuilt to the original style. An electric train is crossing the new arches in this 1947 view. The bold grandeur of the viaduct contrasts well with the clutter of houses below.

5 Early Ephemera and Uniforms

BOLTON AND LEIGH RAILWAY.
FROM BAG-LANE TO
Provided there be room in the Carriages on their arrival.
At   o'clock,   184
No.   Paid   Entered
(Turn over.)

No.

1st Class - Paid   7   0

This Ticket must be shewn to the Guard, or other authorised Officer, in Uniform, on the Passenger entering the Carriage, and delivered up to the proper Officer, also in Uniform, on arriving at the end of the journey.

EASTERN COUNTIES RAILWAY.
(COLCHESTER LINE.)
CHELMSFORD to LONDON.   First Class.
Seven Shillings.
The Company will not be responsible for any Passenger's Luggage, unless Booked and Paid for. Passengers receive Tickets at intermediate Stations on condition that they cannot be forwarded if there be not room on arrival of the Train.   The time of arrival is not guaranteed.

Two other features of the railway scene which constantly come before the eyes of the public, in addition to its trains and buildings, are the posters it publishes and the uniforms worn by its staff. Both tend to have an element of fashion in their design, typical of their period, and study of these helps us to gain a clearer picture of their respective times.

A railway must publicise its services, by means of posters, hand bills and timetable sheets. The majority of such printed matter comes under the heading of *ephemera*; ie to be thrown away once it has served its purpose. Fortunately for us there have always been collectors of such items and a good selection of early railway printed matter has survived to the present day. A few carefully selected examples are reproduced in this book to give a fairly representative picture.

The railways have always been huge users of printed matter; during Victorian days they had considerable influence upon the growth of the printing industry, and also upon advertising.

The design of the earliest printed matter for railways was left very much in the hands of various jobbing printers. They followed the general conventions of the day as seen on theatre and race bills. The printers had a good selection of bold display typefaces which they used alternately on the same item to great effect. Important words, names or dates were emphasised by choice of a suitable character or letterform, and a sort of instinctive good taste seems to have guided the hands of these jobbing printers, who produced many beautiful designs.

One interesting development was the use of decorative line drawings of a steam locomotive hauling a train (usually a 2-2-2 of uncertain build); these were cut by typefounders and widely used by the printers. The same cut could appear on the printed matter of many different railway companies. It was also used on theatre bills and suchlike to draw attention to announcements concerning the time of the last train home! Regrettably the typefounders overlooked the fact that steam locomotive

development was proceeding apace, and they continued to issue the little 2-2-2s long after these had been superseded in reality.

By the year of the Great Exhibition, railway posters and handbills were following a fairly set pattern of design, based upon various typefaces cleverly used together. Printing in two or three colours added emphasis and appeal, and sometimes coloured paper was used. The GNR poster of 1851 (Photo 64), was printed in three colours, with black used to great effect as a shadow on some letterforms. No great change took place in the following 20 years, but many examples of great beauty were produced and the railway stations were considerably brightened by the poster displays that were a feature of them all.

Uniforms were soon provided for certain grades of railway staff, either to distinguish them for easy recognition, or else to suit them for the job they had to perform. Thus we have the extremes of the dandified 'policeman', and the rugged engine driver.

The policeman acted as a hand-signalman at strategic points along the route, and he was easily recognised by his top hat, tail coat and tight trousers. The colours of this ensemble varied from railway to railway; another feature was his truncheon. This was decorated with the arms and initials of the company.

The grit-impregnated clothes of the driver and fireman were intended for protection rather than appearance, and the life they led — constantly exposed to the weather, to heat and steam — largely dictated their uniform. This was usually of strong cloth, with perhaps a waistcoat, with a neckerchief worn loose around the neck, and a peaked cap which could be

pulled well down over the eyes. The cap might be of a weatherproof oilskin texture. Sturdy boots were desirable and in some districts wooden clogs were favoured (a tradition which persisted in parts of north-west England up to the demise of steam!)

The railway guard became a figure of some dignity and importance, with frequent contact with passengers at stations. By the 1850s he usually wore an impressive uniform with a large belt and buckle and peaked cap. He must have been quite a swashbuckling figure as he supervised the loading of luggage, or directed elderly maiden ladies to their correct compartment!

60   Two early paper tickets, 1840s, with coloured backgrounds. The Bolton & Leigh Railway ticket was blue and had space for handwritten entries. The Eastern Counties Railway example was pink and somewhat more sophisticated.

61   Timetable sheet for the L&MR 1831. Note the hyphenated spelling of Rail-Way.

62   Notice of 1838, by an Aylesbury jobbing printer, with great emphasis placed upon the word 'railway'.

63   A classic example of a jobbing printer's instinctive sense of style. The charming little woodcut of a locomotive and train was a stock item and was widely employed irrespective of the railway concerned.

64   By 1851 railways were making extensive use of printed handbills and posters to attract custom. This beautiful example was printed in three colours, with black used for the shaded effects. A bold and completely successful use of varied typefaces.

65   The passenger train guard became a figure of some importance. His handsome uniform is shown in this etching of an LNWR guard of 1852, from *Fore's Contrasts* by H. Alken.

Liverpool and Manchester RAIL-WAY.

TIME OF DEPARTURE
BOTH
From Liverpool & Manchester.

FIRST CLASS, FARE 5s. | SECOND CLASS, FARE 3s. 6d.

Seven o'Clock Morning. | Eight o'Clock Morning.
Ten „ Do. | Half-past Two Afternoon.
One „ Afternoon. |
Half-past Four Do. |

₊ For the convenience of Merchants and others, the First Class evening train of Carriages does not leave Manchester on Tuesdays and Saturdays until Half-past Five o'Clock.

The journey is usually accomplished by the First Class Carriages under two hours.

In addition to the above trains it is intended shortly to add three or four more departures daily.

The Company have commenced carrying GOODS of all kinds on the Rail-way.

January, 1831.

61

AYLESBURY RAILWAY.
FIVE POUNDS REWARD.

Some evil-disposed Person or Persons have lately *feloniously Stolen and carried away*, a quantity of RAILS, STAKES, and MATERIALS, belonging to the Company, for which any Offender, on Conviction, is liable to Transportation for Seven Years.

Several STAKES driven into the Ground for the purpose of setting out the Line of Railway, *have also been Pulled up and Removed*, by which a Penalty of Five Pounds for each Offence has been incurred, half Payable to the Informer and half to the Company.

The above Reward will be paid on Conviction, in addition to the Penalty, to any Person who will give Evidence sufficient to Convict any Offender guilty of either of the above Crimes, on application to Mr. HATTEN or Mr. ACTON TINDAL, of Aylesbury.

By Order of the Directors.

Aylesbury, August 18th, 1838.

May, Printer, Aylesbury.

62

LLANELLY & VALE OF TOWY RAILWAYS.
LLANELLY, LLANDILO, LLANDOVERY & CWMAMMAN
On and after NOVEMBER 15th, 1858.

REGULATIONS.

JOHN THOMAS, PRINTER, LLANELLY.

63

64

GT. NORTHERN RAILWAY.
PETERBORO
OCTOBER.
IN ADDITION TO THE REGULAR
EXCURSION TRAINS
PASSENGERS FOR THE
EXHIBITION

Will be conveyed daily (Sundays excepted) from Peterboro' by the 7.0 a.m. Train, and Back by any Excursion Train. 1st and 2nd Class up to the 20th October, and 3rd Class Passengers up to the 18th October

FARES, UNTIL FURTHER NOTICE.
6s. | 5s. | 3s.

BY ORDER | SEYMOUR CLARKE, General Manager.

65

66 Driver and fireman of LNWR 'Small Bloomer' No 103 (see also photo 29). The gentleman in the top hat was Mr Widdowson, pay clerk between London, Stafford and branches, circa 1860-1870.

66

1870-1914
The Golden Age
of Steam

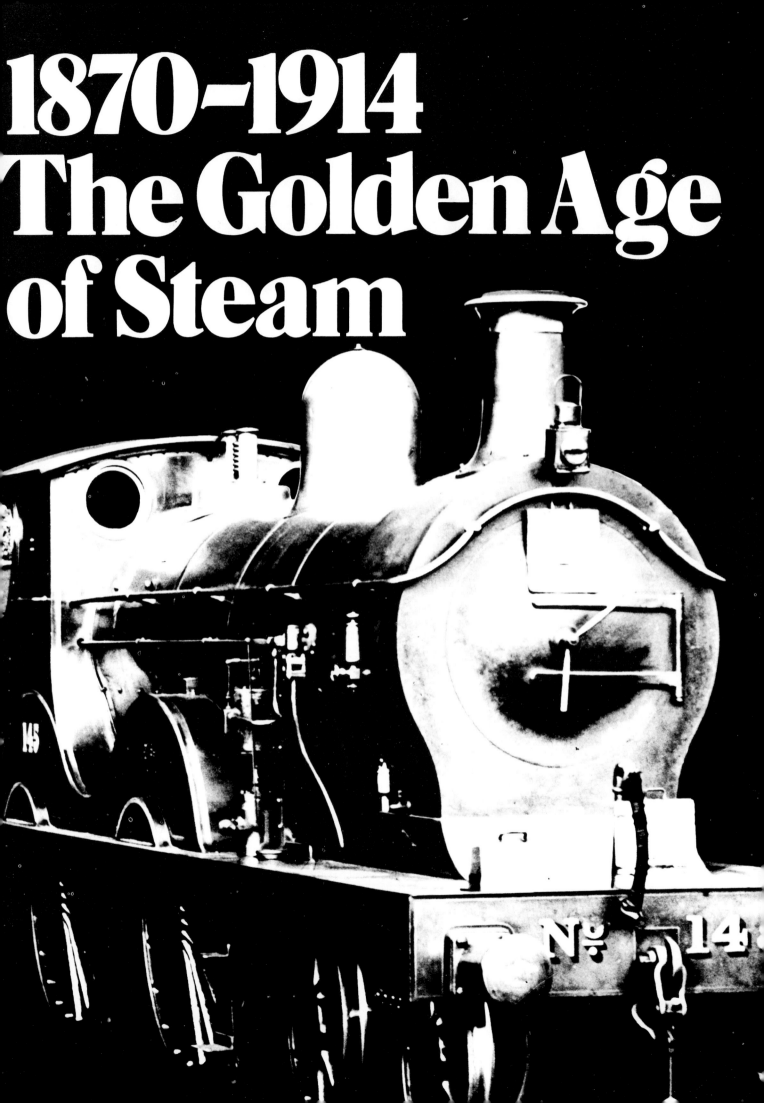

6 The Artist Engineers

The first of Patrick Stirling's 8ft 'Singles', GNR No 1, steamed out of Doncaster Works in April 1870. This was to prove one of the classic steam locomotives of all time, with a combination of grace, symmetry and power which won the hearts of countless admirers. It was a victory for aesthetics, for in fact the 8ft Singles were in some ways not the most successful of Stirling's Single designs, but they were without doubt the most aristocratic of their breed. The combination of outside cylinders, large driving wheel and flowing curves to frames and footplating, produced a wonderful harmony which looked good whether seen travelling at a mile-a-minute, or standing at rest.

A well-known story which reveals Stirling's jealous appreciation of the good looks of his 8-footers, concerns David Joy (of *Jenny Lind* fame), who produced a drawing showing his valve gear adapted for a Stirling 8ft Single. Stirling would have none of it, dismissing Joy with the words: 'Naa, mon, I canna spile my grand engine with the likes o' that machinery outside o' her.'

Stirling was probably very aware of the fact that the British public had become locomotive 'conscious'. They had started to exhibit signs of that strange love for steam engines which is now hailed as one of our national characteristics — and which to this day remains quite incomprehensible to many foreigners! There was now keen interest in both appearance and performance, and rivalry for the popularity stakes was springing-up between the various companies.

Two other engineers besides Patrick Stirling were beginning to show their considerable artistic powers at about this time, one was Samuel Waite Johnson; the other, William Stroudley.

Stroudley must be singled-out for the profound effect he had upon locomotive aesthetics during and after his lifetime. From 1865 till 1870 he had been Chief Locomotive Superintendent of the newly formed HR. Earlier in his career he had worked under Gooch at Swindon, and under Johnson at Glasgow. Whilst on the

HR, Stroudley seems to have been content to rebuild existing locomotives, until 1869, when he produced a very small design of tank engine. But at the end of that year he was appointed Locomotive and Carriage Superintendent of the LBSCR, and moved to that company's works at Brighton. The scene that greeted him there was a sorry story of poor discipline, poor maintenance, and (worse still) poor locomotives. His predecessor, John Chester Craven, seems to have taken it upon himself to supply the railway with an immensely varied collection of engines, with hardly any two alike!

The way in which Stroudley 'cleaned-up' at Brighton has been often retold. He created new discipline and won great respect for himself among the men. Stroudley was a perfectionist, everything had to be 'right', and he thought each problem out from scratch for himself. He allowed no latitude to his contractors, who had to follow his designs exactly as he wished. It was this love of perfection which outwardly manifested itself in the beautiful series of designs he was to produce for the Brighton line, up to his untimely death in 1889. It was probably also this love of perfection which drove him to launch a terrific onslaught upon the great variety of engines Craven had left him to look after. In this action he must have recalled his early contact with Daniel Gooch, for Stroudley, too, was quick to realise the virtues of standardisation, just as Gooch had done when confronted with the varied freaks first produced for the GWR.

In 1872, Stroudley produced a new small tank engine design which he intended primarily to work trains on the South London line. Their snappy performance and small size, soon won them the lasting nickname of 'Terriers'. This diminutive design was destined to have one of the most remarkable careers of any steam locomotive ever produced. It was so soundly engineered that it still refuses to die! There are Stroudley 'Terriers' in steam today hauling passengers over the private lines of preservation societies, whilst several

examples are preserved as museum pieces, including one in Canada.

The 'Terriers' were the smallest of Stroudley's standard tank engines, and yet probably the best loved! For express passenger work the earliest engines Stroudley produced for the Brighton company were some outside framed 2-4-0s and a 2-2-2, which contained parts from certain of Craven's engines. The first 'pure' Stroudley express design was a 2-2-2 Single with 6ft 9in driving wheels, built in 1874. In producing a Single, Stroudley chose not to follow the general swing away from single-wheelers which was by then evident. In fact, only two railways continued the regular construction of Singles between 1870-1875; these were the GNR and the GWR. The GNR Single of the 8ft design referred to at the beginning of this chapter were introduced very slowly, and only 12 were in service by 1875. Construction of 2-4-0 engines was in some favour, and a notable series was the 800 class produced by Matthew Kirtley for the MR in 1870.

Whilst most railways were showing a preference for the 2-4-0, and in some cases beginning to consider the virtues of a bogie express engine, Stroudley defied popular opinion and applied front-coupled driving wheels and a trailing carrying wheel to express passenger engines. His most famous examples were undoubtedly the 0-4-2 'Gladstone' class which first appeared in 1882, and we are fortunate that *Gladstone* herself has been preserved at York Museum.

The essence of a Stroudley design was simplicity, impeccable workmanship and beautiful detailing. This was given added distinction by one of the most beautiful copper-capped chimneys ever produced (incidentally the cap itself is reminiscent of Daniel Gooch's much larger broad gauge chimney caps), with a subtle taper to the chimney proper. The dome was simple in shape, with the Salter safety valves incorporated with the minimum of fuss. A most distinctive feature of Stroudley's engines was the cab design, with broad side sheets and a domed roof. But above all it was the detailing and finish which made a Stroudley design a masterpiece of engineering art. Everything, down to the whistle and the numberplate, was treated with the same sense of tasteful restraint. But lest one should imagine such restraint would produce visual boredom, the complete locomotive was finished in one of the most elaborate colour schemes ever bestowed upon steam. Elaborate yes, but certainly not vulgar! It was a wonderful combination of golden ochre, olive green and claret red, set-off to perfection by rich 'lining-out'. But this is anticipating; a later chapter deals with this more fully.

Stroudley's sense of style and discipline in design won countless admirers and his locomotives were a constant source of inspiration to early railway photographers. Hundreds of photographs still exist of his engines, taken by Stroudley devotees in the days when a camera was a most cumbersome piece of equipment to manage.

His influence can be clearly seen in the designs of some of the men who were associated with him at some period in their career. Of these we should list first Dugald Drummond. He had been foreman erector under Stroudley at the HR's Inverness Works, and he moved to Brighton to become work's manager there until 1875. From there he took many Stroudley features to the NBR, including a preference for standardisation. His first two engines were virtually copies of the first Stroudley Single, and he even used Stroudley's superb livery style! However he avoided the copper-capped chimney, substituting his own plainer, but well proportioned design. But quite soon Dugald Drummond began to show that he was capable of far more than mere pastiche. He accepted the idea of placing a bogie beneath a locomotive — which Stroudley had certainly not considered desirable — and by 1876 he had produced the first of 12 four-coupled bogie express engines; nevertheless the Stroudley influence remained strongly apparent in the neat, simple lines of these engines.

From this batch of NBR 4-4-0s we can trace a whole family tree of magnificent 4-4-0 designs, for a number of railways, built by his brother, Peter, by his successors on the NBR — Mathew Holmes and W. P. Reid — by Lambie and McIntosh on the Caledonian; as well as by himself.

Dugald Drummond moved on from the NBR to the neighbouring CR in 1882, taking with him his characteristic style. Thus the Stroudley influence was gradually spreading, so to continue until the first decade of the 20th century, when Drummond was producing locomotives for the LSWR, where he had been in power since 1895.

Features of a Drummond engine, and of those inspired by him, were the great simplicity of line and neat finish. Their graceful aspect was enhanced by the flowing line of the 'wing-plates' to the smokebox, by the neat simple splashers (often with combined sandbox on the leading driving wheel splasher), by the 'Stroudleyesque' cab, and the beautifully matched straight running plate of both engine and tender. A further point was the balance created by making the centre line of the chimney and the centre line of the bogie one and the same. The engine seemed to be poised upon the rails.

Samuel Waite Johnson, another engineer who possessed a fine aesthetic sense, had worked with David Joy on the drawings for *Jenny Lind* as a young apprentice. By 1870 Johnson was in charge of the Locomotive Department of the GER and he was beginning to show his ideas on locomotive appearance. He produced his first express engines with bogies, two 4-4-0s, and also some bogie tank engines of 0-4-4T design. These, which had side tanks and inside frames, were to be perpetuated by Johnson, and others, for years to come. But perhaps the most interesting of his designs for the GER speaking artistically, was the rebuilding of two of Sinclair's little 2-2-2 Singles as 4-2-2s. Sinclair's engine originally had many 'Crewe Type' features; Johnson gave them quite an elegant new look, and painted them a bright yellow — perhaps mindful of Stroudley's LBSCR golden ochre scheme.

Before his first 4-4-0 was in service on the GER Johnson moved to Derby to take over from Matthew Kirtley on the MR in 1873. Here he found wonderful scope for his powers and he continued with the MR for the next 30 years or so.

At the time of his arrival on the MR, a considerable effort was being made by that company to improve the passenger carriages (see Chapter 7), and consequently there was a need for more powerful engines to haul heavier trains. First of all he produced some 2-4-0s, but in 1876 he repeated the bogie 4-4-0 design he had introduced on the GER; first with 6ft 7in wheels and then a series of 7ft wheels, following with some more engines of the 2-4-0 type.

The true Johnson style is seen in all of these Derby engines, and in terms of constructional quality they ranked second to none, except possibly those of Stroudley. The Johnson engines were full of subtle flowing curves. Each part of the locomotive seemed to merge imperceptibly into the whole; there were no awkward corners or angles. The chimney was a masterpiece and the base met the radius of the smokebox so beautifully that it seemed to *grow out* of the engine, rather than to

have been placed upon it. The same can be said for the dome cover and the polished brass safety valve cover over the firebox (this had some similarity to the safety valve cover used by Patrick Stirling). A Johnson locomotive was a work of art, and when he decided to change the livery from the green of the Kirtley regime to a deep crimson lake, he added the crowning touch to his shapely designs.

Locomotive development in general was progressing steadily, with larger engines being requested to pull heavier trains. Cabs were becoming a feature of new designs, in place of the previous weatherboards and side sheets, although not all the cabs were particularly effective. C. Hamilton Ellis, in his book, *Twenty Locomotive Men*, says of the Johnson cab that it was: 'a pretty little thing, with beautiful curves, and roofs just long enough to send drips down the necks of the enginemen in wet weather'. But if this is a valid criticism of Johnson's cab design, those of Stroudley, Jones, the Drummonds, Stirling and many others, were by now noble affairs and very well thought out from the enginemen's viewpoint.

On the HR, with the departure of Stroudley to Brighton (and with Dugald Drummond soon following), David Jones took over responsibility. In 1873 he rebuilt one of the 'Crewe Type' 2-4-0 goods engines as a bogie engine, and in due course his first express engine design appeared; a 4-4-0 with 'Crewe Type' front end framing. But this design showed that Jones had learned a lot from Stroudley (and perhaps Drummond) and there were many 'Stroudleyesque' features to these distinctive engines; thereby producing a very interesting marriage of styles! Jones used a neat, roomy, cab design derived from Stroudley and in addition he placed a distinctive new style of chimney upon his engines. This had a double casing; the outer one being provided with louvres in front to increase the draught under certain running conditions.

Chimney design in general was becoming more and more attractive. We have seen the shapely chimneys which were the recognised hallmarks of a Stroudley, a Johnson, a Drummond or a Jones design. But there was an alternative convention which although very plain, nevertheless possessed a real dignity; I refer to the so-called 'stove-pipe'. This as its name implies, was utterly straightforward, with no embellishments such as copper, or other, type of cap; yet somehow it was ideally suited to some locomotives. Could a Stroudley engine, or a Johnson, have carried a stove-pipe? It seems sacrilegious to even suggest such an outrage! But William Adams put a stove-pipe on many classic designs, including his lovely series of 4-4-0s for the LSWR. When, at a later date, some of these had their Adams stove-pipe replaced by a Drummond-style chimney, some of their character was lost.

Stove-pipe chimneys had been a feature of Robert Sinclair's locomotives, and they were afterwards copied by Conner and Brittain on the CR and by Adams, Massey Bromley, T. W. Worsdell and Holden on the GER. Although Adams is best remembered for his stove-pipe design, his early locomotives for the North London Railway had a copper-capped chimney rather after the style of Beyer Peacock. When he moved to the GER (following Johnson's move to Derby) he stopped the change-over from stove-pipes to the Johnson style and reverted to stove-pipes for his own locomotive designs for that railway. In 1878 he moved again, this time to Nine Elms on the LSWR and the stove-pipe went with him. (Curiously, W. G. Beattie produced some engines for the LSWR, with stove-pipes, shortly before Adams succeeded him at Nine Elms).

There were, of course, railway companies and engineers who remained outwardly unmoved by the productions of the men so far discussed in this chapter. Of these the LNWR at Crewe Works comes most readily to mind. And here I will no doubt irritate devotees of that remarkable railway when I say that a Crewe engine paid scant respect to appearances! Don't misunderstand me — there were plenty of handsome engines produced at Crewe — but no money was spent on adornment. If Midland engines were glowing crimson lake; Brighton engines were golden ochre; Caledonian engines deep blue, those of the self-styled 'Premier Line' were black — by order of the General Manager. A Crewe design was thoroughly workmanlike, with very simple, robust construction. Things were bolted together, and one *saw* the bolts! No such nonsense was to be tolerated as copper-capped chimneys or smokebox wingplates; almost the sole concession to sentimentality was a neat brass nameplate on the splasher — but how that brasswork shone, and what lovely names they carried!

Another railway that followed very much its own course in locomotive design in the latter part of the 19th century was the GWR. Here we must pause briefly to pay a further tribute to Daniel Gooch. We encountered this remarkable young man in Chapter 1, when, just 'coming of age', he took responsibility for the locomotives of the GWR. He remained with the company, growing in stature as the years passed. He drove personally the locomotive used on the first train journey made by Queen Victoria; he had the intimate confidence of that great man,

I. K. Brunel; but above all he put the locomotive stock of the company into first class order.

When William Dean took command at Swindon (after a period when Joseph Armstrong held office) he continued to build express engines of Gooch type for the broad gauge. The writing was on the wall for the 7ft railway, but it took a long time for it to finally die. Meanwhile the locomotives were getting old, and replacements were needed. It was not economical to design new ones, so for the time being Dean was content to perpetuate Gooch's designs. However, Dean later realised the possibilities of building convertible engines (ie engines which would run as broad gauge types until the conversion of the gauge to 4ft 8½in, whereupon they would be capable of easy conversion to run on the narrower tracks). It would be true to say that some of these 'convertibles' were visually the most ungainly locomotives ever produced — but what a transformation occurred when they were converted! But this anticipates our story; we must first retrace our steps a few years.

By 1880 bogie locomotives were being produced in increasing numbers, although some engineers still did not favour them. A notable innovation of 1878 was the first Mogul (2-6-0 wheel arrangement), introduced by the GER to designs by Adams shortly before he left for the LSWR. The final design was modified in a number of details by his successor, Massey Bromley, and contained certain American features. Between 1880 and 1889 there was considerable pressure upon engineers to economise, and many experiments were tried to achieve this end, including the principle of compounding. In fact, Webb on the LNWR had converted a 2-2-2 to compounding in 1879, and by 1882 Crewe Works was producing three-cylinder compound engines. Four classes of express engine were built at Crewe from 1882-1890, known as the 'Experiment' (one engine only), 'Compound', 'Dreadnought' and 'Teutonic' classes, and there were also some compound tank engines. In appearance, Webb's compound experiments followed typical Crewe practice. In fact the tradition set by Webb for locomotive appearance was to remain with the LNWR for the rest of its separate existence.

In 1884 T. W. Worsdell introduced a compound 4-4-0 for the GER. This had a large continuous splasher over the two driving wheels, but the design of cab, boiler and details (including the stove-pipe chimney) showed considerable Adams influence. Worsdell moved from the GER to the NER, and in 1887 he produced a

series of compound 4-4-0s, in which considerably more of his own personality was apparent. The continuous splasher was retained, but now there was a handsome side-window cab and new boiler mountings, including a lovely polished brass safety valve casing, and a shapely chimney casting.

With the invention of steam sanding apparatus in 1886 there was a return to favour for the Single driver express passenger locomotive, although construction of 2-4-0 and 4-4-0 types was also continued. The steam sanding proved an effective answer to the wheel-slip problem which had bedevilled Single drivers when starting away with a train. A handsome Single was built in 1886 by Neilson & Co, and exhibited at an Edinburgh Exhibition, afterwards being purchased by the CR, with whom it became No 123. This had a number of obviously Drummond features (plus an Adams bogie) but it is in doubt just how much Drummond actually had to do with the overall design. No further engines of the class were built, but No 123 seems to have been a very popular engine, achieving some fame in the famous 'races to the North' in 1888, and today she is happily preserved in Glasgow Transport Museum. A fond memory I recall was to witness her travelling at well over a mile-a-minute, when hauling an enthusists' excursion some years ago. The big single driving wheel seemed to move the train effortlessly, with a special sort of grace.

S. W. Johnson produced a new series of Singles for the MR from 1887, of which there were several varieties, with 4-2-2 wheel arrangement and inside cylinders. These Midland Singles had superbly graceful lines. A new pattern of smokebox door made this feature flush with the boiler cleading plates, and a new chimney was used. This was a smooth casting, but retained the familiar Johnson lines of the old built-up pattern. It became the new standard Midland chimney. Brasswork, highly polished of course, was used to great effect by Johnson. Never overdone, it was applied to the splasher rims, axleboxes, whistles, number and safety valve casing. Few locomotives have rivalled these Midland Singles for sheer beauty of line and perfection of finish.

Johnson's series of bogie Singles culminated in the truly magnificent *Princess of Wales*, which appeared from Derby in 1899. Whilst she possessed the same classic outline as her predecessors, she was a massive engine, and as if to emphasise this Johnson placed a bogie eight-wheel tender behind her. The first of the class, No 2601 *Princess of Wales*, was exhibited at the Paris exhibition of 1900 (11 years earlier one of her smaller sisters had also been exhibited in Paris). No 2601 was the largest Single to run on a British railway.

Mention has already been made of Dean's 'convertibles'. Some of his 2-2-2 Singles began life as convertible engines, with the wheels outside both sets of frames. When converted to 4ft 8½in the wheels went between the double frames, in conventional Stephenson GWR style. History, it is claimed, repeats itself. Certainly this was so with the GWR 2-2-2s. Just as Gooch's *Great Western* had proved to be nose-end heavy and had eventually been rebuilt as a 4-2-2 following a derailment, so also did Dean's 2-2-2 design prove troublesome. One of the class, *Wigmore Castle*, broke her leading axle whilst hauling a train through Box Tunnel. As a result the class was rebuilt to bogie 4-2-2 arrangement, and the following 3031 class featured the same bogie. These were indeed 'ugly ducklings' transformed; many enthusiasts rated them second to none in terms of locomotive aesthetics.

The Dean bogie Singles were certainly an arresting sight, with glittering polished brass, copper and steel. The very large brass dome cover was kept in a highly polished state, and tradition has it that after it had been polished at the sheds, a sack was placed over it to keep it from sooty smuts. When the time came for the locomotive to 'back-down' from the sheds to the station to couple on to its train , the sack was removed to reveal a glittering brass dome which was guaranteed to impress the passengers!

An interesting comparison can be made between the Dean Singles and James Holden's 10 GER 4-2-2s which appeared in 1898. These were the first Holden engines to have a bogie. Hitherto he had built a series of smart little 2-2-2s and 2-4-0s, with quite pronounced Adams characteristics. But when he turned his attention to producing a Single, the Dean influence was unmistakable; so also was that of Johnson! These GER Singles were a strange mixture of styles, but nevertheless they had a certain elegance. The chimney, which was virtually pure Dean, was a departure from the stove-pipe Holden had perpetuated until then.

On the LNWR, Webb persisted with his efforts at compounding, despite the very mixed performances on the line. A larger eight-wheeled class appeared between 1891 and 1984, known as the 'Greater Britain' class, and one of these, the *Queen Empress*, was exhibited at the Chicago Exhibition of 1893. With a very long boiler, they had quite a racy aspect which their performance — alas — did not always live up to. Webb produced further compound designs, and amongst these, his 'Black Prince' class of 1897-1900, a bogie 4-4-0, was a smart,

well proportioned, design.

The period 1890-1900 saw the production of a whole series of classic 4-4-0 types; of these we can only single out a few for mention in this brief essay. Those of Adams for the LSWR had the longest bogie wheelbase in the country, 7ft 6in, and it was this feature which gave them an especially handsome outline.

There were two series, one with larger driving wheels, but basically very similar in appearance. The big sweep of the frames at the front end; the flowing curves of the splashers and the plain but dignified boiler mountings all added up to a finely balanced, harmonious ensemble; one of the all-time classics from the golden age of steam. Other handsome 4-4-0s were produced by Aspinall for the LYR and by Worsdell for the NER. On the Caledonian, J. F. McIntosh produced the first of his 'Dunalastair' class in 1896, in which the Drummond influence was most marked. He put a larger boiler on a basically Drummond engine, and later series of 'Dunalastairs' had progressively larger boilers still. These engines retained the simple, neat lines of Drummond and the NBR also produced some handsome 4-4-0s of Drummond inspiration.

Mention should also be made of the 4-4-0s designed by R. J. Billinton for the LBSCR, in which considerable Johnson influence was apparent. The first series, known as the 'Grasshoppers', comprised graceful, slender-looking engines, but were sadly under-boilered. The later B4 class remedied this defect whilst retaining much the same elegant aspect. Their Johnson-inspired curves were further enhanced by application of Stroudley's golden ochre livery.

Two further 4-4-0 designs of exceptional beauty must be mentioned. One was H. S. Wainwright's D class for the SECR, introduced in 1901. The other was *Claud Hamilton*, James Holden's masterpiece for the GER. Wainwright's design was set-off to perfection by great attention to appearance of both metalwork and livery. His livery was most elaborate and expensive to apply and there was a beautiful copper-capped chimney and polished brass dome. One of the class is preserved at York and to stand alongside this, even in the cold, quiet, museum atmosphere, is sufficient to recapture much of the singularly elegant quality of the design.

Holden's *Claud Hamilton* was No 1900 of the GER. The number was chosen to commemorate the year she was built, when she was shown at the Paris Exhibition, winning the Grand Prix for Holden. The lovely appearance of this engine, in her rich GER blue, with polished copper-capped chimney and

spacious side-window cab, captured many admirers.

These two 4-4-0 designs probably represent the finest examples of a period of British steam locomotive design which placed great emphasis upon external appearance, and upon superb detail. As such, they are the very epitome of 80 years' development in this country, and even by today's sophisticated standards they can be readily judged as fine examples of industrial design. At a time when public taste was still directed towards the picturesque and the fanciful, the British steam locomotive was supreme in establishing acceptable standards for pure machine art. When Holden's *Claud Hamilton* returned from Paris to take an active part in the day-to-day running of the GER, the noise of the motorcar was already making itself heard upon our roads — albeit, as yet, a novelty. Steam locomotives had developed to the degree that we can now consider them classics; motorcars were mere upstarts; but who could foresee the drastic developments of the next 20 years?

Around the turn of the century, there was already a noticeable trend towards still larger engines to pull heavier trains. The Single revival was quickly over (the last Single was built in 1901 to H. A. Ivatt's designs for the GNR) and the 2-4-0 was now considered somewhat undersized; no more were built after 1903. Development of larger engines of 4-4-2 and 4-6-0 types had begun. The 4-6-0 had been introduced to Britain by David Jones on the HR, back in 1894, for goods work. The 'Jones Goods', at it became known, was followed by a large passenger version, the 'Castle' class, introduced on the HR in 1900. The 'Castles' were completed by Peter Drummond, and had several typical Drummond features including the chimney and cab. How fascinating all these variations are, when examined in detail. For example, on these two 4-6-0 designs, both the Jones and the Drummond cabs had their common origins in Stroudley. Jones used his own louvred chimney; Drummond discarded this in favour of his design, which was closely akin to that of his elder brother. Jones used Stroudley style numberplates on the cab side, with raised numerals; Peter Drummond used brass numberplates with countersunk numerals — and so on. The important fact is that in 1900 the Stroudley influence still persisted in quite a large portion of British locomotive design.

This would seem an opportune moment to review the changes which were about to take place in locomotive aesthetics. We have seen, in such classics as the Johnson and Dean Singles, the Holden and Wainwright 4-4-0s, the final essays in late

Victorian, early Edwardian, industrial art. This could be summed-up as a nicely proportioned, well balanced machine, with great attention to detail and finish. Now the call was for bigger engines. The loading gauge was dictated by thousands of existing bridges and tunnels. Boilers could be larger, but engines could not be taller. There were also restrictions upon overall width, except on the former broad gauge lines. So by the early years of the 20th century locomotive engineers were already fully aware of the physical limitations on development they must face. If only Brunel's broad gauge had won acceptance! However, development of the bogie, and of flexible leading and trailing axle designs, permitted engines to be longer, even if they could not be made much wider or taller.

Two schools of thought were apparent in locomotive design in the first decade of the 20th century. Both schools accepted the need for larger locomotives of greater power, but the actual shape these should take was not so readily agreed. One school, which might be termed 'conventional' (without being in any way derogatory), followed the classic conventions of the 1890s producing what were virtually enlarged 4-4-0s, in the shape of 4-4-2s and 4-6-0s. The other school, which might be referred to as the 'modern' school, evolved a new aestheticism which broke away from existing conventions in many ways and which is examined in more detail in Chapter 11.

Early examples of the 'conventional' school of big engines were the two HR 4-6-0 designs already referred to. In addition to these 4-6-0s there was an express engine version produced for the NER by Wilson Worsdell in 1899/1900. But perhaps this period is better described as the era of the 4-4-2 Atlantic type. It was the Atlantic, an elongated 4-4-0 with an additional carrying axle under the firebox, that won so many hearts for its combination of graceful symmetry and increased power. The first 4-4-2s were by H. A. Ivatt for the GNR, and appeared in 1898, starting with the famous No 990 *Henry Oakley* (now preserved). These had somewhat small boilers for their size. The following year J. A. F. Aspinall produced his famous series of Atlantics for the LYR. Colloquially known as the 'Highfliers', they had inside cylinders, and were the largest and most powerful engines in Britain when new. They had very neat and simple lines, with a great impression of size, emphasised by the high pitch of the boiler and the big splashers housing the 7ft 3in driving wheels.

When Ivatt's *Henry Oakley* was placed in service is caused quite a sensation in that it was unlike any British locomotive then running. But perhaps the large-boilered version he produced in 1903 was even more striking, with a wide firebox giving the onlooker a sense of enormous capacity. Two years later, in 1905, the GNR Atlantic design was repeated with only minor differences on the LBSCR by D. E. Marsh, who had previously been chief assistant to H. A. Ivatt at Doncaster. What an amazing course of events Brighton had witnessed! First Stroudley's superb engines, then R. J. Billinton bringing some Johnson influence from Derby, now Marsh introducing Ivatt's Doncaster practices. In 1910 a further batch of Atlantics was produced by Marsh but completed by his successor, Lawson Billinton (son of R. J. Billinton) who slightly altered their appearance, in particular smoothing out the curves of the footplating; a distinct improvement.

Two other Atlantic designs of imposing appearance, and with many features in common, were the Robinson locomotives for the GCR and those ordered from the North British Locomotive Co for the NBR. The Robinson engines were built between 1903 and 1906, and many people consider them to be the most handsome engines of their time. They were massive, but beautifully proportioned, and the Robinson pattern of chimney casing was a veritable masterpiece. Except for the horizontal lines of the flange and lip, this chimney (as fitted to the Atlantics) did not have a straight line anywhere on its outer surface. How perfectly it matched the curves of the engine, which were subtle yet strong. Engine and tender were beautifully matched, and the tender was distinguished by curved solid coal guards. The NBR Atlantics were constructed between 1906-1911, and it seems that they were produced almost straight from Robinson's design. There is considerable similarity between the two, especially about the frames and running plate. The North British loading gauge was restricted in height, and they were forced to place a squat dome and chimney upon the big boiler of their Atlantics. This gave them an impression of being even larger than they really were.

In addition to his graceful 4-4-2s, Robinson produced a number of well proportioned engines for the GCR. Of these, we should mention the inside-cylinder 4-6-0 *Sir Sam Fay*, of 1912, and the huge inside-cylinder 4-4-0 'Director' class of 1913. All his designs bore a strong family likeness, and despite the fact that the last two mentioned had inside cylinders, all had a very modern look which resulted from their massive yet elegant dimensions.

On the GER S. D. Holden produced a 4-6-0 inside-cylinder design in 1911 which was visually an enlarged 'Claud Hamilton'. This had a most impressive side-window cab, with side sheets so long that a complete driving wheel splasher was included in them! It is perhaps worthwhile pointing out that at this time certain railways still persisted with cab designs dating from Victorian days, which did not have side windows — notably the LNWR, where Webb's design was continued unchanged — and the GNR.

On the CR, McIntosh continued to build still larger engines, having shown the way with his famous 'Dunalastair' series of 4-4-0s. These grew into 4-6-0s, with both passenger and goods versions. Through all his designs there ran the same Drummond inspired simplicity, and even his large 4-6-0 passenger engines (of which the best known and best loved was the fabulous *Cardean* of 1906) had the same classic treatment, and a feeling of poise and dignity despite their imposing size. At Crewe, George Whale had taken over from Webb in 1903. He was immediately faced with the unenviable task of operating the line with a locomotive stud comprising of, on the one hand, old and undersized but reliable designs, and on the other hand, larger and newer — but incompetent — Webb compounds. Whale set to work to produce a design for a new *simple* 4-4-0, and his well known 'Precursor' class appeared from Crewe just nine months after he took office. These went straight into mass production off the drawing board, and were very well received by the enginemen. Whale also designed a 4-6-0, the inside-cylindered 'Experiment' class, which was not so well received to begin with, but his successor, Bowen Cooke, improved the design without much alteration to appearance, in his 'Prince of Wales' class. He likewise produced a superheated version of Whale's 'Precursor' 4-4-0 which was known as the 'George the Fifth' class. This had a different driving wheel splasher design and a longer smokebox.

One company that resisted the trend towards bigger engines was the Midland; they never built a six-coupled express engine, or an Atlantic for that matter. But if Derby did not feel inclined to build larger than 4-4-0s, it did attempt to improve their design and performance, and compounding was one outcome of this. Although Webb's efforts at compounding on the LNWR must have made many engineers fight shy of the idea, a system developed by W. M. Smith on the NER had proved to be considerably more successful. Smith's system was adopted by S. W. Johnson on the MR in 1901-1903, for five three-cylinder 4-4-0s built at Derby. Johnson retired in 1904 and his successor was Richard Deeley, who had been his works manager. The following year Deeley brought out the first

67

67　Taken out of honoured retirement for the occasion, Patrick Stirling's masterpiece, GNR No 1 shows off its elegant lines, hauling a special train near Marshmoor on 30 June 1938.

of his modified version of the Smith/ Johnson compound, and this was a fine 'racey' looking machine with neat lines marred only by a rather clumsy chimney. Although Deeley also built some simple 4-4-0s of comparable size, the compounds — or 'Crimson Ramblers' as they became known — proved very successful. We shall encounter them again, in greater detail, in Chapter 11.

Briefly then we have examined some of the highlights of the 'conventional' school of early 20th century locomotive design. Inevitably many worthy examples have been left out, and we can only acknowledge in passing the contributions of Manson, Worsdell and many others who were also producing beautiful locomotive designs about this time.

Besides the significant contribution of Churchward on the GWR discussed in Chapter 11, there was the generally increasing use of superheating; of Belpaire fireboxes; outside cylinders and Walschaerts valve gear. On the GNR H. A. Ivatt had been succeeded by Nigel Gresley in 1911, and whilst Gresley was apparently happy to follow Doncaster practice in locomotive appearance to quite a considerable degree, he showed the way future developments would taken when he produced a class of mixed traffic 2-6-0s in 1912-1913. These had outside Walschaerts gear and most significantly, a high running plate over the driving wheels, so high that there were no splashers.

Finally, although we are primarily concerned with the development of express passenger engines in this essay, mention should be briefly made of a few of the fine designs for tank engines and goods engines which appeared in the first decade or so of the 20th century.

Tank engine designs had progressed to the point where they included types capable of hauling fast main line trains for distances up to about 80 miles. These were mostly six-coupled outside cylinder engines, but there were also 0-4-4T and 2-4-2T classes which were capable of a good turn of speed when required. The 2-4-2Ts of the LYR were used continuously on main line trains and there are accounts of some remarkable runs behind these sprightly engines. The 0-4-4T type was built by Dugald Drummond on the LSWR and Harry Wainwright on the SECR. Drummond's 0-4-4Ts, the M7 class, were built between 1897 and 1911 and were the standard design for LSWR suburban duties. The derivation from his earlier engines on the NBR/CR was quite obvious, but they were probably the best tank engines he produced. Some examples remained in service in the 1960s and they were still capable of putting up a good performance then. They were graceful engines with a good turn of speed.

Wainwright's 0-4-4T, the H class, was also intended for suburban work. They were very solid, sturdy engines with the same beautiful finish that Wainwright put on his big tender 4-4-0s. Built between 1904 and 1915, quite a number survived until the 1960s, virtually unaltered in appearance. My last memories of the class are of a few stationed at Three Bridges where they worked turn-and-turn-about with some Drummond M7s on the line to East Grinstead. The enginemen preferred the Wainwright design, incidentally.

A four-coupled tank engine design by Douglas Earle Marsh for the LBSCR deserve mention for both appearance and performance. Known officially as the I3 class, they had 4-4-2T wheel arrangement and inside cylinders and were built between 1907 and 1913. These were so successful that Marsh was prompted to produce an even larger tank engine for the Brighton company, and in 1910 there duly appeared No 325 Abergavenny. With a 4-6-2 wheel arrangement she was a singularly neat and handsome design; a

second engine No 326 Bessborough had the outside Walschaert's valve gear instead of inside Stephenson's gear, but was otherwise similar. To onlookers this pair must have seemed the ultimate word in tank engine design — surely they could not be enlarged upon yet further? But only three years later Brighton produced an even larger and more imposing design. This was by Lawson Billinton, who retained a good deal of the Marsh style. But the newcomer was really massive, and with a 4-6-4 wheel arrangement it ranked as a powerful express engine by any railway's standards. Only two of the class appeared by the end of 1914, but after World War I a further batch of examples (with some modifications) was produced in 1921-1922.

The design of goods locomotives took full advantage of the improvements made to passenger types. Larger boilers, six- and even eight-coupled wheels and greater flexibility of wheelbase, were the order of the day. We have already encountered the HR 'Jones Goods' and the CR McIntosh goods 4-6-0s. Other railways followed suit with similar bogie engines for fast goods work. The 0-6-0 and 0-8-0 were mostly favoured for slow, heavy, mineral trains and suchlike.

There was an interesting development in 1899-1900 when a batch of 80 American bar-framed 2-6-0 Moguls was imported, owing to the fact that British builders were so overwhelmed with work that they could not accept more orders. The MR had 40; the GNR 20; and the GCR 20. They were typically American in design (such as were used on light railways in the United States and elsewhere in the world), and very simple in layout. The few concessions to British practice included the design of boiler mountings, which varied according to which railway they were delivered. They do not seem to have been popular with our railwaymen, and none lasted more than 15 or so years (compared with the great age attained by many contemporary British goods engines, this was very short).

The 2-8-0 goods type made its debut in 1903 when Churchward produced a design for the GWR. Robinson on the GCR and Gresley on the GNR followed suit with designs in 1911 and 1913 respectively. The Robinson design, which had the solid, robust qualities combined with a handsome outline which was typical of his engines, was adopted for war work, and 521 engines were built for the ROD (Railway Operating Department of the War Office) for overseas military service. What more fitting conclusion to the present chapter than this? A classic British steam locomotive shipped overseas to aid the war effort — this was no ugly weapon of war!

68 A close-up of the 8ft driving wheel of Patrick Stirling's classic single-wheeler of 1870, built at Doncaster. Now preserved by the National Railway Museum.

69 Stroudley's tank engines were every bit as elegant in design and finish as his passenger tender engines. Illustrated is No 239 *Patcham*, of Class D1.

70 The superb 0-4-2 passenger engines designed by Stroudley had few rivals for quality of workmanship and finish in their day. Class B No 215 *Salisbury* is posed in the shed yard at Brighton; in spotless condition.

71 Drummond 4-4-0 No 17 of the CR. This superb photograph clearly shows the neatness and simplicity of design, which characterised both Stroudley and Drummond locomotives. The driver, Mr Soutar, was something of a popular hero of his day.

72 Drummond 4-4-0 No 79, *Carbrook*, posed outside Carlisle Citadel station. A study in sheer artistry.

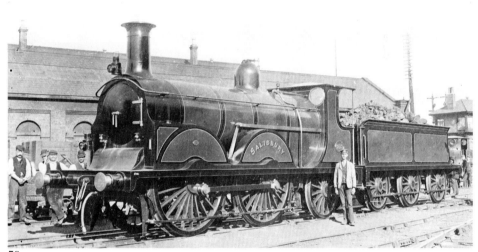

69

71

70

72

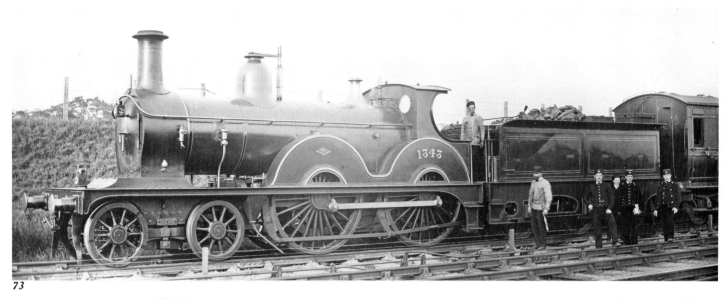

73

74

75

76

73 The classic Johnson style is well shown in this photograph of 4-4-0 No 1343 of the MR.

74 David Jones rebuilt a 'Crewe Type' 2-4-0 as a bogie engine, No 7 of the HR.

75 Broad gauge 4-2-2, *Inkermann*, final version of the original Gooch design, by Dean.

76 Dean produced some convertible engines; illustrated is 2-2-2 No 3026.

77 Webb compound No 315 *Alaska*; LNWR, 1884.

78 T. W. Worsdell's compound 4-4-0 No 779 of the NER, photographed at Edinburgh Waverley. A spacious cab, and single continuous splasher were features of this elegant design.

77

78

79 Perhaps the most graceful of all S. W. Johnson's designs were his single-wheelers. No 1863 very clearly illustrates the subtle flowing lines which were a hallmark of his engines.

80 An 'ugly duckling' transformed. Dean's 4-2-2 *Wigmore Castle*, GWR No 3021. Note the huge polished brass dome cover.

81 There was considerable family resemblance between the Holden GER 2-4-0s and their 0-4-2 counterparts by Adams, for the LSWR. Illustrated is GER No 486.

82 Perhaps the most graceful of Webb's compound designs for the LNWR was his 'Greater Britain' class. Illustrated is No 2054 *Queen Empress*, which was exhibited at Chicago in 1893. She is seen here in special white and purple livery to commemorate Queen Victoria's Jubilee.

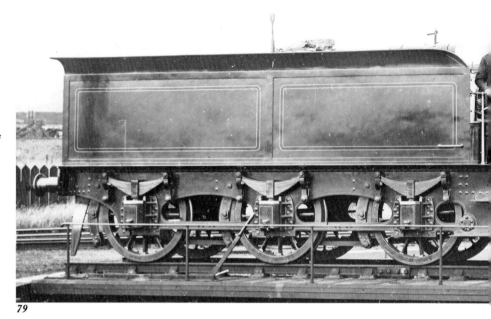

79

80

82

81

83

83 Adams produced two series of classic 4-4-0s for the LSWR, this is No 563, seen on shed at Nine Elms after preservation by the SR. The plain stovepipe chimney suited these engines admirably.

84 Considerable Drummond influence can be seen in the design of the NBR 4-4-0 No 258 *Glen Roy.*

85 R. J. Billinton brought some Derby influence to Brighton. His 4-4-0 designs were graceful engines and must have looked well in Stroudley's orchre livery. Illustrated is No 316 *Goldsmid* of the first small-boilered type.

84

85

86

87

88

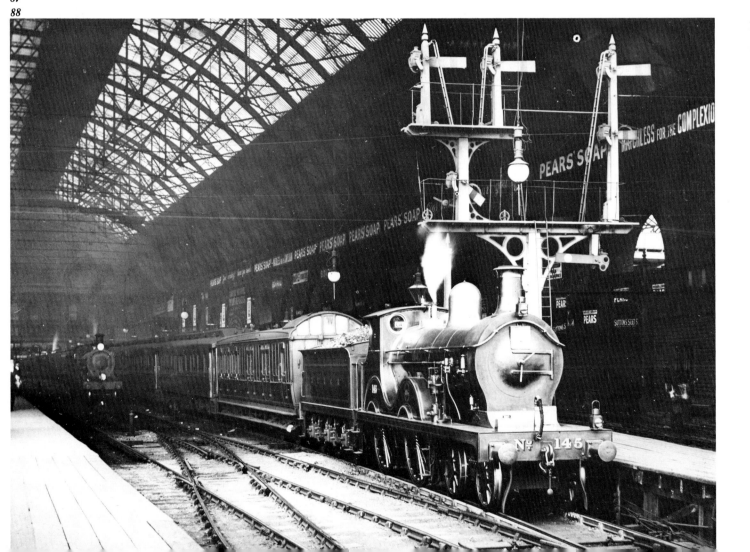

86 Larger-boilered Billinton 4-4-0 No 51 *Wolferton*; immaculate in the LBSCR golden ochre livery.

87 HR 'Jones Goods' 4-6-0, introduced in 1894. An example is preserved at Glasgow.

88 H. S. Wainwright's beautiful D class 4-4-0 for the SECR, 1901. No 145 is seen standing in Cannon Street station about 1908, with the 'Folkestone Car Train'.

89

89   The first British Atlantic design by H. A.
Ivatt, for the GNR, 1898. No 990 (later named
Henry Oakley) is now preserved by the
National Railway Museum.

90   Most graceful of all the Atlantics were
those produced by Robinson for the GCR.
No 265 is seen in all the splendour of the GCR
livery complete with two coats of arms, one on
each splasher, on the engine, plus another on
the tender.

91   LYR 4-4-0 No 1228, designed by Aspinall
and built at Horwich, displays its elegance in

this broadside picture. The flowing line of
the brass beading to the driving wheel
splasher is a particularly attractive feature.

92   The NBR Atlantics had many features in
common with the Robinson engines, although
the squat chimney altered their outline
considerably. No 868 *Aberdonian* was
photographed in matt livery, prior to
varnishing just after completion. This was to
enable photographs to be taken without the
problems caused by shiny reflections.

93   Holden's 4-6-0 and 4-4-0 designs for the

GER. Note the large cab which encloses the
rear driving wheel splasher on the 4-6-0
(second engine) and the general similarity in
style of the two classes. 'Claud Hamilton'
class 4-4-0 No 1507 is seen piloting 4-6-0
No 1812 on an up Cromer express at Gidea
Park.

94   The famous CR inside-cylinder 4-6-0
design by McIntosh; the Drummond style
carried through successfully to a large
passenger engine. Illustrated is No 904. Note
the large bogie tender.

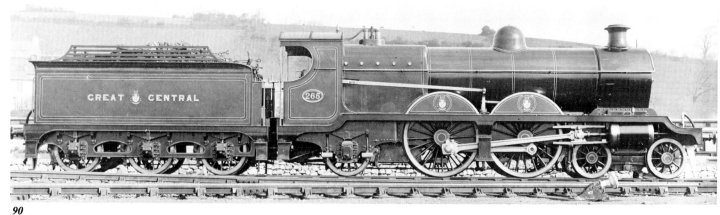

90

91

92

93
94

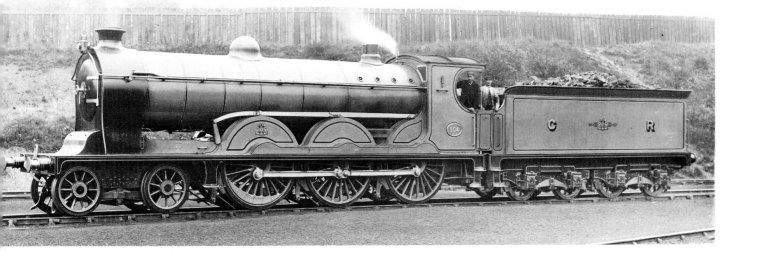

95

96

97

95　MR Compound 4-4-0 No 1012 at
St Pancras station, on a train of clerestory
roofed coaches. The great span of Barlow's
roof makes an eerie setting to the scene on a
misty day.

96　The LYR possessed a fleet of sturdy
2-4-2Ts which were capable of express
passenger performances. They had neat,
simple outlines with nicely balanced
proportions. Illustrated is No 740.

97　One of the most attractive tank engine
designs must surely have been the Adams
4-4-2Ts for the LSWR. A survivor still
operates on the Bluebell Railway. No 49
displays the classic Adams style with plain
stovepipe chimney.

98　Baltic tank engine by Lawson Billinton for
the LBSCR. The LBSCR 1914-18 war
memorial engine *Remembrance*, pictured in
early SR livery at Redhill.

99　Churchward's 2-8-0 design GWR.
Churchward was mainly responsible for the
'modern' style of locomotive appearance on
British railways; as discussed further in
Chapter 11.

100　Robinson 2-8-0 design for the GCR was
adopted by the War Department. Illustrated is
one operated by the GWR as its No 3014.

98

99

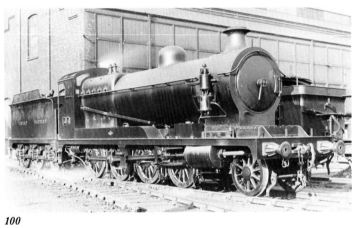

100

7 Sumptuous Carriages

In Chapter 2 we left the railway passenger feeling rather sorry for himself. Despite some advances in construction, the facilities for comfortable travel were lagging sadly behind the mechanical progress in steam locomotion. True, carriages were longer, wider and slightly higher than those current in the 1850s. But in terms of amenity the second and third class passengers had a raw deal. However, in the period covered in this chapter (1870-1914), railway carriage design underwent marked improvement, and transformation from a still primitive conveyance to an elegant room on wheels.

It was the Midland Railway, in the early 1870s, that took the initiative in improving travelling conditions. The Midland's General Manager, James Allport, visited America in 1872 and following this some American-style Pullman cars were imported and introduced to British travellers. Despite their superior construction and better riding qualities — not to mention their ornate and lavish comfort — the all-Pullman trains introduced on the Midland did not come up to Allport's expectations, and the complete Pullman trains were disbanded, the cars being used on ordinary trains, together with conventional British stock. Nevertheless they became a status symbol of luxury which has remained synonymous with the name of Pullman in this country to the present day. A supplementary fare was charged for the privilege of travelling by Pullman car.

More significant than the introduction of the Pullman to Britain, was Allport's decision to abolish second class travel on his railway, and to give third class passengers a comfortable compartment to ride in, with upholstered padded seats and better lighting and ventilation. Naturally this move, acknowledging as it did the changed social conditions arising from mid-Victorian industrial prosperity and greater freedom of travel, was considered revolutionary. Although other companies were more or less forced to follow suit, they remained obstinate in retaining second class accommodation, whilst

making third class travel gradually more tolerable.

The 1870s witnessed a move away from rigid wheelbase four- and six-wheeled stock, towards eight- and even 12-wheelers. Some eight-wheelers had rigid wheelbases, some had a degree of flexibility on the outer axles, and some possessed bogies proper. These latter included the American Pullman cars. The 12-wheeled bogie carriage was pioneered by the MR and when these appeared they were the longest ordinary passenger carriages in the country, measuring 54ft long over body ends. The Pullman cars were also exceptionally large for their period. Six-wheelers were of course commonplace on trains of the 1870s and pot-oil lamps still provided illumination. Trains were frequently composed of a mixture of carriages, with different lengths and wheel arrangements; some possessing bogies, some not. The bogie allowed greater length of carriage to be safely carried around curves, consequently trains tended to be longer and heavier, making it necessary to produce more powerful locomotives (see previous chapter).

In addition to greater length, the height of carriages was gradually increased. At first this was only by a modest 12in or so, along the centre line of the roof; this was achieved by making the roof an arc-shape. This became possible when luggage was no longer conveyed on the rooftop (a somewhat dangerous practice with hazards such as fire or high winds), and separate luggage compartments, or vans, were provided. The guard also no longer travelled precariously on the rooftop; instead he was positioned in an enclosed elevated 'birdcage' compartment, where he could see over the top of the train. As carriages became yet higher, this 'birdcage' was not always possible within the loading gauge, and an alternative look-out was provided by means of ducket side-windows to the guard's compartment, which was situated within the carriage.

The clerestory roof, (which we have already encountered in Chapter 2, on the

GWR 'Posting Carriages'), now reappeared on the GWR and MR (also on the American-built Pullmans). Besides giving additional headroom, the clerestory provided better natural lighting and ventilation. A drawback was the illumination at night. An oil lamp suspended within the raised clerestory tended to cast heavy shadows to each side of the compartment interior. After a while, the MR Carriage Superintendent reverted to arc-roofs, but on the GWR, Dean continued the clerestory. A third and more widespread revival of the clerestory roof was to occur in the 1890s; as we shall see presently.

The year 1879 saw the introduction of the first British dining car. Until that date passengers had perforce either to carry their own refreshment in hampers (which could be quite a lavish meal), or else join the throng clamouring to be served during a special stop at one of the station refreshment rooms *en route*. Many stories exist of the profiteering refreshment room managers who purposely produced their beverage or soup so scalding-hot that the luckless passenger could only sip a mouthful or so before the whistle blew, to summon them back to the departing train. Needless to say the remainder of the liquid was duly resold to the next trainload!

At first, dining or refreshment cars were the preserve of the first class passenger. The cars did not possess gangways at each end and it was not yet possible to 'stretch one's legs' and head for the diner whenever the fancy occurred. Either you travelled the whole way in the restaurant car, or else changed carriages at a stop *en route*. The first dining car was, in fact, a Pullman, the *Prince of Wales*, which was specially rebuilt with a kitchen. Later the GNR (who operated it) purchased it outright and placed it in ordinary stock.

Sleeping cars of varied concept began to make their appearance, and to begin with the designers seem to have been very uncertain what form they should take. The first proper sleeping carriage was introduced on the NBR in 1873, and by 1877 other examples were to be found in use. The most popular early version seems to have been the American Pullman saloon layout, with curtains offering a degree of privacy to each berth. These required passengers to undress whilst on the bed — a complicated manoeuvre for Victorian ladies complete with bustled skirt and tight corsets! The British public, at least those of the wealthier class who could afford to pay for the privacy of a bed on the train, took even more kindly to the idea of having separate compartments to sleep in, linked by a side-corridor. In 1881 the GWR produced this arrangement in a broad gauge sleeping car which had six two-berth compartments, no fewer than three lavatories, plus a pantry. This carriage was a 'convertible', with narrow body running on broad gauge wheels, to facilitate ease of changeover to the 4ft 8½in system in due course.

Mention should be made here of the improvements made in lighting, heating and brakes for passenger carriages. The Pullman cars had very effective double kerosene lamps with Argand burners (but these were a decided fire risk in a wooden-bodied carriage). They also had oil-fired hot-water heating, a remarkable advance in comfort at a time when the British passenger still froze in cold weather despite his footwarming aids. Lighting on certain railways had changed from the poor pot-oil lamps to coal gas, or compressed oil gas, usually carried in cylinders under the carriage. The compressed oil gas was superior to most systems and it was widely used by British railway companies for many years. A serious disadvantage of gaslighting was the grave fire risk in the event of an accident.

Reverting for a moment to the subject of carriage heating; the footwarmer had been 'improved' by substituting soda-acetate crystals for the use of hot water. The sealed canister of crystals was heated in a mobile vat, and retained the heat for a number of hours. This improvement was first made by the LNWR, and subsequently adopted elsewhere.

A notable experiment of 1881 was the application of electric lighting to a Pullman car. This was by means of underfloor batteries (Fauré cells) supplying 12 Edison bulbs. Despite their pioneer nature the arrangements worked sufficiently well to encourage William Stroudley to equip four more Pullman cars. Stroudley disliked the heavy battery equipment and replaced this with a generator, driven by an axle, situated in a guard's van, with an accumulator to light the train when stationary. Some 20 or more Brighton trains were equipped with the system as a result of these experiments.

A most important advantage of electric lighting was that it could be turned on or off as required. This at least solved the problem of passing through tunnels during daylight hours. Prior to this such hazards were often negotiated in pitch darkness, and both robbery and murder had been committed with the aid of these temporary black-outs. But many years were to pass before electricity replaced gaslighting for British railway carriages. The Pullman company were keen on electric lighting, but until the mid-1890s their new cars retained alternative means of light in case of failure.

Brakes for passenger trains were the subject of considerable debate. There was much interest in providing continuous brakes, following a number of serious accidents, but it was not clear what form these should take. One method utilised chains; but more sophisticated systems using either a vacuum, or compressed air were soon sought after, as the chains were both cumbersome and difficult to apply smoothly. A series of brake trials took place on the Newark to Nottingham line of the MR in 1875, with various railway companies competing; these trials involved automatic air-brakes, hydraulic brakes, vacuum brakes and chain brakes. The results favoured the Westinghouse system of air brake, but despite this, many companies chose to go their own way and both vacuum and air brakes were developed. (Could they but have foreseen the events of the 1960s when British Railways were faced with the reversion to air brakes despite a fairly recent decision to standardise upon the vacuum brake!)

An aspect of braking, dear to the passenger's heart was the emergency communication. A cord system between driver and guard had been recommended by a Select Committee of the House of Commons in 1853, but although this was widely adopted the cord was not supposed to be accessible to the passengers. By 1865 recommendations were made to allow passengers access to the cord, and in 1868 under a Regulation of Railways Act, railway companies were obliged to provide an efficient means of passenger alarm communication on all trains making non-stop runs of 20 miles or more. This usually followed the principle of an outside cord, accessible to passengers through the droplights, and connected either to the engine whistle or to a gong mounted on the side of the tender. Upon hearing the alarm sounded, the driver applied the brakes. In 1890 the first move was made towards allowing the passenger to have direct access to the brakes. Approval followed in 1893, and in due course the familiar system of a chain running inside a pipe, with the pipe placed inside the carriage, appeared. Pulling the chain (on dire penalty of a fine for improper use)

began applying the brakes on the train. And so it remains today!

Before passing on to what might justifiably be called the 'sumptuous phase' of British passenger carriage design, I would like to mention the external styling of carriages. British carriages followed pretty rigid conventions, stemming (as we have seen in Chapter 2) from road coachbuilding practices. A number of divisions characterised the side of a wooden bodied railway carriage, above and below the waistline. Below the waist, the panelling was usually plain (later some matchboard sides were produced, including Pullman cars); above the waist the side was as a rule subdivided into three 'quarters' — waist-quarter, window-quarter and top-quarter. The waist-quarter panels were horizontal in emphasis and ran along under the windows. These were topped by the windows and adjacent upright panels, above them came the top-quarter panels which were also horizontal and perhaps included ventilator louvres. The actual shape of the panels varied. Some had very rounded corners, others were rectangular with straight mouldings. These conventions in coachbuilding were to remain virtually unchanged until the coming of steel panelled carriages. The typical British carriage still had hinged doors to each compartment. A carriage produced by the GNR in 1881 broke away from the existing non-corridor compartment layout and provided a side corridor to each compartment. As such, this (and the similar arrangement on a GWR sleeping car, already mentioned) represented the prototype of countless hundreds of carriages built since with this interior layout. As yet there were no gangways between carriages, but toilet facilities were accessible to passengers within the carriage.

The typical Victorian lavatory carriage, prior to the provision of gangways, remained a non-corridor compartment style vehicle with a lavatory accessible only from immediately adjacent compartments.

It was not until 1891 that the through-corridor train made its appearance, with gangway bellows between carriages. The GWR produced a complete train of gangwayed side corridor carriages, and concurrently the GER provided a dining car train with gangways. Perhaps more important still, the GER train allowed meals to be served to second and third class passengers. Before long other railways followed suit, with first and third class diners (by now the second class, long abolished by the MR, was beginning to die out elsewhere). As yet gangwayed corridor trains were by no means universally approved of — the British it seems do not readily alter their habits even when greater comfort is offered — and in some cases only the dining cars were interconnected, with the remainder of the train still composed of non-corridor stock.

Mention of dining cars brings us to what I have already suggested should be described as the 'sumptuous' phase. (C. Hamilton Ellis also favours this descriptive term, in his book *British Railway History*). Sumptuous it indeed was! The late Victorian railway carriage, especially the dining vehicle, had a lavish interior, with rich plush furnishings. To give some idea, take these two contemporary descriptions: the first dated 1897, the second 1899.

From *The Sketch*, 11 August 1897:

'The Midland Railway's new dining-car express trains to Bristol and Bradford are very handsome. The third-class cars have interior fittings of richly coloured and figured mahogany. The seats are upholstered with figured crimson or blue moquette, and shaped so as to give passengers not only a convenient seat while dining, but facility for a comfortable nap after dinner. The roof is panelled with Lincrusta-Walton painted white. The two dining-saloons are connected by the "kitchen carriage", a vehicle containing a large kitchen, of adequate size to provide for the dining of 15 first class and 47 third class passengers. This kitchen is fitted up with all modern appliances for the preserving and well-cooking of every kind of food required, and attached thereto are a conductor's pantry and stores. In the remainder of the new train the first and third class compartments are all constructed in the same superior style, decorated with photographs and mirrors. Ample lavatory accommodation is provided throughout the train.'

The second description comes from the *Illustrated London News*, 8 July 1899:

'New Midland Corridor Train
'The Midland is again making sweeping changes in the class of carriage which has done duty between St Pancras and the north. It has just placed on the road four new trains composed of corridor coaches of the latest type, replete with every comfort, artistic in design, and furnished throughout in the most liberal and ornate manner. The first of these trains leaves St Pancras for Edinburgh at 10.35am, the afternoon 2.10 express running direct from London to Glasgow. The trains from the North leave Edinburgh at 10.5am and Glasgow 1.30pm respectively. Judged from the exterior, the new stock resembles very much the type of carriage which the company are now running on their most

important trains. For some time the shops at Derby have been turning out coaches with raised roofs, which give the carriages an imposing look, and provide more air space than was formerly to be obtained in a compartment built on the old plan. The new corridor carriages are built on two different plans. Those intended for dining purposes have the passage through the centre; in the others the corridor runs down the side. The first class corridor-carriage is divided into compartments holding four persons, two on each side; while the third class is so arranged that six people may be easily accommodated. The interior furnishings for both are all that artistic skill can accomplish. The first is tastefully trimmed with blue cloth with walnut gold lining, and gilded Lincrusta-Walton ceiling. The upholstery of the third is none the less comfortable. The first class dining-coaches have the seats upholstered in red morocco or buffalo hide, and so arranged that they can be pulled forward to make them take the form of a lounge-chair. The new stock has been built in the company's works, under the supervision of Mr Clayton, ably assisted by Mr T. P. Osborne.'

This latter description mentions 'raised roofs', these were of course the clerestory design which came back into vogue, especially on dining cars, in the 1890s. Gas lighting, in huge pendants (of highly polished brass in many instances) allowed the interior to be better illuminated when a clerestory was used, as the pendant hung low enough for the light to reach all corners of the interior. The clerestory was aesthetically a singularly handsome addition to both the interior and exterior of a railway carriage. It somehow bestowed great dignity upon the whole design, and at its peak, it was a thing of coloured or etched glass and polished brass fittings. The row of small glass panels and ventilators did present a problem to carriage cleaners, however, and this was a factor against the design. On the other hand, the clerestory brought better ventilation and natural lighting to the carriage interior. Pullman cars had traditionally been associated with clerestory roofs, but in due course it disappeared from these, as well as ordinary carriages.

As in the case of train brakes, the actual design of gangway connection and coupling was the subject of some difference of opinion. The Pullman company introduced some new cars on the Brighton line in 1888, built in America and assembled at Derby. They had enclosed end vestibules (in place of the open verandah of earlier Pullmans) and a flexible gangway of spacious design between the coaches. The Pullman

gangway was wide, and it simply butted together with its neighbour. There was a buckeye coupler (automatic) which held the carriages firmly together. The GNR adopted this design, using side buffers as well, so that their carriages were capable of being coupled to other stock by the simple expedient of a hinged buckeye coupling, which was dropped to reveal a conventional hook.

The more favoured design of gangway connection was a smaller, lengthy concertina (bellows) type which was joined to its neighbour. Couplings remained the screw-type, first introduced on the L&MR, and long side buffers were fitted. Some 60 years were destined to pass before British Railways finally standardised on the infinitely superior (and safer) Pullman gangway and buckeye coupling.

The American-designed Pullman cars had been highly decorated, ornately furnished vehicles right from the start. They had introduced a new and glittering note to the British railway traveller, with their elaborate gilt work, velvet cloth, walnut panelling and flower-patterned ceilings. They must have startled a good many sober British eyes upon first acquaintance, but there is no doubt of the influence the Pullman car had upon the trend in British carriage design in the last decade of the 19th century. The highly-decorated carriage became a matter of some prestige. By 1899/1900 the major railway companies were producing some remarkable feats of artistic coachbuilding, with elaborate interiors filled with choice Victoriana. Fine woods such as mahogany and oak were chosen for walls and partitions, with delicate gilt inlay. For upholstery, leather and plush velvet in rich reds, purples, greens and blues might be used, or moquettes in similarly bold colours. Ceilings were usually finished with Lincrusta-Walton relief mouldings which would be painted white, or a pastel shade, and then picked out in gilt. Some very elaborate designs appeared for these ceilings and, particularly when used in conjunction with a clerestory roof, they became a truly magnificent feature. Windows, other than the main side windows, often had elaborately etched designs and some coloured glass was used. Glass in doors through partitions and in lavatory windows was emblazoned with the company's heraldry, in etched manner. All the small interior fittings — such as luggage rack brackets, light pendants, handles and door knobs — were in highly polished brass with intertwining floral patterns and forms. *Art Nouveau* influence was detectable in some of these smaller fittings, particularly the lamp-brackets and shades, but as a whole *Art Nouveau* did not greatly penetrate the

101

101 **American coachbuilding practice comes to Britain, with a style and elegance all its own. Pullman car No 8, of the MR, was constructed in 1876.**

British railway carriage designers' conventions.

From about 1900 onwards there was a general trend towards bogie carriages for main line stock, but it should be pointed out that at that time, these were still a minority; the vastly inferior compartment six-wheeler was still a commonplace of rail travel. The clerestory once again began to lose favour; one reason was the cleaning difficulties it presented, already mentioned, another reason was that it was undoubtedly more expensive to construct. Wood was still the principal material for coachbuilding, but steel was introduced for underframes and headstocks and was gradually used for other items. J. Stone produced a belt-driven dynamo and battery system for lighting carriages with electricty which was to become very widely used in due course, but for the present there was still divided opinion over the relative merits of electricity versus gaslighting and many new carriages were gaslit. Train heating in late Victorian years still depended very much upon foot-warmers and even the sumptuous vehicles just described retained this primitive device. After a number of different experiments a system of carriage heating using steam piped through the carriages from the locomotive was satisfactorily established. In 1905 the GWR placed in service the largest railway carriages ever built for a British railway, measuring approximately 70ft in length and 9ft 6in in width, with a high elliptical roof. These quickly gained the nickname *Dreadnoughts* (after a contemporary design of battleship). They had end vestibules and a side corridor arrangement that changed from one side of the carriage to the other, via a centre vestibule. The compartments were accessible only from

the corridor; they did not have doors opening directly on to the platform. This layout was probably in advance of its time and it must have raised some protests from passengers, because the GWR afterwards reverted to the door-to-each-compartment layout for its corridor carriages for the next 30 years or so.

Two years after the appearance of the 'Dreadnoughts' the LNWR produced a very handsome end vestibuled side corridor design for its 'American' boat train between Liverpool and London. Some additional vehicles were also used on the Anglo-Scottish service. These fine vehicles were exceptionally comfortable and vied with the Pullmans used by some other railways. The LNWR had not shown much interest in the Pullman car but these 'American' boat train carriages suggest that they were fully aware of the prestige value of superior design and comfort.

The high elliptical roof found increasing favour because it allowed maximum use of the loading gauge, and gave more headroom to the sides of the carriage. Nigel Gresley employed it on new stock for the GNR from 1906, and there were some very high roofed carriages (known as 'Balloon Roofs') on the LBSCR. Some railways preferred a lower, flattened elliptical design; only the MR was still building clerestories by 1914, for main line stock.

The Edwardian era witnessed something of a reaction against the elaborate carriage interiors of late Victorian years. The trend was towards quieter furnishing (with springs replacing buttoned-in seats) and with far less moulding and panelwork. Ceilings were much plainer (emphasised by the high elliptical shape) and the few elaborate touches that did remain, on luggage racks and lamp fittings, etc, seemed rather self-conscious. The passing of the clerestory must be mourned on artistic grounds, for it was replaced by a far less attractive alternative.

By the year 1914 the British main line carriage had reached the dimensions it was to retain for the next 60 years or more, and the pattern was set for lighting, heating and layout.

Finally, we must turn our attention to the suburban and branch line trains; always they seem rather looked upon as the poorer relatives of the main line express.

Suburban carriages up to 1900 were still of basically mid-Victorian design, with four or six wheels, and often closely coupled into sets without corridors or gangways. From this date bogie carriages began to supersede them but new four- and six-wheeled stock remained in service for many more years on some routes. The bogie carriages were of non-corridor compartment type but some had lavatories accessible to compartments within the carriage. The carriages were coupled into sets as had previously been the case, and a logical development took place in 1911 when Gresley produced some articulated suburban train sets, in which adjacent carriages shared a common bogie placed between them. Comfort for suburban travellers remained decidedly stodgy by comparison with the artistic flights of late Victorian main line stock.

A new factor made itself increasingly felt in late Victorian days, causing not a little anxiety to the railways: the development of electric traction. The introduction of electrified City railways (such as the underground City & South London: Waterloo & City, and Central London Railways, and the overhead Liverpool line) had demonstrated the successful replacement of steam power by electricity for intensive suburban working. But this was not all; electric traction had taken to the roads. The electric tram routes spread fanwise from the hearts of our cities; the railway companies were faced with severe competition for their suburban services. Between 1900 and 1910 the tramcars sapped the railways' traffic to an enormous extent, much of it never to be recovered. Trams became a menace which forced the railways to rethink their suburban train service and design. Their answer — Electrification! Already the City railways had been converting to electricity, but partly because of the extreme unpleasantness of steam-worked trains underground. Now the railway companies began to electrify surface lines on suburban routes. The LYR electrified its first line in 1904 and the North Eastern was converting its Tyneside (North) routes the same year. In 1909 the LBSCR began electrifying suburban lines in London and, at the end of our present period, the LNWR had begun work on electrification on its London suburban routes.

Design of the electric suburban trains showed that the railways were willing to learn from the severe lesson of the tramcar. The interiors had a good deal in common with their road-borne counterparts, except on the LBSCR, where the conventional compartment-type carriage was retained, although some had an internal side passageway within the carriage (a rather quaint arrangement). The side passageway variety were confined to the south London line because they were somewhat wider than normal LBSCR stock.

These early electric trains, operated as multiple units, were to prove very successful although they did not by any means detract from the success of the tramcar. Another idea for improving the economics and appeal of lightly loaded services, was the steam 'rail-motor'. This consisted of a very small tank engine with a coach body attached to it. Many varieties appeared, and for the record I append a list of those in service in 1913:

Unfortunately 'rail-motors' were not an unqualified success because of their limited capacity and power. If they built up traffic to the extent that a trailer could be required they were not always powerful enough to haul the extra load. Nevertheless they are an interesting example of Edwardian awareness of growing competition from the roads. The very term 'rail-motor' perhaps chosen unconsciously, reminds us that the motorcar was already on the scene, although as yet something of an expensive novelty. The railways still had a virtual monopoly of passenger business over routes of more than 30 miles or so. They had been brought to harsh reality by the electric tram regarding their suburban services — but no one could have foreseen the incredible mechanical progress that would be made both on the roads and in the skies during the terrible years of war that lay ahead. In August, 1914, the British steam railway reigned supreme, and its passenger carriages presented a

civilised means of transport. Very shortly they would be pressed into service to assist in retaining that civilisation. Picnic saloons became hospital trains, with emergency operating theatres. But let us close this chapter with the happier vision of the tremendous progress in carriage design achieved between 1870 and 1914 — the golden age of steam railways.

102 Engraving of the interior of a MR Pullman Parlour car, with sumptuous furnishings and great sense of space and light, emphasised by the tall windows and raised clerestory roof.

103 The new deal for third class passengers. MR 1875 third class compartment, with stuffed seats and improved lighting and ventilation. (From a mock up in the National Railway Museum.)

102
107

103

Rail-Motor Cars on British Railways
Based upon the Annual Reports for 1913, and other sources of information

	Steam	Petrol	Petrol-electric
Alexandra Newport & South Wales	1		
Barry	2		
Belfast & County Down	3		
Caledonian		1	
Cardiff	2		
Freshwater Yarmouth & Newport		1	
Furness	1		
Glasgow & South Western	3		
Great Central	3		1
Great Northern	6		
Great Western	99		1
Kent & East Sussex	1		
Lancashire & Yorkshire	17		
London & North Western	7		
London & South Western	24		
London & South Western share of joint stock	2		
London Brighton & South Coast	2		
London Brighton & South Coast share of joint stock	1		
Midland Great Western		1	
North Eastern		5	
North Staffordshire	3		
Northern Counties Committee	2		
Port Talbot	1		
Rhymney	1		
South Eastern & Chatham	8		
Taff Vale	16		
	205	8	2

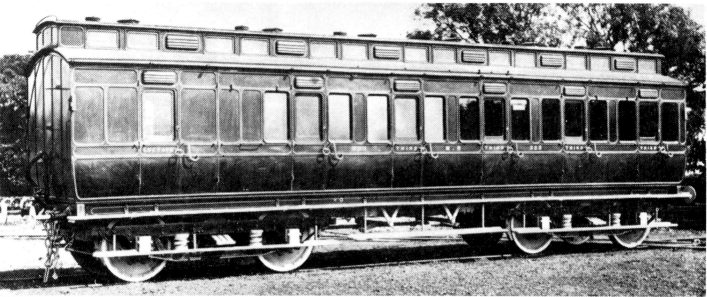

104

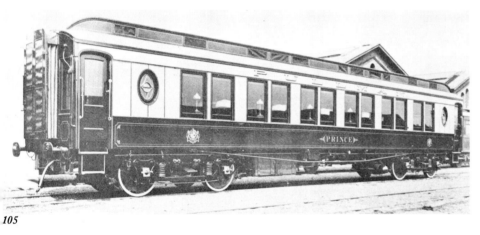

105

106

104   MR clerestory brake third of the 1870s.

105   Pullman car *Prince*, of the Brighton line with enclosed end vestibules and gangways. Some of the original American flamboyant styling has given way to a more restrained British approach, producing a carriage of majestic appearance.

106   Interior of an early 1900s third class saloon for the GNR with large gaslight pendents within the clerestory. Note the leather padded ends to the seat backs.

107   Clerestory composite second and third class gangwayed carriage, GWR 1900.

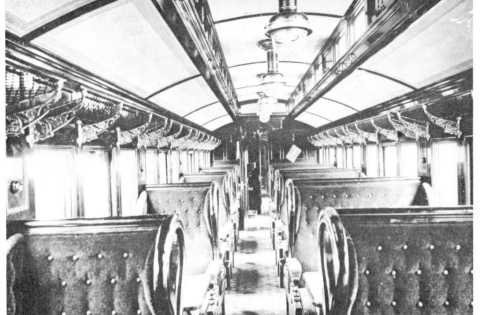

108

1870-1914 The Golden Age of Steam

108 Third class dining car, corridor train, introduced by the MR 1894, with considerable Pullman influence.

109 GNR dining car, circa 1900. Note the wirework basket racks, and ornate seats in cast iron and plush.

110 Parlour car portion of the Pullman car *Princess Patricia*, used on the LBSCR 'Brighton Limited'. This was prefabricated in America and shipped in 1905 to Britain for final assembly. The carriage was fitted with electric lighting.

111 LNWR 12-wheeled dining saloon No 290. A magnificent example of coachbuilding.

112 The interior of No 290 was elaborate and ornate, and one suspects also very comfortable.

109

110

111

112

113

114

115

116

117

113 MR non-corridor lavatory third, with clerestory roof. The door to the lavatory is between the seats on the right.

114 Interior of a first class sleeping car berth, MR, 1907. A 12-wheeled, 65ft car No 2778.

115 Open third class saloon of the GCR,

early 1900s, with low elliptical ceiling replacing the clerestory, and fitted with electric lighting.

116 The GWR 'Dreadnought' dining cars were noteworthy for some elaborate furniture, in carved walnut, with Morocco leather upholstery; illustrated is the interior of coach No 1575, built 1905.

117 GNR non-corridor composite suburban carriage of the early nineteen hundreds. These four-wheelers were designed to operate in close-coupled rakes.

118 NER Tyneside suburban electric train, in latter-day condition and LNER livery, photographed at Pelaw station.

118

119

120

121

122

119   The MR operated an electric train
service between Lancaster-Morecambe and
Heysham.

120   Interior of a LYR electric train of 1904,
built to work between Dingle (on the Liverpool
Overhead Railway) via Seaforth to Southport.

121   Interior of a NER Tyneside electric train
showing layout probably influenced by
tramcar design; complete with period
commuters! Circa 1904.

122   GWR steam rail-motor No 84,
photographed on a Henley-Twyford-Reading
service, in 1925. The engine portion was
completely encased within the carriage body
(leading end in this picture).

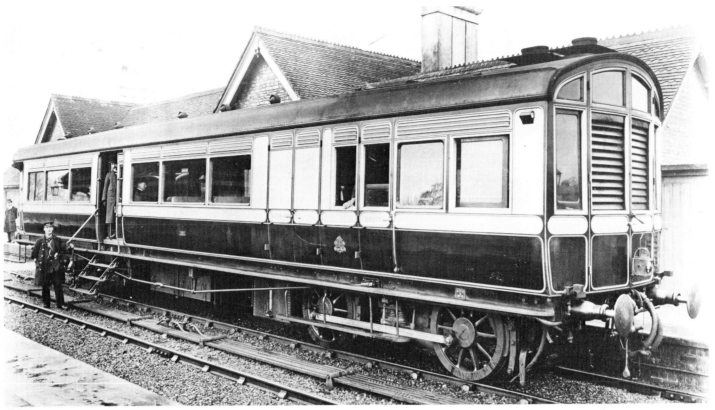

123

124

125

123 LNWR rail-motor, seen at Bicester station, also with the engine unit enclosed within the coachwork.

124 The engine unit is more visible on this LBSCR example although it is housed in an enlarged cab extending almost to the chimney. No 2 is shown on a south coast local duty.

125 Internal combustion made a tentative venture upon rails in the early 1900s, as seen in this LBSCR petrol-electric four-wheeled railcar, with saloon layout. The GWR and GCR experimented with similar types.

8 Late Victorian Architecture

By 1870 the greatest years of railway architecture were over, and already the reaction of late Victorian industrial vulgarity was setting-in. Some singularly bleak stations were constructed in the last decades of Queen Victoria's reign, and much of the pioneer enthusiasm which had earlier produced so many classics, was gone forever. The latter-day extensions to earlier buildings were all too often vastly inferior in design. To take Euston for example: each new addition to cope with increased business seemed to assist in turning the place into a rabbit-warren. Where new stations were built, as extensions were opened, a dreary sameness seemed to characterise them.

True, there were some splendid exceptions. There were still a number of great iron roofs to be completed, for example at Darlington (1877), York (1877) and Manchester Central (1880), and on a somewhat smaller scale, the lovely Bath Green Park (1870).

When York was opened it was the largest station in the world, and the impressive interior, with its great roof curved from end-to-end, remains — in the present writer's humble opinion — the finest example of its kind ever constructed. It represents the climax of the big iron and glass overall roof trainsheds first introduced by Dobson at Newcastle.

Another magnificent exception to the general dreariness were some of the later bridges. The tragic story of the original Tay Bridge design, by Bouch, is far too well known to need repeating. Its collapse during a gale on 28 December 1879, whilst a train was crossing, was a disaster due to a combination of bad design, bad workmansip and bad maintenance. But it had stood up long enough to prove indispensable; a second Tay Bridge design was commissioned just 19 months after the collapse of the first. The longest viaduct in the world when built (just as Bouch's design had been before it), it was designed by W. H. and Crawford Barlow, and stands adjacent to the stumps of the disastrous first attempt. It is an impressive effort, but undeniably ugly.

Without doubt, the classic of late Victorian railway bridge design is the world-famous Forth Bridge, which even today is an awe-inspiring structure with a truly majestic sense of scale; it is still one of the largest bridges in the world. Design of this masterpiece was the responsibility of Sir John Fowler and Benjamin Baker, in consultation with T. E. Harrison and W. H. Barlow. Baker was taking no chances of a repetition of the Tay Bridge disaster; he conducted a series of experiments on the site to study the effects of wind pressures. The final design, opened to rail traffic on 4 March 1890, by the Prince of Wales, was of cantilever principle.

Mention was made in Chapter 4 of the verandahs, which, supported on cast-iron columns or cantilevered out, became a characteristic of the ordinary-sized British railway station. These verandahs were frequently very fine, and a great deal of ingenuity was shown in the design of the wooden valances and cast iron pillars and brackets. The repetitive motifs cut-out by skilled carpenters became one of the more attractive items characterising railway architecture. Many and varied were the designs these men produced, and their pretty silhouette quality lends a great deal of attraction to what could otherwise be a commonplace item. Some were very simple, some possessed intricate repeats; all were quite beautifully executed. On many late Victorian stations these decorative valances were almost the sole redeeming feature.

A blight which settled upon railway architecture during the 1870s and 1880s, and from then onwards, was the enamel advertisement which was screwed to all available prominent surfaces — walls, fences, cutting sides, etc — to catch the eye. Passengers were urged, in coloured enamel, to buy this or that ink, soup, soap, tonic, and suchlike. Some of these signs seem to be indestructible; one still sees them occasionally, used to patch up a shed or fence in a back garden adjacent to the railway line! They were a manifestation of the increasing spirit of commercialism — how George Stephenson or Brunel would

have loathed them. Certainly they would *not* have been tolerated!

On country stations the platforms were often enlivened by small gardens, or even hanging baskets and tubs of flowers beneath the verandah. Pride in the job was such that these station gardens often became real showpieces, with the station name worked in different coloured blooms or perhaps topiary hedges in a row behind the platform fencing. Of course, life on these stations was often very leisurely and there was plenty of time to attend to such things 'between trains'. There is no doubt that the wayside British station often possessed great character and charm and such touches sadly are missing on present day stations; only occasionally does one see a glimpse of something like it nowadays.

Station hotels, in large cities and towns, were frequently places of some magnitude and importance, and some impressive examples were constructed. In some cases they enhanced the station proper, in others they dominated it even to the extent of hiding the station from view. The Euston hotel, now demolished along with the station, began as two buildings flanking the main entrance to the station (through the Propylaeum). In due course the two halves were joined, and as a result the Great Arch was absurdly hidden from view.

When the GCR reached London in 1899 it erected a large hotel in Marylebone Road, right in front of the station. The hotel was quite dignified, if not exactly an architectural masterpiece; but the trainshed beyond was a poor, uninspired affair. The great days of railway station building were over. The rebuilt joint Victoria stations of the Brighton and Chatham companies, standing alongside one another, were both poor architectural essays with a general air of decadent classicism.

By 1914 many of the earlier stations had been submerged beneath latter-day additions, or even completely replaced, in order to cope with the greatly changed traffic conditions. There were increasing signs that railway architecture was in the

126

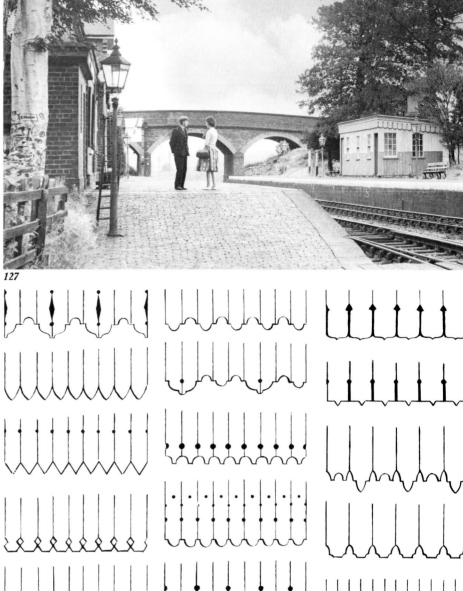

127

doldrums, basically because the demand for new buildings had dropped almost to nil. Added to this were the effects of constant exposure to soot and industrial grime, becoming increasingly evident to the eye. Nevertheless standards of maintenance and of day-to-day cleanliness were very good. The drastic effects of World War I were yet to be felt.

126 **GWR coat of arms and Art Nouveau numerals on the façade of Windsor & Eton Central station.**

127 **Rural station scene: Caythorpe on the Grantham-Lincoln line.**

128 **A selection of decorative effects used for the valances of station roofs and wooden awnings. Drawing by the author.**

129 **Cromford station, MR. A compound 4-4-0, No 1021, thunders through, but the gentleman reading the paper appears not to notice! Note the advertisements affixed to the fences.**

128

129

130 The cathedral-like structure of the roof, Liverpool Street station, GER.

131 Details of the Derby Friargate station, made by Andrew Handyside & Co Ltd in 1878, with the Arms of Derby in cast iron.

132 The magnificent Forth Bridge, by Fowler and Baker, opened 1890. Photographed in 1955, as a Kings Cross-Aberdeen express was crossing.

9 Fine Liveries and Decorations

Without doubt, the period 1870-1914 included the finest examples of locomotive and rolling stock liveries. The increasing competition between railway companies, plus a growing awareness of public interest in their activities, made them place great emphasis upon the appearance of their trains. The great junctions and joint stations were the meeting-places for trains of many different companies, and the value of ready identification of *their* trains, as opposed to those of competitors, did not escape them. Even small companies operating purely local services were sufficiently proud to want their own individual livery.

A major junction, such as York or Carlisle, presented a glorious galaxy of colourful liveries, with engines of one company replacing those of another before the train went forward on the next stage of its journey. What fascinating places these were; the Victorian equivalent of today's international airports — but far more exciting to watch!

Space does not permit me to list in detail all the many and beautiful liveries produced during these years; in any case specialised books have been published on the subject. Rather, I would take a few of the classic liveries and leave these to speak for the rest. But first, a word about the general application of liveries to trains.

The basic reason for painting and varnishing a locomotive or carriage was preservation, not decoration. Locomotives had to be proofed against rust and corrosion; carriages against deterioration of woodwork. Beneath the final glossy appearance some very important groundwork was essential, no matter what final colour was chosen for the stock. An extract from *The Construction of the Modern Locomotive* by George Hughes, dated 1894, is worth quoting in full:

'. . . The engine is then handed over to the paint shop.

Here it first receives a thorough scouring all over with sandstone, and is afterwards washed down with turpentine, to thoroughly cleanse it from all rust and dirt. It is then given one coat of oil lead colour, which consists of white lead and common black, mixed with boiled linseed oil, turpentine and terebene drier. This coat gives adherence to the stopping and filling, which consists of white lead, Indian copal varnish and gold size. The whole surface of the engine is gone over first, and the worst parts filled up with a thick stopping, using putty knives and then followed with a thinner stopping worked on with trowels. The rivets are then brushed round with a thinner filling, which softens that put on with trowels, and makes the whole a smooth surface. A cheaper material is mixed with the white lead and used after the first coat of lead colour, when the surfaces are worse than usual and a great quantity of material is required. It is then stained with one coat of vegetable black, mixed with gold size and turpentine, which acts as a guide for the rubbers-down. A smooth surface is then got up by wet rubbing with Schumachersche's Fabrick. Afterwards it receives the first coat of paint, which is a dark lead, mixed in a manner similar to the light lead colour used before filling up. This is followed by a coat of the best drop ivory black, which is mixed with gold size and turpentine, bound with varnish. The third consists of the best drop ivory black mixed with varnish, upon which the lining out is done. It is then ready for the varnish, the first two coats being flattened down with pumice powder, horsehair and water, followed by a third coat; best engine copal varnish being used in all cases. The cab is filled up inside in a similar manner to the rest of the engine, and painted with three coats of buff or stone colour, which consists of white lead, Turkey burnt umber, orange chrome, mixed with boiled oil, turpentine and terebene driers. It is then stencilled, lined out, and given two coats of clear varnish. All the motion work, where not bright, and the bufferbeam, receives three coats of vermilion and varnished. Wheels, framing, smokebox and brake gear receive one coat of drop ivory black and two coats of the best Japan black. The whole operation occupies about three weeks, including one week for the varnish to set, and it is such that it will not be required to be repeated for five years.'

In Chapter 6 I mentioned the beautiful livery produced by William Stroudley. The basic colour, a warm golden ochre, had the slightest hint of green about it. Even so there is confusion over the description Stroudley used. He called it his 'Improved Engine Green'. Any suggestion that he was colour blind or suffered from defective vision is ludicrous. My own belief is that the name arose quite simply because when Stroudley first applied his new colours to some HR locomotives he used the current workshop parlance of Inverness, where engines had previously been painted dark green. The term 'engine green' had come to mean the colour used for locomotives; Stroudley *improved* upon it. Another name for it was 'Scotch Green'.

Stroudley brought his new livery to Brighton from Inverness, and ironically Dugald Drummond took it back north of the border when he moved from the Brighton company to take over on the NBR. Stroudley's scheme relied upon elaborate lining-out for its rich effect. The ochre was enhanced and enriched by the careful choice of colours used in juxtaposition. Basically the scheme comprised as follows: first the main body colour, a rich golden ochre with slightest tendency towards green; next to this a white line, then a black band, then a red line, edged by a panel of dark olive green. Boiler bands were black, with a red line on each side, then a band of olive green with finally a white line next to the ochre. Frames were claret colour, with a black edge with yellow line on the inner side and red line on the outer. Wheels were ochre, with black tyres and olive green axle ends. Locomotive names were in gold-leaf on the ochre, shaded to the left by a graduated emerald green to red on white, and to the right by black. Buffer beams were claret, with a panel of vermilion bordered by a black stripe lined with red and yellow. Coupling rods were often claret coloured; the inside frames, guard irons and leading sand pipes were vermilion. The chimney and smokebox were black; the top of the chimney having a polished copper cap. Cab roofs were lead white, and the tops of tenders were finished with red lead. The numberplate (see later) was brass with a dark blue background. Anyone wishing to see a really authentic contemporary version of Stroudley's magnificent livery is advised to inspect the lovely model of his 0-4-2 *Como,* in the Brighton Museum. Stroudley's goods engines were painted in dark olive green and black. Those fitted with through brakes had a vermilion line on each side of the black line.

Other companies' liveries for their passenger engines were only slightly less elaborate. The CR had a lovely prussian blue, lined black and white with crimson lake frames. The GER had quite a different royal blue, with black separated by a vermilion line. Many companies favoured green, ranging from sage green to bright apple green or deep brunswick green. In each case the associated 'lining-out' was carefully chosen to enhance the body colour. Reds of differing hues were also employed, ranging from brick reds to deep crimsons and magentas. Black was a most efficient finish for steam locomotives; the LYR and LNWR both used it, with attractive lining-out. The important point to remember is that the black was beautifully finished and varnished, so that it possessed a richness and a definite warmth, quite opposed to the lack-lustre black engines of the mid-20th century.

The wonderful MR crimson lake livery, introduced by S. W. Johnson, depended upon a painstaking building-up of successive coats of paint and varnish to achieve its glowing warmth of tone. Synthetic modern paints, speedily applied, cannot reproduce the same intensity of colour today.

One could go on, ad infinitum, describing the many superb locomotive liveries of the period, but one final example must serve. This was introduced by Wainwright on the SECR around the turn of the century. It was the last of the truly elaborate liveries. Basically it comprised a brunswick green body colour, with a fine yellow line, a broad band of pale sea green, a fine red line and a border of black. The frames were light brown edged with black separated by a red line, with an adjacent yellow line. The chimney cap was polished copper, and the dome cover polished brass. Wainwright's livery was most attractive, but expensive to apply. By 1912 it was modified to reduce the cost; all brasswork and copper were painted over, and the lining-out was simplified. The great days of locomotive liveries were drawing to a close. Stroudley's ochre had already given way

to Marsh's umber brown on the Brighton line, and the HR was painting its engines plain green, totally devoid of lining. Some railways managed to retain their schemes up to the 1914-18 war, but before then the general trend was already towards simplified and less expensive liveries.

Finally a word about cleaning. Victorian and Edwardian locomotives positively gleamed and the effects of constant polishing and cleaning greatly enhanced their liveries by producing a rich patina on top of the varnish coats. Engine drivers were responsible for their own engines and there was no shortage of apprentice cleaners at the shed. A dirty locomotive was unthinkable; it was cleaned outside and in, regularly, above and below the frames and inside the frames. Metal fittings were kept burnished and oiled to prevent rust, and copper and brass were highly polished. Pride in the job was reflected in the sparkling exterior of even the humblest tank engine, whilst the large main line steam locomotive was a joy to behold.

Carriage liveries were also colourful and varied during this period, with the same careful attention to finish before they left the workshops. Some companies preferred to retain the natural wood finish, preserving it with coats of varnish and enhancing it with lining-out. Others preferred to use a painted scheme, either of one colour overall, or else a two colour scheme above and below the waist. Panelling was emphasised by lining-out the relief mouldings. It would be impossible to list all the hundred or more carriage liveries in use during this period, so I must content the reader with a description of what was undeniably one of the most popular, the so-called 'chocolate and cream' of the GWR.

As applied during the 1890s this was an elaborate and beautiful livery. The waist panels and lower panels, including underframe, were windsor brown (also the body ends); above the waist, the panels were creamy-white. The mouldings had a broad black band and a thin brown line on their flat outer surfaces, with gold-leaf on the curved sides. Mouldings of the droplights and quarterlights were varnished natural wood. Roofs were white, and ironwork was black (other than the brown underframes). The numerals were in gold leaf shaded with black.

A typical feature of practically all carriage liveries during this period was the way the mouldings and panelling of construction were turned into decorative features. Sometimes these lining-out schemes became so prominent that they diverted attention from a relatively sombre body colour. On some railways the carriages were painted in the same colours as the locomotives, or in colours very

similar. On others a definite contrast was achieved; but always with pleasing effect. The standards of taste and craftsmanship exhibited were often quite superb.

Just as in the case of steam locomotive liveries, the cost of applying the elaborate late Victorian schemes to carriages was proving somewhat exorbitant by 1905. Despite this many liveries remained unchanged up to the outbreak of World War I. A good many hearts were broken when, in 1908, Churchward changed the GWR livery to a chocolate-lake overall scheme, with yellow and black lining-out, and so it remained until 1922.

A feature of railway liveries during the period 1870-1914 was the greatly increased use of identification marks by the various companies. Sometimes this took the form of an elaborate monogram of their initials; sometimes the name was displayed in full (perhaps without the word *railway*) and coats of arms were widely used. Of the latter, some examples were true heraldry and some were rather dubious; all added an undeniable richness to the scene. The granting of coats of arms to railway companies was permissible, as they came under the heading of companies which dealt with services rather than goods.

Many of the railways' heraldic devices were very complicated in origin and meaning, and the present author does not profess the specialised knowledge to expound upon them at great length. On some, the 'arms' of earlier amalgamated companies were linked together. Often the coats of arms of major counties or cities served by the railway were included. Suggestions of speed by means of allusion to Mercury*; by showing a locomotive, or wheels, were also a feature of some. Heraldry certainly lent an air of distinction to the locomotives and carriages with a very decorative and colourful effect. A few examples are illustrated, and I would rather that these spoke for themselves.

Typical locations for coats of arms, on locomotives, were on driving wheel splashers, cab side sheets or tender sides. Sometimes they were flanked by the name or initials of the company. Particularly attractive were Robinson's Atlantics on the GCR, where the coat of arms appeared no less than three times on each side — one on each driving wheel splasher and one on the tender!

The numbering of locomotives, for record purposes, became a general policy. Gone were the days when locomotive fleets were so small that they could be remembered by individual characteristics, or name alone. Naming was still in some favour, although the tendency now was to name the passenger engines and not the goods types, and on a few railways (such

---

* Mercury — messenger of the Gods.

as the MR) the practice had virtually died out. Both names and numerals presented opportunity for enriching the overall livery by suitable choice of letterforms, and style of application. It was typical of the thoroughness of the Victorian 'Artist Engineers' that these details should receive very close attention.

Polished brass plates were particularly favoured, both for their permanence and attractiveness. They usually took the form of a casting with raised figures and lettering, with the background painted red, blue or black or left polished. Alternatively the polished brass plate could remain the outer surface, with countersunk lettering filled with black wax, or paint, for contrast. A further, and rather attractive, method was to cut out, or cast, the individual letters and numbers and affix these separately, either directly on to the cabside or boiler sheets, or else to a plate. This last method allowed greater freedom for spacing words, and easier replacement if accidentally damaged.

The actual styles of lettering used were frequently of great character and beauty, and they seemed to belong to the steam age, with the bold shapes and brassy finish. The earliest nameplates were usually lettered with 'serif' letterforms of Egyptian type. (Heavy slab serifs, probably slightly curved on the inner sides.) Stephenson's two GWR broad gauge engines *North Star* and *Morning Star* had this style of lettering. On the GWR the Egyptian slab-serif style, first seen on these two locomotives, was to remain in constant use throughout the separate existence of the company, with only very minor modifications.

Sanserif types were becoming popular by the 1850s, and many railways adopted these for name and numberplates, probably partly because they were easier to draw and cast. One curious tradition was that of Crewe Works on the LNWR. Nameplates had sanserif lettering, countersunk on a brass plate; whereas the numberplates had raised Egyptian slab-serif numerals (incidentally, of more subtle beauty than their GWR counterparts).

Date and place of construction were sometimes incorporated into either name or numberplate and sometimes cast or engraved upon a separate small brass plate. The practice of casting brass numberplates flourished under the influence of Stroudley and Drummond. Stroudley's numerals were most distinctive. He first introduced them on the HR (where David Jones continued to use them) and they became a characteristic of the LBSCR. The style was a very 'fat' curved serif form, with a most peculiar '7' which was in fact just like a '2' upside-down. Drummond

favoured countersunk numerals of sanserif type upon an oval brass plate.

Scarcely less rich in character were the painted version of names and numerals. These would frequently be executed in gold leaf with elaborate shading countershading. Thus an illusion of the letters standing in relief would be created (very similar to the traditional fair-ground styles); here again both heavy serif and sanserif types were used to great effect. Stroudley, already noted above for his beautiful brass numberplates, preferred to have the names of his engines painted on to the golden ochre colour scheme, and so it was with a number of other railways where the Stroudley influence was felt, such as the NBR and HR.

Perhaps the most delightful of all the embellishments of Victorian and Edwardian locomotives were those done by the enginemen and shed staff themselves. These took two forms, one fairly permanent, and one decidely to the contrary. The permanent form included burnished decorative shapes on smokebox doors and buffers, or polished rivet heads or other constructional details. Painstaking scraping away of layers of paint was a prerequisite to these decorations. Once the bare metal was exposed it was burnished until it shone bright. Many Scottish locomotives had thistles or stars burnished upon the smokebox doors, according to the individual fancy of the enginemen. (Much to the author's delight, he can recall this tradition still flourishing in some areas of Scotland in the mid-1950s.) Brass filigree was also widely applied.

The other form of embellishment was akin to the idea of dressing-up horses for a ceremonial parade. A true sense of occasion seems to have prevailed in railway circles during this period. A funeral, Coronation, Diamond Jubilee or other royal event was the excuse of elaborate preparations. Garlands of everlasting flowers were arranged along boiler sides, or placed in wickerwork baskets. Portrait busts were mounted upon bufferbeams, along with coats of arms and various royal devices. The whole engine was cleaned and polished until it shone like a new coin, and to crown it all the coal was whitewashed!

No less favoured were visiting foreign princes, politicians, famous generals, or even soldiers returning from the Crimea. Whilst the annual Stationmasters' and Inspectors' excursion to the seaside was an opportunity seized to garland an engine in truly festive spirit. No carthorse ever looked as gay as these 'iron horses'.

Picture if you would St Pancras station on a dull morning. All about you are the handsome crimson lake trains of the MR, with important destinations. What

133

startled eyes must have been raised from their newspapers, as an engine steamed slowly into view to couple on to that insignificant train of carriages belonging to the LTSR. The headboard read as usual Southend and it was one of the company's typical 4-4-2T locomotives, No 61 *Kentish Town*. But what a spectacle it was for this was the time of the coronation of King Edward the VII. On this occasion No 61 defies any further description on my part. (See photo 158).

The MR of course frowned upon such frivolities! Its own royal engine was distinguished purely by a cipher on the cabside (see photo 160).

Finally, a trivial thought. I have often wondered how much of the decoration was lost *en route*. The spectacle of *Kentish Town* leaning into the curves as she sped alongside the Thames estuary towards Westcliff and Southend, with garlands of flowers flapping wildly in the slipstream and busts of Their Majesties jogging merrily to the beat of the exhaust, leaves me happily speculative!

133 **Victorian locomotives were kept spotlessly clean. A typical example of the care lavished upon their finish is GNR 2-4-0 No 759, seen here. Note the decorative effects worked into the tallow on the tender sides.**

134 **LSWR crest on the splasher of an Adams 4-4-0.**

135 **Detail of the lining out and maker's plate on a Fletcher locomotive, NER.**

136 **Coat of arms of East Lancashire Railway, removed from the frontage of Bury Bolton Street station, prior to reconstruction.**

137 **Hull & Holderness Railway coat of arms.**

134

135

136

137

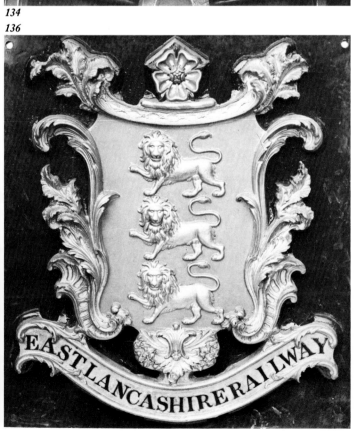

EAST LANCASHIRE RAILWAY

HULL & HOLDERNESS RAILWAY

138

139

140

141

142

143

138 Coat of arms of the L&BR on the gates, Euston station prior to rebuilding.

139 Garter emblem used on NER passenger coaches.

140 MR coat of arms on Compound 4-4-0 No 1000.

141 The MR frequently employed the Wyvern as its symbol, even using it on the etched glass window of carriage toilets.

142 LBSCR coat of arms.

143 GWR coat of arms.

144 One of the most elaborate coats of arms belonged to a minor company, the Manchester, South Junction & Altrincham Railway.

145 LYR coat of arms.

146 SER coat of arms.

144

145

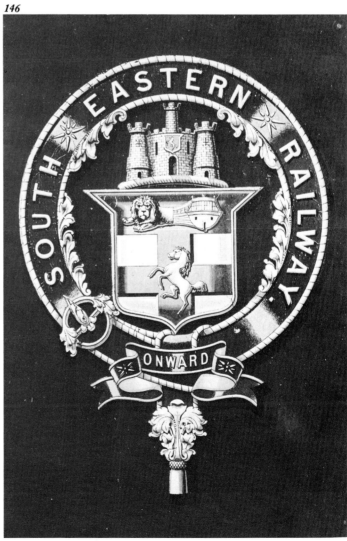

146

147

148

149

147   NER worksplate.

148   GWR worksplate.

149   LBSCR worksplate on
No 82 *Boxhill*.

150   NER numberplate.

151   Numberplate on Fletcher
locomotive No 910, NER.

152   Drawing of LNWR numberplate.

150

151

152

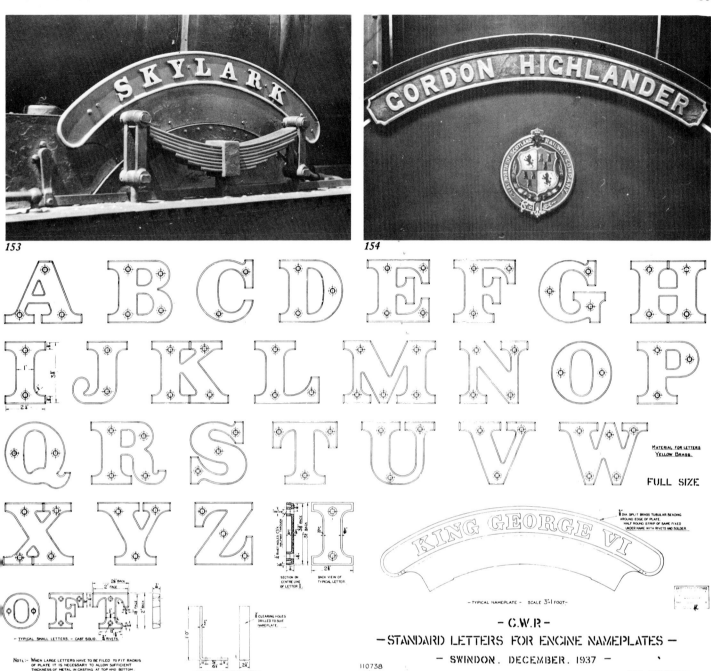

153 GWR nameplates were characterised by a distinctive Egyptian slab-serif letterform from the earliest days. Illustrated is the nameplate on a 'Bird' class 4-4-0.

154 GNSR nameplate on 4-4-0 *Gordon Highlander*, using a sanserif style.

155 Blue-print of GWR alphabet for locomotive nameplates. Shown reduced from full size. Although dated 1937, it is almost certainly a tracing of a much earlier drawing.

156 Decorated front of NBR Atlantic, *Highland Chief*. Such decoration was usually done by the engine driver in his spare time, by burnishing the steel parts to a bright finish or adding brass filigree.

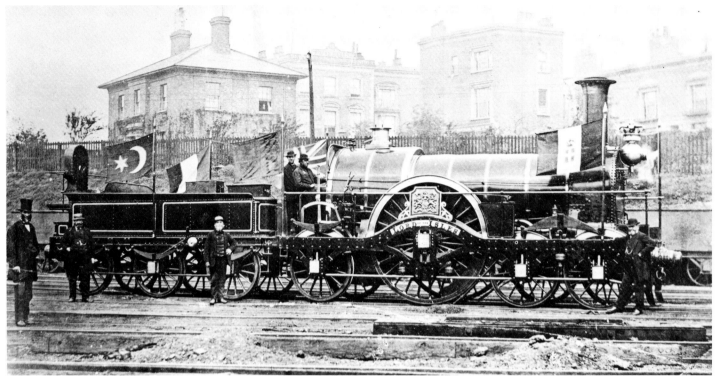

157

157 GWR locomotive *Lord of the Isles*, decorated 24 June 1873, for soldiers returning from the Crimean war.

158 LTSR 4-4-2T *Kentish Town* specially decorated to celebrate the coronation; 9 August 1902.

159 LBSCR Marsh Atlantic No 39, named *La France* and decorated with red, white and blue ribbons, to work a special train conveying the French President from Portsmouth Docks to London.

160 The MR royal engine, with cipher on

cabside. It was No 502, a standard inside-cylinder 4-4-0.

161 FR 4-4-0 No 36 decorated for Royal Train duty.

162 Royal engine decoration; typical of those carried by locomotives in pre-Grouping days.

158

159

160

161

162

10 Ephemera, Liveries and Uniforms

We have already seen in Chapter 5 how the early railway printed matter was left very much to the instinctive taste of the individual printer, with remarkably happy results. In the 1870s and 1880s this situation remained much the same, although greater standardisation of typefaces became apparent. Printing upon coloured papers was increasingly used for excursion handbills to attract attention to these items; whilst posters were often in two or more coloured inks, but still basically all-lettering designs.

The development of colour printing for pictorial reproduction (particularly the chromo-lithographic process) offered new scope for publicity. Pictorial posters could be produced in attractive quantities for widespread display, and this was a feature of the railway publicity from Edwardian days, with many famous contemporary artists being employed to produce specially commissioned pictures.

As mentioned in Chapter 8, the advertisement hoarding became a typical feature of railway stations from late Victorian years onwards. Enamel signs were coming into use, but for the more ephemeral publicity the printed poster remained supreme. Another feature was the large hand-painted poster, advertising special excursions (produced in insufficient numbers to warrant the cost of printing) displayed outside large stations. Railway companies advertised their services widely in these highly competitive days, and it was commonplace to find their posters on stations hundreds of miles from their own routes. Thus the GNSR might well advertise its services in Cornwall; and so on, for these were the days of 'through carriages' taking passengers right to their destination without a change en route.

Printed matter, by nature of its ready production, always tends to follow most readily the current trend in artistic taste. By way of contrast, a more sober approach characterises the applied letterforms of cast-metal signs and notices. The railways produced many types of warning signs and other notices in heavy cast-iron, because of their vulnerability to vandalism or accidental damage. Mileposts and gradient posts are other instances where a high degree of permanence was considered desirable. In fact many of these signs have proved very permanent indeed, and it is not uncommon to come across them in use today. Countless examples have become the treasured possessions of railway enthusiasts or museums. An interesting sidelight is that those signs which were produced in enamels, rather than cast-iron, have suffered far more from the effects of small boys with stones, over the years. One feature against the choice of cast-iron is that it is impossible to alter the wording. Hence there are still signs bearing the names of railway companies that ceased to exist over half-a-century ago. The usual expedient is to paint-out the name and pretend it is not there!

Station names were often built up from cast-iron letters screwed to wooden boards, and small versions of these might be found on seat backs, on the platforms. Some railways favoured painted name signs, but these required greater upkeep. Gas lamps often had the station name in the glass, perhaps reversed out of a deep blue, so that the light shone through the name at night. In Edwardian years the GWR produced some very elaborate *Art Nouveau* lettering for the name signs outside stations, in metal, affixed to the frontage. A feature of most direction signs was the use of cast-iron 'pointing' fingers, or hands, to show the direction to be taken, rather than the arrows favoured today.

Uniform design became very important by the 1870s, as stations grew larger and services more frequent. It was essential for the passengers to be able to identify the appropriate staff, whilst the staff themselves now numbered so many that identification of seniority of rank or grade became imperative. Different styles of headgear and dress identified the various grades, with the top-hat remaining the status-symbol of superior officials. The porter was a very active participant in the railway travel scene of those days; for families were large and luggage was heavy. Much careful shepherding and loading of parents and children, plus trunks and hampers, promised good rewards. The porters' dress, complete with velveteen or corduroy trousers and waistcoat, ideally served him.

The railway guard had become a very dignified figure by the 1850s (see Chapter 5) and he remained so throughout our period. The LNWR guard illustrated in photo 176 should be compared with the dapper character illustrated in photo 65. Could they in fact be one and the same? It is quite feasible. Certainly the style of uniform had but little changed over the intervening 50 years or so.

Finally, the engine driver. I have not illustrated him separately in this chapter, as several examples of typical driver's dress are to be found elsewhere in this volume. He remained, throughout the period, in clothing ideally suited to his duties, with very little decorative consideration except possibly a cap-badge.

163

Poster: GREAT WESTERN RAILWAY · ROYAL AGRICULTURAL SHOW AT KILBURN · SPECIAL FAST EXCURSION TO LONDON · SATURDAY, July 5th, 1879

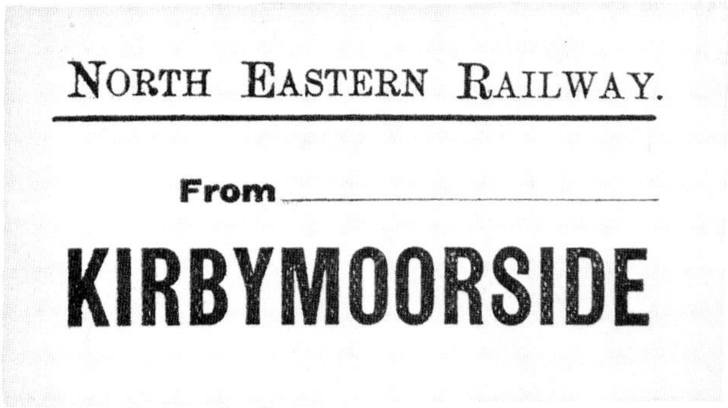

NORTH EASTERN RAILWAY.

From _____

KIRBYMOORSIDE

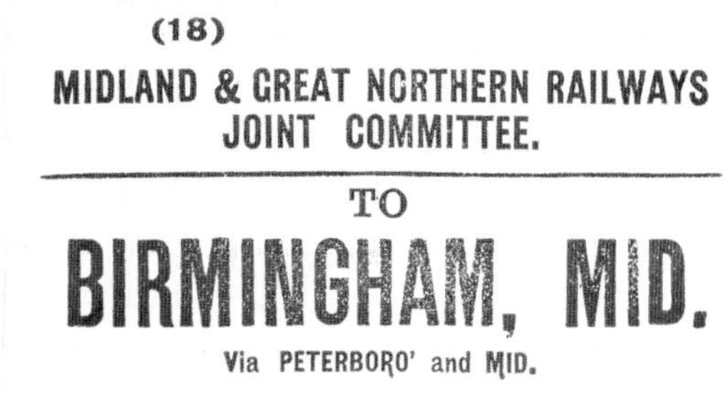

164

(18)

MIDLAND & GREAT NORTHERN RAILWAYS JOINT COMMITTEE.

TO

BIRMINGHAM, MID.

Via PETERBORO' and MID.

London and South Western Ry.

787

TO

BIDEFORD

G. W. R.

BOURNEMOUTH

(WEST)

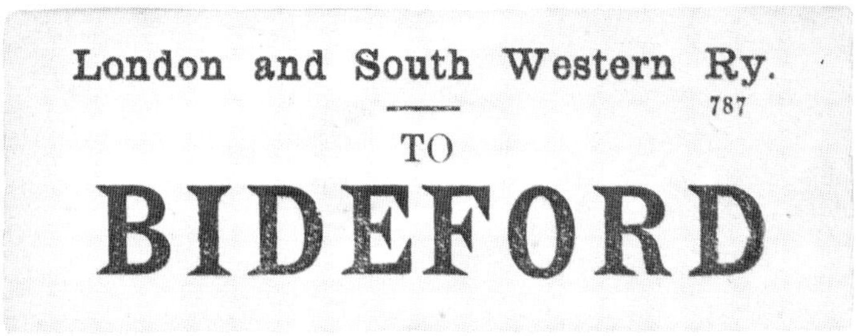

163   Poster of 1879, GWR, printed in Bristol.

164   A characteristic feature of rail travel in late-Victorian and Edwardian days was the large quantity of luggage conveyed. Illustrated are some typical paper labels.

165   Handbill, 1886, LNWR.

166   Poster of 1888, LBSCR.

But what an impressive figure he was (the equivalent of any racing driver, airline pilot or even astronaut, today), and the combination of a hot steam locomotive and a sweaty, coal dust covered driver and fireman at the end of a long journey, scarcely required the frills of a uniform to add romance — *it was there in plenty, as every small boy knew!*

165

N.E.D.—No. 292.

LONDON AND NORTH WESTERN RAILWAY.

SADDLEWORTH WAKES.

A Cheap Excursion
TO
BLACKPOOL

WILL RUN AS UNDER
On SATURDAY and MONDAY, AUGUST 21 and 23, 1886.

STATION.	Time of Starting.	Fares.	
		Going on Saturday & Monday and Returning the same day at 7.40 p.m. from Talbot Road.	Going on Saturday and Returning up to the following Tuesday by Ordinary Trains.
	a.m.	Cov. Carriages.	Cov. Carriages.
Saddleworth .	7.5	2/9	4/6

The Tickets will be available only as shewn above.
Tickets not Transferable.

CHILDREN UNDER TWEL E YEARS OF AGE HALF FARE.

All information regarding E rsion Trains on the London and North Western Railway, can be obtained o ...pplication to Mr. G. E. MAWBY, District Superintendent, Exchange Station, Manchester.

EUSTON STATION, LONDON, July, 1886.

G. FINDLAY, General Manager

McCorquodale & Co., Limited, Printers, London—Works, Newton

166

London, Brighton and South Coast Railway.

NOTICE.

On and after the 1st October next

THE NAME OF

CATERHAM JUNCTION

STATION

WILL BE

ALTERED TO

PURLEY.

(By Order)   A. SARLE, Secretary & General Manager.

JULY 2nd. 1888.

Waterlow and Sons Limited. Printers. London Wall, London.

167

168

169

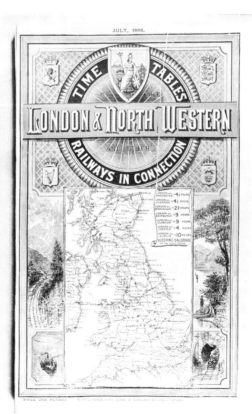

167   MR poster of 1903, printed in two colours.

168   The pictorial poster was well established in 1913, when this design was produced by Graham Phillips for SECR.

169   Two typical timetable covers. LYR design of 1912, and an earlier (1888) LNWR cover complete with map.

170   When in peril or distress, read the notice and follow the instructions carefully! GNR carriage notice.

170

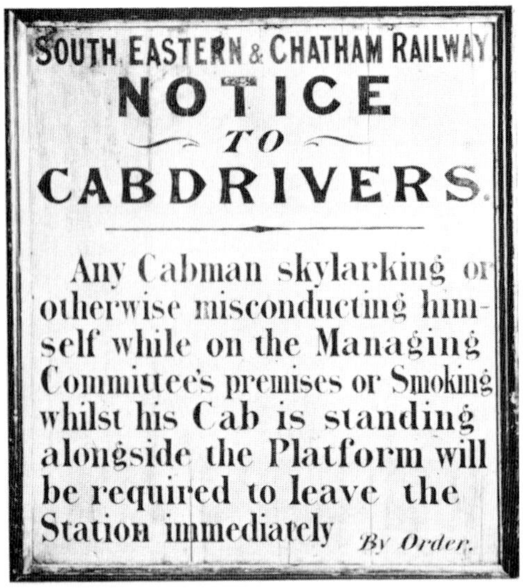

171

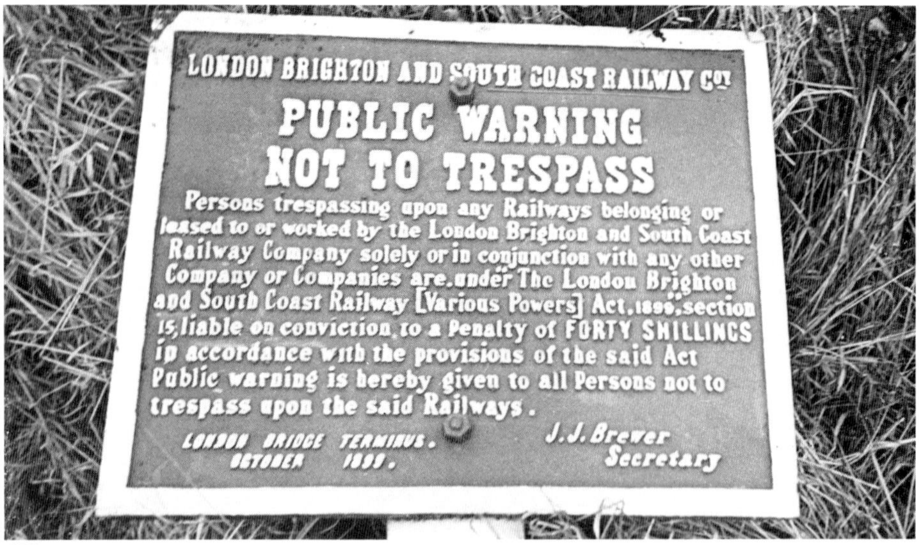

172

171   Painted notice, SECR.

172   Cast iron notice of 1899, LBSCR.

173   A very neat cast iron notice of 1896, GNR, still in use in the 1960s.

174   Great Western and Central Joint Committee notice.

175   LBSCR staff 1881. Left to right: ticket collector; ticket inspector; station superintendent, station inspector, guard and policeman.

176   LNWR guard (compare with photo 65).

177   Midland Railway guards.

173

174

175

176

177

178

178 Porters on the SER, with typical close-coupled suburban carriages. The gentleman peering intently through the window is believed to be the photographer.

179 A facility for passengers which was probably greatly appreciated. Euston 1905.

180 Three tickets of typical design. A LBSCR 'Commercial Travellers' ticket, a LSWR excursion ticket and a later LSWR excursion ticket.

179

180

1914–1939
Steam's Finest Years

11 'Modern' Steam, 1914-1932

Although the late-Victorian steam locomotive probably represented the highest degree of artistic engineering, it was in the years between the two world wars that the reciprocating steam locomotive achieved its finest mechanical form. The emphasis was now definitely upon technical development of steam, with aesthetic appearance taking second place, and to a large degree it was as a result of technical innovations that the shape of the modern steam locomotive evolved. Nevertheless a fine sense of finish and workmanship survived, and this was to bestow considerable benefit upon the finished products of the majority of designers, however much they seemed to break away from established conventions.

The development of larger boilers, with superheating, and more efficient valve gear (with perhaps three or four cylinders), was gradually to increase the physical dimensions of the modern steam locomotive until these factors were to restrict the designer because of the problems of the stringent British loading gauge. One can only speculate what might have been had the magnificent 7ft gauge of Brunel been perpetuated by the Victorians rather than the less ambitious 4ft 8½in favoured by Stephenson.

The 'modern' British steam locomotive — to use a term which conveniently distinguishes it from its graceful Victorian counterpart — was to all intents and purposes born at Swindon, when George Jackson Churchward was appointed to succeed Dean as head at Swindon. Prior to this, in his office as Works Manager and chief assistant to Dean, he had built the first outside-cylinder 4-6-0 for the Great Western. It is commonly believed that he was basically responsible for the design. This was No 100 (later named *William Dean*), and it marked the beginning of a completely new aesthetic convention for British express passenger engines. J. N. Maskelyne, in his book *Locomotives I Have Known*, recalls that when No 100 appeared, locomotive enthusiasts everywhere were profoundly shocked by her appearance. Certainly the style introduced by Churchward was

completely new to British eyes; principal features being the domeless boiler with brass safety valve casing, Belpaire flat-topped firebox with a medium high running plate with small splashers. In her outline we see the precursor of the modern express passenger engines produced by Swindon, and others, for the ensuing 50 years or so. Henceforth Swindon engines were unmistakable, and a proud tradition arose regarding their appearance. The tapered boiler barrel (which appeared on a second 4-6-0, No 98), polished copper-capped chimney and brass safety valve casing became the hallmarks of Swindon, just as Webb's chimney and cab had done at Crewe.

Churchward experimented with both 4-6-0 and 4-4-2 wheel arrangements to determine which was best for future development, and he even purchased three of the well-known De Glehn compounds from France for comparison. Eventually he decided in favour of the 4-6-0, and some engines which started life as 4-4-2s were rebuilt accordingly. He produced both two-cylinder and four-cylinder designs. The four-cylinder type, known as the 'Star' class, was strikingly modern for its time and by far the most successful four-cylinder 4-6-0 built in the period under review. Drummond, on the LSWR, experimented with four-cylinder 4-6-0s but not with any great success. His engines seemed huge but clumsy and very indifferent performers. Drummond 'saved his face', so to speak, by producing a really fine 4-4-0 design in 1912, of Class D15, which may perhaps be considered as his masterpiece. Had Drummond been content to produce a two-cylinder 4-6-0 he might have come up with a winner comparable to McIntosh's *Cardean*! But we digress.

Churchward's design, the 'County' class of 1904-1911, in which the new lines were very well handled perhaps prepared most people for the shock when in 1908 Churchward built *The Great Bear*, the first 4-6-2 to run on a British railway. A huge and heavy engine that was ahead of its time in conception, it was nonetheless prophetic. It remained the only Pacific

type every built at Swindon, and the sole example in Britain for 14 years.

Aesthetically, Churchward's engines broke completely away from the established classic conventions, and many people were profoundly shocked by the 'new look' they presented. It is interesting to note Churchward's own observations on the subject, made before members and guests of the Institution of Mechanical Engineers in 1906. To criticism from James Stirling, retired Locomotive Engineer of the SER, who had said, 'they are novel in shape and expensive in construction: they may be good but they are certainly not "bonnie", to use a Scotch expression', Churchward replied as follows:

'I know that I have been accused of spoiling the appearance of the British locomotive as much as any man in the country, but I take exception to the statement. In my opinion, there is no canon of art in regard to the appearance of a locomotive or machine, except that which an engineer has set up for himself, by observing from time to time types of engines which he has been led from his nursery days upwards to admire. For instance, people like to see a long boiler, with an immense driving wheel about 8ft in diameter, just like the old GWR broad gauge engines. Engineers must admit that the time has gone by for studying appearances in the construction of the locomotive boiler at any rate.'

Although this statement would appear to suggest that Churchward had little time to spare for attention to the external appearances of his new locomotives, it is worthwhile placing on record that he did, in fact, subsequently authorise some detail changes which considerably improved the appearance of later construction. In particular, a more pleasing design of running-board was adopted.

By 1914 Churchward had largely succeeded in his major ambition to create a high degree of standardisation between various categories of locomotive. His express passenger 4-6-0s were setting-up consistently good performances in everyday service, and amongst the other successful types he had introduced was a powerful 2-8-0 goods locomotive of sound modern design. He had also revived the 2-6-0 Mogul wheel arrangement, using it for a mixed traffic concept, ie a locomotive suitable for a variety of duties. The mixed traffic locomotive was destined to become increasingly popular on British railways, as we shall see later.

The Mogul had achieved considerable popularity in North America, and apparently the decision to introduce a mixed traffic version of the GWR stemmed from the favourable impression of the type gained by one of Churchward's personal assistants, Holcroft, who had visited Canada in 1909. Earlier Mogul designs in Britain (notably an American-built batch imported in 1899/1900 to meet a temporary shortage of new locomotives following a builder's strike), were intended for goods traffic. The new Churchward version had 5ft 8in driving wheels, which gave it a fair turn of speed when employed on passenger duties. Known as the 43xx class, it was first introduced in 1911.

Significantly the following year had witnessed the introduction of a second new Mogul design, on the GNR. This was the maiden design of Nigel Gresley, after his appointment to succeed Ivatt as Locomotive, Carriage & Wagon Superintendent at Doncaster. This was also a mixed traffic engine and, with outside Walschaerts valve gear, and a high running-board which exposed the driving wheels, it gave some clue of what was to emerge under the Gresley regime in the years ahead, although a number of traditional Ivatt features remained visible, in particular the design of the cab and tender.

Nigel Gresley had been an apprentice at Crewe, under the formidable F. W. Webb, and later he had worked under Aspinall at the LYR works at Horwich, but little influence of either of these men was visible in the design of his first locomotive for the GNR, and it seemed that Gresley was prepared to break new ground in search of greater power and efficiency.

At the end of 1913 his second design appeared; this was a somewhat larger 2-8-0 goods locomotive, but the same style was followed and it was repeated yet again when he introduced a second and more successful version of the pioneer Mogul with a larger boiler, in early 1914. Thus, at the commencement of the period dealt with in this chapter, Gresley had felt his way with new mixed traffic and goods locomotives but as yet had not shown his intentions for express passenger power.

While Churchward and Gresley were shaping the modern steam locomotive in the pursuit of their quest for greater power and efficiency, a number of other engineers were producing what may be termed transitional designs which still retained many of the classic features of late Victorian/early Edwardian practice, and which were in many instances visually very attractive. In particular I would cite the later designs of J. G. Robinson for the GCR; the Cumming 'Clan' class 4-6-0 for the HR; and R. W. Urie's express 4-6-0 for the LSWR. This latter design, introduced in 1918, had an austere outline, with stovepipe chimney and a high running-board, grafted upon the solid Drummond tradition of Eastleigh.

In 1913 Bowen Cooke built the first really big express engine the LNWR possessed. This was his four-cylinder 4-6-0 No 2222, *Sir Gilbert Claughton*, a fine looking engine which attracted much attention. Yet even this had the old familiar Crewe 'hallmarks' of chimney and cab design, but she had outside Walschaerts valve gear, and we might justifiably describe her as the LNWR contribution to the 'modern' school of design.

Another locomotive engineer in the forefront of the 'modern' school during the important years between the outbreak of World War I and the 1923 amalgamation, was Richard Maunsell; appointed to succeed Wainwright as Locomotive Superintendent of the SECR in 1913. Maunsell had been a pupil of Ivatt on the Great Southern & Western Railway of Ireland (before Ivatt moved to Doncaster) and later spent some time at Horwich. Scarcely had he arrived at Ashford before war interrupted the normal routine of the establishment, but he was to make some remarkable changes to the locomotive stock of that railway in the years ahead. Perhaps it is not an exaggeration to state that the break from classic Victorian conventions was nowhere more abrupt than at Ashford. It is difficult to believe that the same works that produced the beautiful D class 4-4-0 of Wainwright's design in 1901 was responsible for the rugged Maunsell designs of 1917.

These pioneer Maunsell locomotives, a mixed-traffic Mogul and an express passenger 2-6-4T, aroused considerable interest in railway circles. Their sturdy outline with taper boiler was clearly Swindon-influenced, but many features were equally obviously based upon MR practice. That this should have come about was perfectly feasible since Maunsell relied upon a new team of assistants which included several ex-Swindon men, whilst his Chief Draughtsman was James Clayton from the MR Derby drawing office. Technically many of the advanced practices of Churchward were incorporated, such as the taper boiler, high working pressure,

top feed smokebox regulator and long lap valves. Somewhat understandably their outline did not greatly appeal to many observers at the time, but they were in every sense very 'modern' locomotives and their appearance — as well as their performance — survived the test of time, and the Moguls still seemed surprisingly undated in the mid-1960s, when finally succumbing to the scrap merchant's torch.

The two prototypes which Ashford produced in 1917 remained the sole members of their respective classes until after the armistice; but they had appeared at an interesting moment in history. For at that time the Association of Railway Locomotive Engineers (ARLE) was engaged in the preparation of standard locomotive designs for postwar use on all British railways, under Government sponsorship. Amongst those involved in the detailed discussions were Churchward (GWR); Fowler (Midland); Maunsell (SECR); Hughes (LYR); Gresley (GNR) and Pickersgill (Caledonian). Drawings for two proposed standard types were agreed upon and produced at Ashford drawing office, and both showed considerable Maunsell influence although the parallel boiler and Belpaire firebox was more typical of Derby.

The work put into these standard designs did quite a lot to break down the design inconoclasm of the individual drawing offices, and it is recorded that Churchward made a significant contribution to their final appearance on paper. However, it is interesting to read Gresley's opinion of the scheme, which he included in his Chairman's address to the Leeds Branch of the Institution of Locomotive Engineers, on 11 May 1918. It is worth quoting in full:

'On the proposed standard locomotives:
'The present is, in my opinion, the most inopportune moment for the introduction of the standard engine. After three-and-a-half years of the greatest war the world has ever known, we are hard put to carry on the railway transport of the country. To add to the difficulties by the introduction of several new types of standard engines, having new standards for such parts as brake blocks, firebars, valves, piston rings, and a hundred others, which constantly require renewal, and of which stocks have to be kept in the various depots all over the country, would be the height of folly and could only result in disaster.'

Perhaps, in view of the fears expressed by Gresley, it was just as well that the plan never proceeded beyond the drawing board; the threat of Nationalisation receded and with it the standard engines. However, the Government subsequently chose the Maunsell Mogul design for construction at Woolwich Arsenal to maintain employment after the 1918 armistice. Subsequently the class was nicknamed 'Woolworths', and although most were employed on the SECR, and later the SR, some examples went to Ireland and the Metropolitan Railway (or to be more accurate — the parts went, and were then assembled into locomotives).

Apart from the ARLE standard design proposals just discussed, there were not many opportunities for locomotive engineers to prepare new designs during the war years, although thoughts were no doubt frequently turned to the likely requirements of the postwar railways. The often formidably heavy wartime train loads had emphasised the need for larger and more efficient locomotives, with greater reserves of power. This need had already been felt by the traffic people, prior to 1914, as more and more bogie carriages were introduced to replace previous four- or six-wheeled stock. Existing undersized steam locomotives were frequently flogged to the limit by their valiant drivers in an effort to keep to schedule, and double-heading was resorted to more often, with all the added expense of two engines and two crews to work one train.

Nigel Gresley gave some thought to the problem in 1915, and he outlined proposals for a Pacific development of the Ivatt Atlantic. This would have had four cylinders and a parallel boiler of the same diameter as the large Atlantic. Although this proposal proved a false starter, we know from the surviving drawings that it would have borne considerable resemblance to his prewar designs, retaining a number of pronounced Ivatt features, such as the design of the cab, the chimney and the tender.

Once the war ended the railways remained under Government control, with the very real possibility of some form of consolidation facing their managers, until the decision to amalgamate all the main line railways in regional groups was announced in August 1921; to be accomplished by 1 July 1923. Such circumstances cannot have been the most conducive in which to plan a policy for locomotive design, although in fact some notable types appeared between 1919 and 1923. In a number of instances existing locomotive designs were improved by the fitting of superheaters, or other technical improvements intended to boost their performance.

The powerful mixed traffic engine had more than proved its worth in wartime service, and further development of this type took place after the cessation of hostilities. At Swindon, Churchward

produced a large 2-8-0 design in 1919 which had 5ft 8in driving wheels and a boiler similar to that used on his 'Star' class express passenger engines; it proved capable of putting up some creditable performances on Paddington-Bristol expresses, as well as working heavy freights.

Two fine tank engine designs deserve mention. First, the Hughes 4-6-4Ts, which were four-cylinder locomotives based upon his LYR 4-6-0 tender engine design. They possessed a very fine outline and an additional point of interest lies in the fact that they were the last true Horwich design to emerge before takeover by the LMSR. Another tank locomotive of massive dimensions was the H16 4-6-2T introduced by Robert Urie on the LSWR in 1919. In appearance this followed the same rather austere lines that he had bestowed upon his 4-6-0 tender engines, with some characteristic Drummond touches retained.

It would be quite impossible to make mention of all the deserving locomotive designs produced for British railways, in the course of this story, and I must beg the indulgence of the reader if any particular favourite should appear to have been overlooked. My intention is to delineate the major changes affecting the development of steam locomotive design and appearance, and it was in the work of a few men that the major influences prevailed. Thus it is certainly not invidious to single out the names of Churchward, Gresley and Maunsell as the leading figures in establishing the modern British steam locomotive.

Having said this I am faced with something of an enigma. I have already shown how Churchward regarded the subject of locomotive appearance, and it must be admitted that it is by no means certain that either Gresley or Maunsell were empirical in their views upon the subject of locomotive appearance. Unfortunately we will never really know just how much of the final appearance of their locomotives resulted from the 'eye' of the great men themselves, and how much resulted from careful consideration at the drawing board stage by their principal assistants. In many cases a great deal of the detail design was entrusted to the care of the Chief Draughtsman, once the outline proposals had been agreed upon. To what extent the appearance of the finished product resembled the original thoughts it is practically impossible to assess. One thing we can rest assured upon is that the engineers would not have readily given their blessing to any design which appeared visually unsatisfactory to them, since after all it was their name and reputation that was at stake. Nevertheless it is certain that Churchward, Maunsell

and Fowler, to name but three, were quite prepared to leave decisions of this sort to their assistants when it suited them. Gresley, I strongly suspect, was rather more concerned that his engines should appear the way he wanted them; as a boy he spent long hours drawing locomotives in pen-and-ink, displaying considerable artistic talent.

In May 1918 Gresley had introduced his first three-cylinder locomotive. This was a 2-8-0 goods design, but the complicated valve gear arrangement was not very satisfactory, and to meet an immediate postwar need for heavy goods locomotives the Great Northern constructed a further batch of two-cylinder 2-8-0s. However, Gresley pursued the three-cylinder concept, and after some correspondence in the technical press he accepted much advice from Holcroft, who had patented a much simpler conjugate valve gear for three-cylinder engines whilst at Swindon in 1909, although the GWR had never employed it. Henceforth, Gresley announced his decision to employ the three-cylinder layout whenever practicable.

A new and powerful Mogul design appeared in 1920, known as the 1000 class (later K3), and with this class Gresley initiated the big engine policy of the Great Northern, which was carried on into LNER days. Big they certainly were, with three cylinders and the largest boiler in the country — no less than 6ft in diameter — and they proved very successful in service. Outwardly the K3 class had a curious combination of modern and traditional features. The front-end had outside steampipes to the outside cylinders, which combined with the huge boiler and running board raised clear of the driving wheels were very modern aspects. But the cab and tender still remained solidly in the Ivatt tradition. The contrast of old and new elements remained unchanged on a batch of three-cylinder 2-8-0s, the 477 class (later 02), which appeared in 1921.

The Great Bear, Churchward's prodigy of 1908, still remained the only Pacific locomotive constructed for a British railway, although Swindon never enthused over it and it was eventually converted to a 4-6-0, in keeping with GWR policy for express passenger engines. However, in America the Pacific type had undergone some significant development during the years 1910-1916, in particular on the Pennsylvania Railroad, whose K4 type was the result of intensive testing and research. Gresley, it will be recalled, had shown interest in a Pacific design in 1915, although this never got off the ground. Nevertheless he was fully aware of the advances made in the K4, as a full account appeared in the journal *Engineering* in 1916, and he made good use of some of the features when once again working upon Pacific proposals for the GNR.

In April 1922, the prototype Gresley Pacific No 1470 *Great Northern*, emerged from Doncaster. Not since Patrick Stirling's beautiful 8ft Single had steamed from the same works 52 years earlier had such a classic design graced the scene. A new era of powerful express passenger locomotives had dawned, and although there remained many technical improvements to be made before the new locomotives were really satisfactory performers, there is no doubt that Gresley placed the GNR in the forefront of development when he introduced No 1470. Aesthetically the A1 class (and the improved A3 of later years) was a masterpiece of artistic engineering. It possessed superb poise and a fine sense of scale to the various elements comprising the overall shape. Gone at last were the Ivatt cab and tender; in their place an excellent new side-window cab and a large, but compact, high-sided eight-wheel tender of handsome design.

A particularly fine feature of the A1 was the superb workmanship revealed in every detail; each item had a straightforward clean-cut finish which evidenced great care at every stage from drawing board to final manufacture. In this respect the Gresley design was to represent for all time the peak of British steam locomotive development, although there were to be considerable technical advances in the years that followed.

Another Pacific design made its debut in 1922, designed by Sir Vincent Raven on the neighbouring NER, and five were produced at Darlington Works. These were huge and undeniably impressive machines with a long boiler which earned them the nickname 'Skittle Alleys'. But compared to Gresley's design they seemed clumsy, with a decidedly top-heavy front end. This was not surprising, because the Raven design was really an enlarged version of the very successful three-cylinder Z class Atlantics, whereas the Gresley engines were a completely new conception. Comparison of the two designs clearly illustrates the turning-point which steam locomotive development had reached; henceforth it was the search for still great efficiency and power which shaped the new designs, and the final vestiges of graceful prewar practice were put aside. The 'modern' aesthetic, depending as it did on the overall proportions of a large boiler with squat chimney and mountings, exposed valve gear and driving wheels and a relatively high running board, had replaced the 19th century predilection for carefully concealed working parts, with ornate flourishes upon basically very simple outlines.

The creation of the Big Four railway companies in the 1923 amalgamation inevitably had considerable effects upon the course of locomotive development, for whereas in the pre-Grouping railway companies there had been considerable variety in the designs of the numerous individual locomotive engineers, there were now only four such posts to be filled. The choice of suitable candidates was no easy task for the new managements, and inevitably some engineers were bitterly disappointed at not being selected, whilst others took the simplest course and retired from the scene.

Significantly both Maunsell and Gresley succeeded to the positions of Chief Mechanical Engineer on the new SR and LNER respectively. On the GWR C. B. Collett had taken over from Churchward in 1921, and he remained in the post after the Grouping. Collett was essentially a staunch supporter of the Churchward school of locomotive design and therefore there was little likelihood of any disruption of GWR locomotive policy. Maunsell brought many advanced Ashford practices to the Southern, but he also seemed prepared to adopt a number of the design features of Robert Urie, who retired when the LSWR ceased to exist. Gresley continued with his big engine policy from GNR days.

The situation on the LMSR — largest of the newly formed Big Four — was far less satisfactory. Strong pre-Grouping loyalties and rivalries persisted, and a stable policy for locomotive design failed to emerge as a matter of course. There was no one of the calibre of Gresley, Maunsell or Collett within the new company and the current practice at Crewe, Derby, Horwich and St Rollox fell far short of the standards of Swindon, Ashford and Doncaster. On the LNWR, Beames had carried on with out-dated traditional designs (although, under the LMS he did apply outside Walschaerts valve motion to some 'Prince of Wales' class superheated 4-6-0s), whilst Hughes on the LYR produced some moderately successful four-cylinder express 4-6-0s. On the MR, Fowler persisted with the small engine policy of that company which resulted in modest-sized compound 4-4-0s being the largest express power available. Ironically, Fowler had produced some successful large 2-8-0 locomotives for the S&DJR, in which he combined the boiler of the standard superheated compound 4-4-0 with outside cylinders and Walschaerts valve gear. He also employed the latter feature on a large 0-10-0 locomotive constructed in 1919 for banking duties on the formidable Lickey incline. But for everyday service on the MR proper there was nothing comparable to these specialised Derby designs.

Despite the fact that he was approaching old age, it was Hughes of the LYR who was appointed as the first Chief Mechanical Engineer of the newly formed LMSR and to begin with there was some degree of Horwich influence which culminated in the appearance of a new mixed-traffic Mogul, although by the time this was constructed Hughes had retired and Fowler was in command, at which point the influence swung away in the direction of Derby. The Horwich Mogul had outside cylinders of large dimensions located very high up and at a steep angle, together with outside Walschaerts valve gear. The resulting appearance, with a very high running board stepped down from the cylinders towards the cab, earned the class the curious nickname of 'Crabs'.

With the appointment of Fowler to succeed Hughes in 1925, the swing towards Midland practice was quickly demonstrated; for example, at this time the above-mentioned 'Crabs' were approaching completion at Horwich. Fowler insisted upon replacing some features with Midland items; this included the tender, which as a result did not match the width of the cab! Derby was the home of small, neat engines designed to handle light loads, or to double-head heavier ones. This was Midland policy, and it now became LMS policy despite the fact that both Horwich and Crewe had constructed considerably larger engines. Immense numbers of medium sized locomotives derived from Midland practice were constructed for the LMS and distributed to most parts of the system, where they were sometimes received with considerable hostility.

For express passenger work Fowler produced a standard compound 4-4-0 derived from Deeley design. It must be admitted that for their size they were fine engines and put up some remarkable performances when handled by crews that appreciated their characteristics, but viewed against contemporary developments elsewhere they were sadly underpowered. Although there had been a proposal by Hughes for a large Pacific design — no doubt inspired by the advent of the Gresley and Raven engines — nothing larger than the Hughes 4-6-0s was actually constructed during the early days of the LMSR, and for the first years of its existence the company was handicapped by a shortage of large express passenger locomotives; of which more anon.

A further milestone in the remarkable story of locomotive development at Swindon occurred in 1923, when C. B. Collett introduced the first of the famous 'Castle' class four-cylinder express passenger 4-6-0s. True to Swindon practice, they were a development of Churchward's 'Star' class and incorporated all the lessons learned, and improvements in manufacture, that Swindon had carefully fostered. The pioneer engine was No 4073 *Caerphilly Castle*, and externally it followed exactly the existing GWR style, with taper boiler, copper-capped chimney, brass top-feed and safety-valve cover and a sturdy workmanlike overall appearance, with immaculate detail finish. It was moreover, to prove an extremely efficient and capable design. Engines of the class were built, to unchanged specification, at intervals from 1923 to 1939; with a further series, slightly modified, constructed between the end of World War II and 1950. Technically they proved superior to Gresley's Pacific design when comparative trials were held, and Gresley subsequently modified certain features which greatly improved the performance of his engines.

I have already made brief mention of the two-cylinder 4-6-0 locomotives introduced by Robert Urie on the LSWR in 1918, which were very much in the solid Drummond tradition. For the SR, Maunsell took the basic Urie design and applied an improved front end and higher boiler pressure, to produce his well known 'King Arthur' class 4-6-0. This was a most attractive design when first introduced by Maunsell but the later addition of smoke deflectors did not enhance its appearance. But although the 'King Arthur' class were excellent performers, they were only medium-size engines by contemporary standards and before long a larger express passenger design was requested to meet the requirements of the traffic department.

Accordingly Maunsell, together with his chief draughtsman James Clayton, evaluated the designs of the GWR 'Castle' and the LNER Pacific, before deciding upon a four-cylinder 4-6-0 layout. In 1926 the first of the new 'Lord Nelson' class appeared, and it was for a short while the most powerful express engine in the country, thereby bestowing some much needed prestige upon the SR. The design was definitely in the Maunsell/Clayton tradition created at Ashford; it had a Belpaire firebox and sturdy but handsome outline. Like the 'King Arthur' class it was later spoiled by the addition of smoke deflectors.

On the LMSR the Midland influence still prevailed under the leadership of Sir Henry Fowler. In his excellent book *Locomotive Panorama* (Vol 1), E. S. Cox — who was personally involved in the developments of this unsettled period in the locomotive affairs of the LMSR — confirms the widely held impression that Fowler himself had very little to do with the design of the locomotives credited to his name.

Cox states that although the operating staff were apparently satisfied with the existing MR types, there had been the idea of a new larger engine in the mind of Fowler for some time. In 1924 a diagram was prepared for an enlarged three-cylinder compound 4-6-0, and this in turn, was developed into a scheme for a large compound Pacific. Detailed design work was put in hand for this (and a corresponding 2-8-2 for freight service), and construction had actually commenced when the dramatic instruction to stop all work on it was issued by the management. Briefly what happened was that whilst Fowler was developing his compound Pacific other interested parties had arranged to borrow a GWR 'Castle' class for trials, in order to press home their belief that a locomotive of similar design was what the company needed, rather than the complicated compound design favoured by Fowler. The management were suitably impressed by the performance of the 'Castle' locomotive and actually expressed their desire to have 50 locomotives built to the GWR design; but loading gauge and other difficulties intervened. Finally the decision was taken to adopt a 4-6-0 type, with three cylinders, having a maximum size boiler, high steam pressure and superheating, and long lap valve gear.

The new locomotives were required for service in time for the summer traffic of the following year; there was no chance to construct a prototype. In the autumn of 1926 an order was placed for 50 locomotives to be constructed by the North British Locomotive Co, utilising both their Glasgow works to build 25 apiece; such was the urgency of the situation. North British was to be responsible for the detail designing and the locomotives were to be constructed straight off the drawing board. A complete set of drawings for the 'Lord Nelson' class was borrowed from Maunsell during the design stages, but it appears that little more than the design of the cab and firebox was actually incorporated into the new locomotive. There were many Derby standard features, plus quite a lot which can probably be credited in a roundabout way to Swindon.

Thus, under somewhat remarkable circumstances, the hybrid 'Royal Scot' was conceived. The first engines were delivered in 1927; not quite in time for the summer traffic as had been hoped, but in time to institute regular non-stop running between Euston and Carlisle in the autumn of that year. They had been designed and constructed in a remarkably short time, and it is a tribute to all involved that they proved themselves to be splendid locomotives in everyday service. At last the LMSR had a large, modern passenger locomotive — but what

involved politics had led up to its construction!

These must have been exciting times for the enthusiast, for only a few weeks prior to the completion of the first 'Royal Scot' another large express passenger 4-6-0 locomotive had made its bow, this time at Swindon. This was C. B. Collett's masterpiece, the four-cylinder 'King' class 4-6-0, which was to prove the ultimate development of the Churchward four-cylinder 4-6-0 concept. The 'Kings' were immensely powerful for their wheel arrangement and their tractive effort was equal to that of the larger Pacific designs produced by the other railways in later years. Visually the 'King' was a fine design with a great feeling of power, which depended upon excellent proportions rather than sheer size. They make an interesting contrast to the 'Royal Scot' class in this respect. Aesthetically the 'Royal Scot' was much the poorer of the two, with an oversize smokebox and a mere pimple of a chimney, and a slab-sided firebox breaking across the centre driving wheel splasher. In contrast, the proportions of these features on the 'King' were well-nigh perfect.

Mention should be made of some excellent smaller designs of the period, intended for intermediate duties or for operation on routes with loading-gauge or weight restrictions.

In 1928 Gresley introduced his 'Sandringham' class three-cylinder 4-6-0s for operation over the lines of the former GER from Liverpool Street. The restrictions of weight and size were further complicated by the length of the track on turntables, and Gresley had to fit very short tenders to the batch for the GER lines, but when a later series was constructed, for the former GCR route, a larger tender was employed which considerably enhanced the appearance of these neat machines.

For intermediate service in the north-east and Scotland Gresley decided upon a three-cylinder 4-4-0 design. The D49 class had a slender appearance, but they were

181 GWR 4-6-0 No 2902 *Lady of the Lake*; an early 'Saint' class locomotive. The new look in locomotive design, introduced by J. G. Churchward at Swindon, shocked many enthusiasts at the time. But there was no denying the excellence of his locomotives in service.

182 A later 'Saint' class 4-6-0 No 2922 *Saint Gabriel*, showing the cleaned up appearance of the front end footplating, running plates and cab. This was undertaken by Churchward's assistant H. Holcroft at his chief's request, to counter criticism about the appearance of his engines.

183 Churchward's solitary Pacific *The Great Bear* of 1908. A design in advance of its time.

capable of putting in some hard work, in
the hands of a competent crew. As modern
derivations of the classic British 4-4-0
they deserve mention in our story; but we
must return to the Southern and the work
of Maunsell to consider the finest modern
4-4-0 design.

The 'Schools' class was produced by
Maunsell in 1930, so as to meet traffic
requirements on the severely restricted
Hastings line of the former SECR. A
combination of heavy gradients, severe
curves and restricted tunnel clearances
dictated a 4-4-0 design rather than a 4-6-0.
The result — produced from a synthesis
of parts of the 'Lord Nelson' and 'King
Arthur' classes — was a veritable
masterpiece for its size, and extremely
handsome into the bargain.

181

182
183

184

184 Churchward's taper-boiler mixed traffic Mogul of 1911 for the GWR, with much detail design work by Holcroft. A 43xx 2-6-0 is seen here leaving Reading on an excursion train to Cheltenham.

185 Rebuilt four-cylinder 4-6-0 No 5999 *Vindictive* in LMSR livery. Designed for the LNWR Bowen Cooke's 'Claughtons' may be described as Crewe's contribution to the 'modern' school of design, and were probably

the most impressive to look upon in this later large-boilered form, as seen here.

186 Transitional steam design. Robert Urie's two-cylindered Class N15 4-6-0 of 1918 for the LSWR, which perpetuated many Drummond features whilst having a more modern layout. No 749 is illustrated in SR works grey livery before the class was named and incorporated in to the 'King Arthur' class.

185

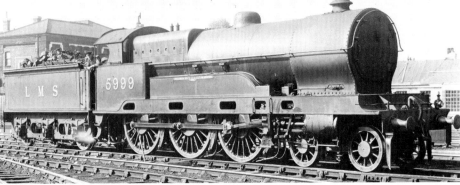

186

187

187 R. E. L. Maunsell's successful prototype Mogul for the SECR, No 810 of 1917, which displayed a sturdy modern outline with some pronounced Swindon features.

188 Robert Urie's powerful H16 class 4-6-2T of the 1921-2 period for the LSWR. These engines remained visually unaltered throughout their lifetime, and No 30517 is seen here in later BR service, hauling empty stock from Waterloo to Clapham Junction, through Vauxhall in July 1951.

189 Gresley's large-boilered Mogul introduced on the GNR in 1920. Note the Ivatt style cab and tender. No 1002, in immaculate condition, is illustrated.

188

189

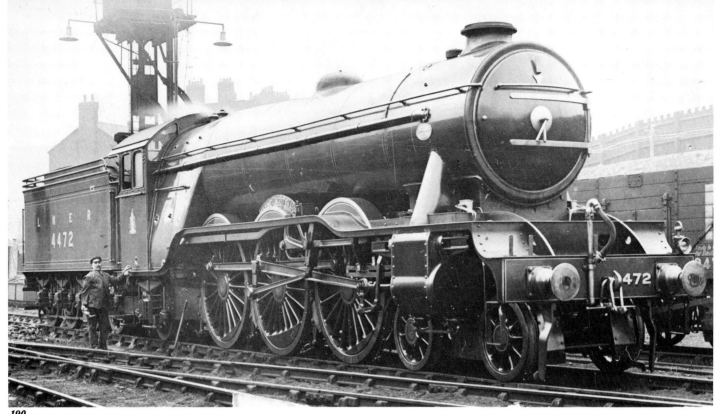

192

190 No 4472 *Flying Scotsman* in special exhibition livery with LNER coat of arms on cabside. This view clearly shows the original boiler mountings and cab design; later reduced in height.

191 The fine 'Castle' class of the GWR, which was constructed over a period of 27 years with only slight modifications. With all the characteristic hallmarks of Swindon practice it was a development of Churchward's 'Star' class 4-6-0. Illustrated is No 4079 *Pendennis Castle*, in original condition, leaving Kings Cross while on trial on the LNER.

192 The Hughes/Fowler LMSR Mogul design; nicknamed 'Crabs' on account of the very high running-board over the cylinders.

193 The 1922 Pacific design by Sir Vincent Raven for the NER, which makes a most interesting comparison with the Gresley design. Although undeniably massive in appearance, the Raven design somehow lacked the poise and elegance of the Gresley Pacific. No 2402 *City of York* was photographed in LNER days at Edinburgh Haymarket shed.

193

194
195

196　　　　　　　　　　　　　　　　　　　　　*197*

194　R. E. L. Maunsell's finest design: the 'Lord Nelson' class of 1926. No 855 *Robert Blake* is depicted in original condition.

195　Sir Henry Fowler's 'Royal Scot' class 4-6-0, produced after study of the Maunsell 'Lord Nelson' design. No 6161 *The King's Own*, is seen on display at the Liverpool &

Manchester Centenary Exhibition in 1930, with Gresley's 'Hush Hush' 4-6-4, a 'King' class 4-6-0 and a 'Lord Nelson' 4-6-0 in the background.

196　'King Arthur' class 4-6-0 No 777 *Sir Lamiel*; developed from the Urie N15 design. Pictured at the head of the 'Atlantic Coast

Express' after the addition of smoke deflectors.

197　C. B. Collett's masterpiece. The four-cylinder 'King' class 4-6-0; ultimate development of the Churchward/Collett period on the GWR. No 6008 *King James II* presents a dramatic picture as it is turned on the table outside Paddington, circa 1949.

198
199

198 'Sandringham' class 4-6-0 design by Nigel Gresley, introduced 1928 for operation over the lines of the former GER. No 2864 *Liverpool*, one of the engines named after football teams, was photographed at Central station, Manchester in June 1938.

199 Class D49 three-cylinder 4-4-0, introduced 1927 by Nigel Gresley for the LNER. Illustrated is No 250 *Perthshire*.

200 The fine 'Schools' class 4-4-0 by R. E. L. Maunsell, produced from a synthesis of parts from the 'Lord Nelson' and 'King Arthur' classes. No 904 *Lancing* was photographed before the addition of smoke deflectors, which somewhat marred their pleasing lines.

200

12 The Quest for Speed

The appointment of W. A. Stanier as Chief Mechanical Engineer of the LMSR in 1932 was a major turning point in the locomotive affairs of that company. Stanier was a GWR man, imbued with all the sound principles and practice of Churchward and Collett, and he wasted no time in applying many Swindon features to the new locomotives he was requested to design, although he was also careful to give proper consideration to the current thinking of Derby and Crewe.

The first Stanier design to emerge was a mixed-traffic Mogul, and as had been widely prophesied, the Swindon lineage of the engine was unmistakable, with Belpaire firebox, top feed and domeless taper boiler, although the tender design was pure MR. To some extent these Moguls were probably designed to allow Stanier to feel his way, since it would have been quite practicable to have constructed another batch of the well-tried Horwich 'Crabs' instead. The first engine of the class, No 13245, appeared in 1933 from Crewe works. A diagram reproduced (photo 202) shows it to have been fitted originally with a GWR style safety valve casing. E. S. Cox tells us that Stanier left quite a lot of such details to the imagination of his drawing office staff, and in their initial diagrams they included this unmistakable piece of GWR adornment. Stanier however, made it quite clear that he did not wish to produce carbon copies of Swindon practice, and ordered the casing to be redesigned. However, through some misunderstanding, the first engine duly sported the offending item, which was quickly replaced on Stanier's instructions!

In 1933, just 17 months after Stanier took office, his first Pacific was completed, the fourth design of this wheel arrangement to appear in Britain. In view of his association with Swindon, some people had envisaged a locomotive roughly resembling *The Great Bear,* but what finally came before their eyes was far more majestic in appearance. In fact, although undoubtedly 'Westernised', it was the 'King' class 4-6-0 it most closely resembled, rather than the Churchward

Pacific. As originally constructed the handsome lines of the Stanier 'Princess Royal' 4-6-2s were spoilt by a rather small Midland-style tender, and it was after this feature had been replaced by a new high-sided design that they looked at their best. Another detail which Stanier was apparently content to leave to the discretion of his drawing office staff, was the final appearance of the chimney. Stanier (no doubt adhering to his refusal to copy such items from Swindon practice), passed the final drawings for production with the engine sporting a short stovepipe chimney of Caledonian style; however some last minute doubts led to the drawing-up of the now well-known attractive Stanier flared-lip design.

Designs for a new standardised series of locomotives to replace the motley collection in existence, was the remit given to Stanier, and certainly no better choice of man could have been made. Under Churchward and Collett the GWR had established just such a range of locomotives of highly competent design and performance, and Stanier was well versed in all the problems this had involved. For the LMSR he produced 11 new standard designs, to which no less than 1,224 steam locomotives were constructed between 1933 and 1939, and for which most of the design effort was concentrated within the first three years.

A Stanier engine — whether it was a Pacific, a heavy goods locomotive or a modest tank engine — possessed great visual character, with a straightforward finish which gave it the same robust lineage that the engines of Swindon and Ashford displayed. There were no ornate touches in the classically Victorian copper and brass traditions of Swindon, but basically they were blessed by an excellent overall sense of balance and proportion. Subsequent technical improvements, such as an improved boiler with separate dome and top feed, in no way detracted from their appearance, whilst the later design of high sided six-wheeled tender suited them admirably. Of all his designs it is probably the mixed-traffic Class 5 4-6-0 (the 'Black Five'), which epitomises his work. Based

upon the GWR 'Hall' class, this two-cylinder maid of all work proved immensley popular and successful; no less than 842 were constructed between 1934 and 1951.

Without doubt the 1930s witnessed the heyday of the British steam locomotive in terms of efficiency and performance in everyday service. Technical knowledge had advanced considerably, as a result of more sophisticated means of testing and research, and all four main line companies built up studs of efficient modern steam locomotives to suit their traffic needs. However it was at this time that the railways really began to feel the full impact of competition from the rapidly expanding motor industry. Something had to be done, and done fast, to recapture both the imagination and the patronage of a public more inclined to enthuse over events on the roads, or in the air, than upon the railways. The answer seemed to lie in speed; if speed could be developed beyond the capacity of existing locomotives and stock there seemed real hope of reviving the supremacy of rail travel.

If steam locomotion was to be employed, there were problems of wind resistance to overcome, whilst both performance and brake power would need improvement. For a while a better solution seemed to lie in the development of high-speed diesel railcars, as there had been some significant developments with these in Germany. This prompted Gresley to explore the feasibility of ordering some similar trains from German builders, for operation on the LNER. But it was realised that a more luxurious standard of amenity could be provided by using locomotive-hauled carriages and it was accordingly decided to introduce a new version of the classic Gresley Pacific, with enhanced performance and a streamlined outer casing.

On two previous occasions Gresley had broken away from the established Stephensonian conventions of boiler and smokebox cladding, by applying semi-streamlined casings; first on his 4-6-4 'Hush-Hush' Yarrow-boilered engine

No 10000, of 1929 (which created something of a stir because of the lack of a visible chimney), and again on his magnificent *Cock o' the North* 2-8-2 of 1934. Of the latter class (P2), the first two had an arrangement of smoke deflecting screens at the front end similar to the design of No 10000, but later ones had a wedge shaped streamlined nose. This wedge shape, which was first applied to the new class A4 streamlined Pacific design, was based upon the front end of the French Bugatti railcars (which Gresley and Bulleid had gone to inspect personally), and it had proved most effective in wind tunnel tests made upon models.

Streamlining of everything, from cigarette lighters to automobiles or cinema kiosks was in vogue by the mid-1930s, and the publicity value of streamlined locomotives and carriages could not have been bettered. But it would be a deep injustice to suggest that such thoughts were uppermost in the minds of Gresley or Bulleid when finalising the shape of the new Pacific. They were chiefly concerned to cut down wind resistance and their streamlining was based upon scientific principles. However, Gresley did bestow a special silver-grey livery upon the first four locomotives, which were designed to haul the 'Silver Jubilee' high-speed train introduced in the autumn of 1935. Later engines appeared in an equally striking garter blue, with the carriages painted in two shades of blue.

The various record-breaking exploits of the Gresley A4 class culminated with the capture of the world speed record for steam traction, 126mph by No 4468 *Mallard* in 1938. More relevant to our present story is the deep impression that their striking appearance made upon the public. Streamlining had caught their fancy, and inevitably it was not long before other railways followed the LNER example; not always with such happy results. In fact, the GWR had anticipated the LNER in 1935, and had committed a grievous error of judgment in applying a semi-streamlined shape to some of their classic 4-6-0s; whilst even a London Transport Piccadilly Line tube train appeared with streamlined ends!

The LMSR were understandably anxious to recapture some of the prestige and limelight which the LNER high speed streamliners had stolen during 1935/36, and they achieved this by introducing the 'Coronation Scot' train in 1937; true to the fashions of the age they indulged in streamlining for the locomotive and train.

The Stanier Pacific introduced for this service had a more bulbous streamlined form than the Gresley A4, and it is on record that this was adopted more to please the directors than through any

201

scientific aim. The added weight and cost of the streamlined casing did not really seem justified to Stanier and although a batch of streamlined engines was first constructed, another batch duly appeared without the casing, and these non-streamlined engines proved to be magnificent machines to gaze upon, with truly massive proportions which seemed to stretch the loading gauge to the limit.

Before concluding this chapter, brief mention should be made of one or two other classic locomotive designs of the period. On the LMSR under Fowler's direction the Derby drawing office produced a splendid 2-6-4T for passenger duties, in 1927. This displayed a simple neat outline, and proved capable of a remarkable turn of speed. When Stanier took office he perpetuated the wheel arrangement, substituting his taper-boiler, and several hundred were constructed by the LMSR. The initial batch of Stanier engines had three cylinders, but no great advantage was discovered, and subsequent orders were for two-cylinder engines. The 2-6-4T design by Maunsell, which had first appeared in prototype form in 1917, was ordered in 1923 for use on the SR. These handsome engines, named after rivers in SR territory, suffered a dramatic rebuilding to 2-6-0 tender engines, following the Sevenoaks derailment of 1927, when it was decided that they were unstable runners as tank engines on Southern Railway tracks. These Maunsell 2-6-4Ts and the later Stanier designs for the LMSR showed considerable Swindon influence, and may be said to be developed from Churchward's tank engines, which in improved form were built by Collett and Hawksworth for the GWR.

201 Still finished in workshop grey (for photographic purposes) and as yet un-named, William Stanier's pioneer four-cylinder Pacific No 6200 *The Princess Royal* at Euston for official inspection. No 6200 entered service only 17 months after Stanier took office.

For heavy freight service the LMSR introduced a 2-8-0 locomotive, designed by William Stanier, in 1935. When war broke out the Government adopted the design for overseas service, and orders were placed for 240 of the type equipped for oil-burning. Eventually no less than 666 were in service on British Railways, including examples built at Brighton, Darlington, Ashford, Eastleigh and Swindon. Once again a classic steam locomotive, designed for the peacetime needs of a British railway, was pressed into service as a machine of war; history had been repeated.

Although no one could have foreseen it, the outbreak of World War II marked the end of the finest years of steam locomotive design in Britain. In such classics as the large Pacific designs of Sir Nigel Gresley and Sir William Stanier a fine combination of aesthetic and engineering qualities had been achieved, without sacrificing the everyday requirements of the maintenance staff (although there was some dislike of the streamlined casings from this point of view). In the remaining years of steam locomotive design and development a far more utilitarian approach was to be perforce adopted, as we shall see in a later chapter.

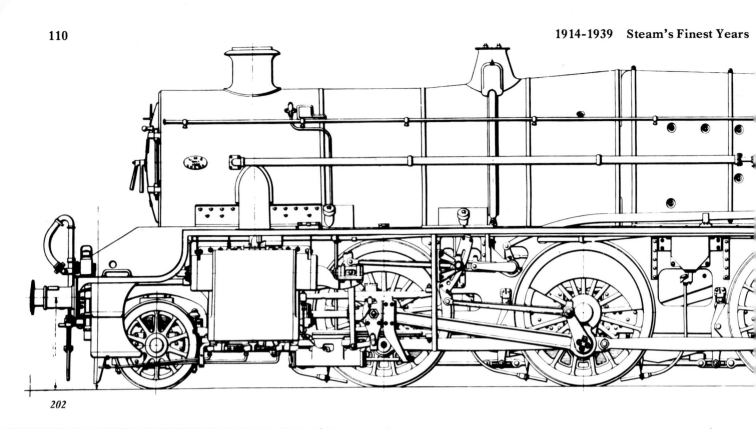

202

203

202   W. A. Stanier was to revolutionise the locomotive affairs of the LMSR. When pioneer Mogul No 13245 first emerged from Crewe Works it sported a typical GWR safety valve casing. This was quickly removed on Stanier's orders as he made it quite clear he had no desire to produce carbon copies of Swindon practice. This design gave but little clue to the great locomotives that were to follow.

203   The classic mixed traffic design by Stanier for the LMSR. The ubiquitous 'Black Fives' of which no less than 842 examples were constructed between 1934 and 1951. No 45225 makes a pleasing picture in early BR days, finished in lined black livery.

204

204   The 'Hush-Hush' Gresley experimental
high-pressure locomotive with Yarrow water-
tube boiler. The only 4-6-4 tender engine ever
introduced on a British railway. Painted
battleship grey No 10000 was photographed
hauling empty stock during trial running. The
front end design and smooth cladding were
portents of the later Gresley and Bulleid
Pacific designs. The apparent lack of a
chimney aroused considerable comment.

205

206

207

205 Nigel Gresley's powerful design of 2-8-2 for express passenger work on the heavily graded route between Edinburgh and Aberdeen. This view of No 2002 *Earl Marischal* shows the original front end design, before fitting with additional smoke deflector plates.

206 Experimental semi-streamlining application to GWR 'King' class 4-6-0 No 6014. The aim was to cut coal consumption by lowering wind resistance.

207 No 2509 *Silver Link* in ex-works condition, photographed prior to the press demonstrations, whilst working the 5.45pm Kings Cross-Harrogate at New Southgate.

208

209

208 The LMSR streamlined train of 1937, the 'Coronation Scot' was hauled by the new Stanier Pacifics. The original livery was blue and silver for both locomotives and train. Later this was altered to crimson lake and gold as seen here on No 6227 *Duchess of Devonshire* photographed at Polmadie shed, Glasgow.

209 The handsome non-streamlined version of the Pacific. No 6231 *Duchess of Atholl* is seen heading north through the London suburbs in original condition with single chimney.

210 Possibly the most handsome of all the British streamlined locomotives were the later series of Gresley 2-8-2s, with the Bugatti wedge-shaped nose and double-chimney. Here No 2003 *Lord President* heads through Princess Street Gardens, Edinburgh, looking in fine fettle.

210

211

211 Stanier's 'Turbomotive', an experimental steam turbine-driven version of his 'Princess Royal' 4-6-2 design, possessed an attractive appearance which was praised by American designer Raymond Loewy. No 6202 is seen panned by the camera at speed.

212 No 4771 *Green Arrow*, first of Sir Nigel Gresley's powerful mixed traffic 2-6-2 locomotives of Class V2, of which four were introduced in 1936 followed later by a further 180. This design had a well balanced powerful

appearance. No 4771 is seen when new, leaving Kings Cross on the 3pm fitted freight in October 1936.

213 Churchward introduced the taper-boilered 2-6-2T to the GWR. Later versions were built by Collett and Hawksworth. A Collett engine, No 6116 is illustrated.

214 The Maunsell 'River' class 2-6-4T, for the SR with Swindon features. No 807 *River Axe* displays their handsome lines.

215 The Stanier three-cylinder 2-6-4T, design; also showing Swindon influence in its outline. No 2501 was photographed on St Pancras suburban duty.

216 The standard LMSR Stanier 8F 2-8-0 which was adopted for service overseas in World War II. No WD300 was photographed in official works grey complete with Westinghouse air brake, intended for use on the continent of Europe.

212

213

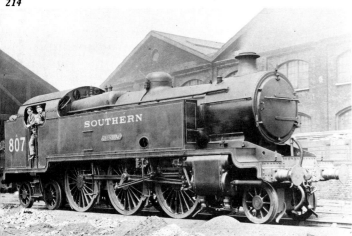

214

215

216

13 Steam Coaching Stock Progress

By 1914 the basic styles of steam coaching stock which were to be perpetuated for the following 20 years or so, were already established. This was the commencement of a period of relative stagnation in carriage design, and far too many Edwardian practices were still commonplace in the 1920s.

The clerestory roof, which had given such a handsome appearance to *fin-de-siecle* carriages, had proved both expensive to construct and awkward to maintain and keep clean. At the commencement of this period, only the MR was still constructing new clerestory carriages. High elliptical roofs were a typical feature of most new construction, and by 1917/18 the MR had come into line with this trend; all their later designs for main line and suburban stock had high elliptical roofs.

Although application of electric lighting was steadily increasing, a few companies still persisted with gas-lit stock, despite the fire hazard that this presented in wooden carriages. No doubt as a result of increasingly strong public anxiety following two disastrous MR accidents in which fire had broken out, the LYR introduced a remarkable 'fireproof train', with gas-lighting, in 1914. This attempt to perpetuate an out-dated amenity did have one significant feature; the carriages were of all-steel construction. In fact it was the first completely all-steel main line train to run on a British railway. At about the same time, the GWR ordered construction of an experimental all-steel fireproof carriage, but war intervened, and it did not actually enter service until 1921.

These early essays in all-steel construction were to prove premature; in 1914 most new carriages had bodies of wooden construction mounted upon steel underframes. However, on some railways by 1918 steel panelling over a timber framework was beginning to supersede the all-wooden construction partly due to the rising cost of wood, but mainly to reduce the fire risk.

The railway companies had invested in extensive oilgas installations, and this factor probably explains the reluctance of some of them to change to electricity. Many carriages survived their entire working life with gas lighting, and gas was employed for cooking purposes on numerous kitchen and restaurant cars. As a matter of interest, there were still a large number of gas lit carriages in service when the railways were Nationalised in 1948. On the GWR for example, no less than 389 were still in service at that time.

Carriages were now normally fitted with steam heating apparatus, with some form of regulator to allow the passenger to switch it on or off. Steam was piped through from the locomotive, and hot as well as cold water was now provided in lavatories.

The layout of carriage interiors followed remarkably set patterns, varied only to suit the type of duties for which the stock was intended. For main line services the typical carriage was gangwayed at each end with a vestibule leading to a side corridor running the length of the carriage. Lavatories were usually situated at the ends, whilst the side corridor gave access to the compartments. Each compartment had its own bodyside door and there were a number of doors on the corridor side of the body. To each side of the compartment door were quarterlight windows, while the door itself had a droplight, usually with a ventilator above.

For suburban duties non-corridor compartment stock was almost universally employed. Exceptions to this were the carriages for some outer-suburban duties (journeys of around 50 miles), which were of non-corridor design in the sense that they did not possess gangways between carriages, but had a short internal corridor providing access to a lavatory. Another version provided a lavatory between two compartments, and it was left to the powers of observation of the traveller whether or not he or she noted this feature, and chose the correct compartment before the train started.

The open saloon layout was employed chiefly for dining cars and the public apparently preferred the privacy of a compartment and the convenience of an adjacent door, for normal travelling.

The restrictions on manufacture imposed during the 1914—18 war period did not encourage design progress for coaching stock, and an inevitable period of stagnation followed the return to peacetime. There was a considerable backlog of repair work to be overcome before the workshops could resume a normal routine of new construction and overhaul. For example, the GWR sold over 200 of their new 'Toplight' carriages, of Churchward design, to the Government for war service, and Swindon converted the carriages to form ambulance trains for operation at home and on the Continent. After the war the majority were repurchased from the Government and restored to their original condition at Swindon.

The average length of a British main line passenger carriage in immediate postwar years was between 50-60ft, and it was usually mounted upon two four-wheel bogies. Exceptions to this were the 70ft Churchward carriages for the GWR, whilst many sleeping and dining cars were mounted upon six-wheel bogies.

The methods employed for coupling carriages together and the design of flexible gangways between carriages were not standardised. The GNR continued to use the excellent Pullman-type gangway, with automatic couplers, which it had introduced around the turn of the century. Despite the undoubted superiority and greater safety of this design, most pre-Grouping companies persisted with the screw-coupling and bellows gangway. An operating problem arose because of this refusal to standardise (a Royal Commission had, incidentally, advocated such a policy as early as 1900) when through workings of carriages were very much in fashion. Special gangway adaptors had to be designed and fitted to carriages used on these through services.

Another feature developed by the GNR was the articulated train set; Gresley had introduced this in 1907. The bodies and underframes of adjacent carriages were pivoted upon a common bogie, thus reducing both the weight and initial cost of stock. The riding qualities of articulated stock proved to be very good, but disadvantages included their inflexibility when a train had to be remarshalled to cope with changed traffic needs, and increased difficulties in the unhappy event of more than one bogie becoming derailed. Nevertheless Gresley continued to build articulated sets of both main line and suburban stock, as we shall see later.

Two carriage designs produced in the final pre-Grouping years deserve brief mention. One was the 'Continental' stock of the SECR (so named because they had a rather Continental appearance, and were often employed on boat trains). This was 62ft long and only 8ft wide, with flat sides on which vertical matchboarding was used below the waist. This very distinctive method of wooden construction had been a feature of some earlier stock built for the NER and GCR, and was also a characteristic of wooden-bodied Pullman cars. Entry to the 'Continental' stock was by end doors, a prophetic feature which must have seemed strange to eyes accustomed to the door-to-every-compartment layout. The other late pre-Grouping design was for the LSWR. These carriages foreshadowed the trend towards plain exteriors which became a feature of steel-panelled carriages in later years. Presumably because of their plain aspect and the massive appearance of their double-framed bogies, they gained the curious nickname of 'Ironclads'.

Interior treatment of carriages built in the last 15 years of the pre-Grouping era tended to show a marked reaction against the ornate decor of late Victorian days. The passing of the clerestory has already been commented upon, and it is a regrettable fact that the elliptical roof did not contribute to either the external, or internal, appearance of carriages with anything approaching the same degree of success. Internally, the plain high ceiling lacked character, and no amount of Lincrusta-Walton relief mouldings could disguise this, whilst the design of lamp pendents — apart from a brief *Art Nouveau* influence — was mundane in the extreme.

The elaborate carved wooden mouldings and inlaid panels of the sumptuous coaches constructed around the turn of the century gave way to dark polished veneers, and the buttoned-in plush with deep horsehair padded cushions was replaced by more utilitarian seating, with more springs but a curiously harsh appearance. The design of such features as luggage racks, ventilators, commode handles and the aforementioned lamp pendents, was plain and uninspired, with brass or pseudo-bronze finish. A sombre, restrained interior treatment characterised much new construction and it seemed that a good deal of the glamour

had gone from the main line carriage by the early 1920s. The situation remained much the same for a further 15 years.

This dreary and conservative attitude to carriage furnishings and amenities could hardly have happened at a worse time; just when competitive modes of transport were developing into a serious threat. The choice of decor for new construction seems to have been regarded as virtually anyone's pigeon, provided they expressed some supposed flair for such things. It was often the wife of the chief mechanical engineer, or a company director, or some member of the drawing office staff, who finalised the interior. Consequently the furnishings of a railway carriage were chosen on a basis of personal preference (just as one chooses such items for one's own home), rather than with any proper understanding of the specialised requirements of travel.

One company that went very much its own individual way in affairs of carriage decor was the privately-owned Pullman Car Company, whose cars were operated over a number of important British routes. Their attitude to interior design underwent very little change between Edwardian years and the 1960s, and may best be summed-up as a somewhat decadent classicism upon a foundation of solid workmanship. The company emphasised the personal service they offered — a form of hotel lounge-cum-dining-room on wheels — and the Pullman cars were very popular with a section of the travelling public prepared to pay extra for the service and the guarantee of a seat; no standing was permitted in a Pullman. As examples of coaching stock design the Pullmans were soundly constructed and incorporated some fine materials, but aesthetically they were curiosities, and did much to foster an out-dated image of luxury rail travel, as the years passed.

Mention has already been made of the flat-sided carriages constructed for the SECR. This was a company which owned several routes with a restricted loading gauge — hence the flat sides. There were one or two flat-sided designs produced for lines which did not require special narrow stock, notably the GCR and NER, and Pullman cars adopted a similar profile. But in general, carriage bodysides had some degree of curvature — or tumblehome — the origins of which can be traced back to road stagecoach design. On early railway carriages the tumblehome was usually below the waistline, with a flat side between waist and roof, whilst some had a continuous tumblehome from roof to solebar. The next development was to provide a profile which was widest at waist level with a gentle fall out from roof to waist and a pronounced tumblehome

from waist to solebar. This latter profile, which was visually most satisfactory, was widely employed for carriages constructed between 1914 and 1951.

Inevitably there were changes in the design policy for some constituents of the new companies after 1923, depending upon which pre-Grouping concern the new carriage and wagon chief had emanated from. Thus it was largely MR practice that affected early LMSR coaching stock, as R. W. Reid was an ex-Midland man, whilst Gresley brought his GNR practices to the new LNER. On the SR Maunsell seemed less content to perpetuate the designs of his former company, and set to work to produce a new range of carriages for main line duties. Only on the GWR with C. B. Collett in charge, did the Grouping appear to make no difference to design policy. Taking them in the order just listed, it would be pertinent to discuss briefly the early coaching stock designs of the Big Four.

On the LMSR it was decided to continue with wooden-bodied carriages mounted on steel underframes, constructed on a mass-production basis; a decision which involved the reorganisation of Derby Carriage Works for the purpose. The general style of the first Reid carriages followed Midland practice, although they were to the standard 57ft length of the former LNWR. On the LNER Gresley also continued with wooden-bodied stock, with his characteristic teak finish, domed roof ends and excellent double-bolster bogies. He also introduced further articulated stock, including a number of twin sleeping cars and triplet restaurant/kitchen cars.

For the SR, Maunsell's new designs were steel-panelled, and featured Pullman-type gangways and buckeye automatic couplers. These designs were destined to remain virtually unchanged until the outbreak of World War II. The GWR, as noted above, continued as though nothing had happened. In fact, some degree of shake-up might have proved beneficial, for in many ways the standard 57ft steel panelled carriages of the 1923-29 period were the poorest ever produced for that company.

Mention has just been made of Maunsell's decision to standardise on the Pullman-type gangway and automatic coupler. The LNER also carried on these features from GNR practice, but the other two new companies remained faithful to the inferior screw-coupling and bellows arrangement, although the GWR carried out experiments with automatic couplers and improved gangways in the early 1920s.

For suburban duties the non-corridor concept remained in favour for steam coaching stock, and here the main changes were in methods of construction rather than improvements in amenity. Specialised stock for dining purposes followed much the same general trend towards sombre furnishings, although their open layout was less claustrophobic in effect. On the LNER, Bulleid (who was responsible for many coaching stock innovations during the Gresley regime) introduced a new austere interior treatment for first class sleeping cars which aroused quite a lot of adverse comment in the national press.

The LMSR eventually followed suit with a similar functional style for their sleeping cars; in fact the pattern was adhered to for the next quarter of a century. Between 1924 and 1927 the LNER constructed a number of new first class sleeping cars which gave an excellent quiet and steady ride due to their wooden bodied construction and Gresley bogies. In 1928 the same company introduced a long-awaited new facility for third class passengers by the provision of four-berth sleeping compartments, and the LMSR and GWR also introduced this facility at about the same time. The accommodation these cars provided could scarcely be described as luxurious, with four bunks, two up and two down, each provided only with a rug and a pillow. But it was better than trying to sleep through a long night journey in a semi-sitting-up position, which had until then been the lot of the third class passenger.

I have already referred to the LMSR decision to proceed with all-wooden carriage construction on a mass-production basis. However, in response to a request to help the British steel industry, in 1926 the company ordered over 200 all-steel carriages (plus approximately 300 all-steel brake vans), to be constructed by outside manufacturers. Thus they went from one extreme to the other, although Derby continued to build wooden-bodied carriages for a few more years.

The new all-steel carriages coincided with another significant change of policy. They were third class with a saloon or open-layout and with doors at the bodyside ends. Hitherto, public opinion had seemed heavily in favour of the side-corridor compartment layout, but these new open thirds started a new trend for the third class, although first class remained chiefly in compartments, except for dining purposes.

An unusual feature of early LMSR open stock was the provision of two windows to each seating bay, in the style employed on Midland Railway dining cars around the turn of the century. The wooden bodied stock soon followed the pattern of the open carriages by providing end doors for the side-corridor layout, in place of the

traditional door-to-every-compartment. One interesting feature of the all-steel flush sided carriages was the livery, which followed the same elaborate panelled-out style used on the wooden bodied stock. The interiors of both wooden and steel construction remained in the conservative style, becoming if anything even more ponderous in effect.

The comparative merits of all-steel versus all-wood carriage bodywork apparently exercised Gresley's attention at about the same time, as he ordered 34 all-steel third class carriages from the Metropolitan Carriage & Wagon Company. Externally these resembled his teak stock; internally they had an open layout, like the new LMSR vehicles.

The next improvement, which followed naturally from the change to end doors for side-corridor stock and the introduction of open-layout third class carriages, was in bodyside window design; with agreeable results. A single large window was provided to each bay, or compartment. On early examples the entire window could be lowered for the passenger to lean out, Continental-fashion, but before long common sense prevailed (in view of the restricted British loading gauge) and this practice ceased, as we shall see later. A separate rotating glass vane ventilator was situated above each large window, and could be adjusted by the passenger to either open into, or away from, the slip-stream of the train.

On the LMSR compromise was reached by the adoption of steel-panelled timber framed coaches from about 1930, bringing that company into line with current SR and GWR practice but Gresley continued to favour teak despite his all-steel experiments, mentioned above.

Soon after 1930 there were some encouraging signs of an improvement in attitudes to coaching stock design, although by that time there were large numbers of carriages in service constructed to the dreary standards of the previous decade. It was a feature of British rolling stock that it had a built-in longevity, and the average carriage of the 1920s probably lasted 30 years in regular passenger service. Thus no widespread changes could be made overnight; a fact which in some respects weighed heavily against the railways in an increasingly competitive era.

In 1928 Gresley had considered it desirable to improve the interior design of the carriages built for the inauguration of the non-stop 'Flying Scotsman'. He realised the need for more attractive decor, if passengers were not to become restless during the $8\frac{1}{4}$hr journey without a break. His personal friend Sir Charles Allom, a furnishing specialist, was invited to produce suitable schemes for the decor,

and a significant change was the employment of painted interiors instead of the customary dark polished veneers. The carriages were furnished in a style described as Louis XIV, over which I would prefer to draw a discreet veil. But at least Gresley had broken away from the general trend, and there was better to follow. Other innovations in the 'Flying Scotsman' train included a hairdressing saloon and travelling newsvendor; whilst in 1932 a cocktail bar was added, followed later still by a coach fitted-out as a cinema.

On the GWR some superb saloon carriages were introduced in 1931 for the Plymouth boat trains. The 'Super Saloons', as they were officially designated were the GWR equivalent to the Pullman cars, but considerably more up to date in conception. Trollope & Sons were employed as contractors for the interior furnishings and fittings. In external appearance these handsome vehicles foreshadowed the 'Centenary' stock of 1935 described later.

William Stanier took over as Chief Mechanical Engineer of the LMSR in 1932, and a number of important changes were introduced for coaching stock, from that date forward. New methods for mass-produced construction resulted in a flush-sided steel panelled carriage, with a neat appearance. The protruding ventilators and window frames of earlier stock were eliminated, and a new and improved design of deep wide window was adopted, incorporating a sliding ventilator in the upper portion. A noticeably brighter finish was adopted for the interiors, with a rather rectangular emphasis to the wooden seat structures and partitions, while the moquettes used had jazz patterns which did much to enliven a basically functional interior, although sometimes the optical effects of such patterns became almost hypnotic in the course of a long journey!

Increasing awareness that the lucrative excursion and special traffic business was being sapped by the motor coach operators, prompted some determined action on the railways' part from 1933/34 onwards. On the LNER Nigel Gresley produced special open tourist stock, which featured remarkably ugly — but surprisingly comfortable — bucket seats, and a plain interior lit by naked lamp bulbs. Externally the tourist stock was at first panelled with plywood (as the cost of teak was rising steadily), but this did not weather at all well and was later replaced by steel sheeting; the livery was apple green and cream.

The GWR at last broke away from the drab phase of the previous 10 years or more ('Super Saloons' excepted), and in 1935 produced new excursion stock of considerably altered interior treatment. In fact the mistake was made of being too fashionable, and the effects dated very quickly. Perhaps best described as 'Odeon, cinema foyer 1935', the GWR magazine described them as follows: '. . . there is a complete absence of curves in the design of the fittings, the decorative effects being obtained by angular and rectangular designs'.

At about the same time, the buffet car became increasingly popular with railway operators as an alternative to the traditional full dining car service, particularly for medium-distance journeys. Buffet cars were usually employed with the open excursion stock.

For main line services proper, the GWR produced some truly splendid carriages for the 'Cornish Riviera Limited', in their centenary year, 1935. Known appropriately as the 'Centenary' stock, it was singularly handsome and took full advantage of the generous loading gauge of that company, with a body width of 9ft 7in and recessed end doors. The interior was attractive with greatly improved finishes, including high quartered oak panelling with walnut inlay for the first

class and gaboon mahogany for the thirds. The seats were upholstered in new standard moquettes and pleasant colours were chosen for the curtains and carpets, while oval mirrors replaced the institutional faded photographs of spas and holiday resorts above the seats. Standard GWR carriages built from this date onwards incorporated a number of the improvements of the 'Centenary' carriages, although externally they were of less generous dimensions.

Finally in this chapter we should consider the prestige trains of the 1935/39 period, although it is essential to realise that these trains were exceptional in the amount expended upon their design and finish. It would be incorrect to leave the reader with the impression that the standards set by these were typical of those generally applying to late 1930s steam coaching stock designs.

In 1935 Nigel Gresley produced the first of his striking high-speed streamlined trains, the 'Silver Jubilee. As recounted in chapter 12, the steamlined trains were introduced in a determined bid to win back public enthusiasm for rail travel, by

emphasising superiority of speed and amenity, at a time when competition from road and air was growing more serious. The 'Silver Jubilee' was formed of steel-panelled carriages in articulated twin-sets, with a triplet dining set. Externally they set a new standard in style and finish, with silver grey Rexine covering the steel body panels and all fittings, including window frames, lettering and numerals, in stainless steel. Mainly to reduce air resistance the body panels were carried down between the bogies, and rubber fairings concealed the gap between carriages.

Two years later, two more streamlined trains were introduced by the LNER and named the 'Coronation' and 'West Riding'. For these the general concept remained the same, but a number of interior layout changes were made. All the carriages were of open layout, with a clever arrangement of partitioned bays for the first class. Decor of the sets was devised with the assistance of White

217 **Gresley first class restaurant car for the LNER 'East Anglian' service, 1929. A sombre interior with ponderous leather upholstery.**

217

Allom and the interior was by no means as
successful as the external appearance.
Although many admirable features were
included, the overall result seemed more
like a boudoir than a railway carriage;
Gresley overstepped the mark in his desire
to create something new.

The 'Coronation' train included a
beaver-tail observation car for the summer
months. This had a tapered streamlined
end based upon the French Bugatti
railcars, and in fact vision from the rear
windows was remarkably restricted.
Livery for the two 1937 trains was
changed to two shades of blue, again with
stainless steel trim. Fixed double-glazed
windows were installed and a form of air-
conditioning and heating employed.

Further carriages for special LNER
services, this time in East Anglia, were
constructed in 1937/38. Although these
had interiors based upon the streamlined
carriages, externally they followed the teak
construction which Gresley had by that
time employed for 31 years; in retrospect
this seems a curious thing for the
company to have permitted after all the
favourable publicity the streamlined stock
had won.

It was hardly surprising when the
LMSR unveiled a streamlined train to the
press in 1937; after all, the LNER had
stolen a march on them which must have
rankled the LMSR directors. I strongly
suspect that board room pressure resulted
in the appearance of the original
'Coronation Scot' train before Stanier was
really prepared, at least on the coaching
stock side. The LMSR stock seems in

retrospect to have been a somewhat hasty
improvisation when compared to the
Gresley train sets. Existing main line
carriages were taken into the workshops,
refurbished and fitted with pressure
ventilation, and outshopped in a new blue
and silver livery.

All the available facts point to the 1937
'Coronation Scot' carriages being nothing
more than a stop-gap whilst designs for a
completely new train were finalised and
authority obtained for its construction.

By 1939, the LMSR had announced its
intention to introduce a brand-new
'Coronation Scot' train in 1940, and some
of the carriages were already constructed.
These new carriages were articulated
twins of semi-integral construction.
Internally they displayed considerable
advance upon the 1937 stock, although the
decor was rather consciously 'Hollywood
Cinema' and the external livery was
altered to maroon and gold.

To publicise the new train, the LMSR
shipped a Stanier Pacific and a number of
the new carriages to North America to
participate in the 1939 New York World's
Fair. While the train was on exhibition
tour in the September of that year, war
was declared in Europe. The locomotive,
badly needed for war service, was later
successfully shipped back across the
Atlantic but the coaches were marooned
until 1946. The new 'Coronation Scot' of
1940 remained forever a dream. The
streamliners, so recently the pride of
Britain's largest railway systems, were put
in mothballs; there was no suitable work
for them during the grim war years.

219

*218 First class compartment of LMSR
semi-open carriage, 1928; with two-a-side
seating allowing everyone a corner seat.*

*219 Pullman detail: A Japanese lacquer wall
panel. LNER 'Sheffield Pullman' carriage.*

*220 Over 200 all-steel carriages built by
outside contractors were introduced by the
LMSR during 1925/26. Illustrated is an open
third, No 5296 of 1925. Note the window
arrangement, with separate slotted glass
ventilators above. Despite the all-steel flush
sides the livery retained the elaborate
panelled effect associated with wooden-
bodied stock.*

*221 The three-bay open section of an LMSR
semi-open first of 1928. Typifying the very
conservative approach to carriage design of
the period, with restrained decor relying
mainly upon dark wood finishes and closely
patterned upholstery, for effect. Design of
light fittings, ventilators, luggage racks and
commode handles (usually in brass finish)
was decidedly weak.*

*222 The GWR's mid-1930s approach to
carriage decor included this 1935 centre-
corridor excursion third, with severe
rectangular styling.*

218

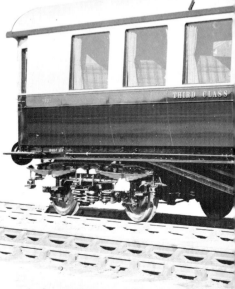

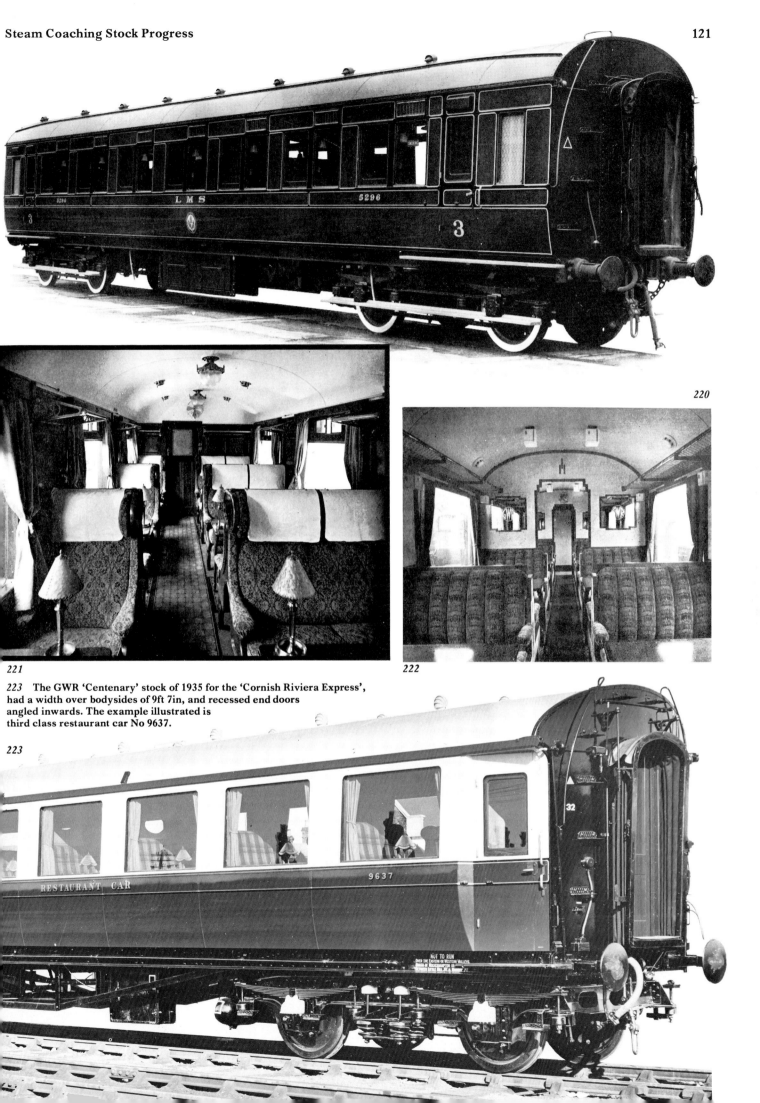

220

221

222

223 The GWR 'Centenary' stock of 1935 for the 'Cornish Riviera Express', had a width over bodysides of 9ft 7in, and recessed end doors angled inwards. The example illustrated is third class restaurant car No 9637.

223

224

225

226

227

228

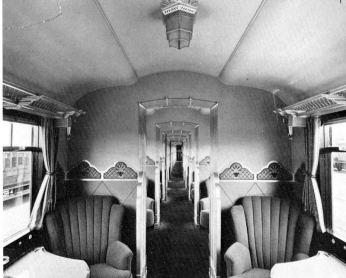

229

224   The low-backed bucket seats of Gresley's 1934 Tourist stock were more comfortable than appearance suggested. Note the use of naked lamp bulbs.

225   Jazz patterns for carriage seat upholstery. The effects upon the eye could become disturbing in the course of a long journey! This example was to be found in the third class open section of the electric 'Brighton Belle' Pullman train.

226   Streamlined Beaver-tail observation car of the LNER 'Coronation' train of 1937. In fact,

the rearward vision was somewhat limited by the external styling. This postwar picture shows the car in store and somewhat dilapidated, but its retains the applied stainless steel lettering and trim, and the original livery.

227   Rubber fairings concealed the gap between the coaches on the LNER streamlined trains, and the bodyside panelling was carried down between the bogies, to reduce wind resistance. Carriages were articulated in sets of two or three. Note again the neat Gill Sans lettering and stainless steel trim.

228   Interior of one of the first class saloons, LNER 'Coronation' train, showing the arrangement of partitioned four seat alcoves. The mock-clerestory treatment of the ceiling is interesting.

229   Open third No 8996 of the 1937 LMSR 'Coronation Scot' train; in blue and silver livery.

230   Interior of refurbished dining car for the SR Waterloo-Bournemouth services, 1938. Note the strip lighting in the ceiling, but very dated ventilators and upholstery patterns. A curious mixture of styles.

230

231

232

233

234

231   First class sleeping car berth, LMSR,
1935. Continuing the functional trend
introduced by the LNER and very much
dependent upon the bright metal finishes of
the various small fittings to give a sense of
style.

232   First class compartment of the LMSR
'Coronation Scot' 1939 train. The telephone
was linked to the dining car for meal orders.

233   Rear coach of the 1939 'Coronation Scot'
photographed during the American tour. The
train, in crimson and gold livery, never ran in
public service in Britain, and the carriages
were stranded in the USA for the duration of
World War II.

234   The cocktail bar portion of the Lounge
Car on the 1939 LMSR 'Coronation Scot' train,
with a considerable degree of 'Hollywood
Cinema' styling.

14 Alternatives to Steam

Electrification of suburban routes in answer to the challenge of the road-borne electric tramcars was gaining increasing favour by the commencement of the second decade of the present century. By 1914 some ambitious new schemes were being developed, and although war delayed or disrupted their introduction, it was becoming increasingly evident that suburban electrification was a paying proposition. Ironically it was seldom at the expense of the tramcars that suburban railway electrification blossomed, rather it was as a result of new traffic created as the city populace moved out to new homes in suburban areas served by the electric trains.

In May 1914 the LNWR opened the first portion of its North London electrification scheme, which by 1927 had developed into a comprehensive system ranging from Richmond to Broad Street and Euston to Watford and Rickmansworth. South of the Thames, the LBSCR, which had been encouraged by the gratifying results obtained from the South London line (reopened to electric traction in 1909), extended electrification to Selhurst via the Crystal Palace. The outbreak of war curtailed their plan to extend as far as Cheam. In 1915 the LSWR electrified the line from Waterloo to Wimbledon via East Putney, and further electrified sections were opened in the following year. Another company which had obtained Parliamentary powers to electrify some of its routes was the SECR, but financial resources were at a low ebb, and the powers were not in fact used until after the formation of the SR.

There was considerable diversity between the actual methods of current collection, and the voltages, favoured for the electrification schemes of the pre-Grouping companies. For example, the MR and the LBSCR both had overhead catenary, while most of the others favoured conductor rails laid along the permanent way (although the LYR experimented with overhead contact on the Bury-Holcombe Brook branch in 1913). This diversity was to create some headaches when further electrification

schemes were being drawn-up by the Big Four railway companies, in particular on the SR, as we shall see later.

The design of the electric trains also varied somewhat, with the companies situated north of the Thames generally in favour of saloon style carriages with end doors and vestibules, akin to American practice, while the LSWR and LBSCR both employed non-corridor compartment stock. In fact the LSWR trains were composed of converted steam coaches, and in retrospect it seems that the failure of both these constituent companies to provide electric rolling stock of improved amenity and appearance has had long-term effects upon the suburban rolling stock policy of the SR electric system. From the outset there seems to have been a rather naïve faith in the ability of electrification to encourage patronage without the need to make any significant improvements in the comfort provided by the rolling stock. The retention of the traditional non-corridor layout, with slam doors to every compartment (despite the fact that it would have been quite practicable to have employed air-operated doors, which the LBSCR at one time proposed) was to remain policy throughout the existence of the SR and for 20 years of Nationalisation. It would certainly be true to say that compared to their contemporaries south of the Thames, the electric rolling stock of the northern companies was of superior design and layout. In particular, the stately saloon cars of the LNWR were splendid examples of the coachbuilder's art.

Before proceeding with the story of electric train design after World War I, mention should be made of one or two other interesting attempts to replace the conventional steam locomotive-hauled train by alternative forms of motive power. We have already observed the phenomenon of the Edwardian steam rail-motor, designed in an effort to improve the economics and appeal of lightly loaded services which might otherwise have succumbed to road competition. Consisting of a tank locomotive with a passenger carriage articulated to the rear,

the rail-motors had proved somewhat under-powered and unable to cope with any form of additional load.

However there was something of a revival of the rail-motor in the mid-1920s, in particular on the LNER and LMSR. This was the result of the adaptation for rail traction purposes of the Sentinel type of high-speed chain-driven steam propulsion unit, hitherto successfully employed on road wagons. The first example was produced for the Jersey Railways in 1923, in conjunction with the Metropolitan-Cammell Carriage & Wagon Co Ltd, who were responsible for the carriage and underframe portions. This prototype proved successful in service in the Channel Islands, and aroused sufficient interest for the LNER to test a similar rail-motor in Yorkshire during the following year. By 1927 a similar design of rail-motor had been produced by the Clayton Wagon Co Ltd of Lincoln, and both Sentinel and Clayton versions were ordered for service on the LNER.

A more sophisticated version, produced by Sentinel in 1928, featured a six-cylinder engine with poppet valves and gear drive, and the first example for the LNER was named *Nettle*. This followed the general style for the bodywork portion, with a saloon seating 59 passengers, electric lighting and steam heating. Subsequently 50 rail-motors (or perhaps railcars would be a more accurate description) to this design were purchased by the LNER. In all, by 1933, the LNER were operating no less than 90 steam railcars of various types.

The original livery for the LNER cars was imitation teak finish painted upon the metal bodysides; this was later changed to red and cream, followed by apple green and cream. They were named after horse-drawn mail coaches (except three Sentinel cars which were never named), and some amusing examples included *Bang up, True Blue, Wonder, Railway, Red Rover* and *Waterloo*! Of all the names, I think that carried by car No 2136 was the ultimate in unconscious humour; it was simply called *Hope*.

The inherent disadvantage of the

Edwardian rail-motors was also present in the Sentinel and Clayton designs of the 1920s and 1930s, namely their inability to cope with unexpected heavy traffic, such as could arise on summer weekends or other holiday periods. In fact they became so popular in some areas that they could not cope with the additional patronage they created, and had to be replaced by conventional steam trains; whilst in more sparsely populated areas even the employment of these undoubtedly more economical railcars could not compete with the door-to-door convenience of rival road services.

A lightweight Sentinel-Cammell steam railcar was purchased by the SR in 1933 for operation on the Brighton-Devils Dyke branch. This had a most distinctive appearance, with a vee-shaped front end reminiscent of early LSWR electric stock. When the Dyke branch was closed there was little suitable employment for so small a unit; eventually the body finished its days as an air raid shelter at Ashford Works during World War II.

There had been a number of essays in the adaptation of petrol and petrol-electric drive to rail traction since Edwardian days, and several examples operated on the Colonel Stephens group of light railways. These were simply road motor coaches adapted for running on rails. A more ambitious venture was the LMSR Ro-Railer, which was tried on the Stratford-upon-Avon & Midland Junction line. This was a conventional style motorbus with an ingenious arrangment of dual road and rail wheels which could be quickly substituted — one for the other — thus allowing the vehicle to make a journey partly by road and partly by rail. This concept had (and still has) much to offer in terms of flexibility and although the LMSR did not develop its initial attempt, the idea has been revived again more recently, alas without much success. (A BR attempt to use road-rail freight containers was abandoned in favour of the now well-proven Liner train principle, despite construction of a quantity of special new vehicles).

Further enterprising attempts to produce a more efficient method of operating branch rail services than the conventional steam push-pull train (of which considerable use was made), were the Michelin pneumatic-tyred railcars brought over from France in 1932 and 1935. The earlier example had an articulated layout formed of a conventional lorry-type cab and bonnet tractor unit, flexibly coupled to a lightweight passenger saloon. The dimensions were those of a large road vehicle rather than a railway carriage and there was some disparity in height between the entrance doors and the

traditional raised British railway station platforms.

The second Michelin railcar, known for publicity purposes as the Coventry Railcar, was of more purpose-built dimensions and capacity. It was a 56-seater, with a 240bhp petrol engine and mechanical transmission driving one of the two eight-wheel bogies. The wheels were fitted with pneumatic tyres which had steel flanges. In the event of a sudden loss of tyre pressure a warning hooter sounded in the driver's cab, whilst a metal rim inside the tyre prevented more than a very small loss of wheel diameter should the tyre become completely deflated. The Coventry Railcar was tested on the LMSR, and attained a maximum speed of 66mph on a demonstration run from Leighton Buzzard to Euston, when observers present were favourably impressed by the steady and silent running qualities. However no orders were placed by British railways for pneumatic-tyred railcars, although development work continued for some years on the French railways. Externally the Coventry Railcar followed French practice, with the driver situated in a sort of conning tower on the roof, whilst the interior was a spartan high-density saloon with seating of road coach standards.

Although the LMSR made an abortive attempt to operate a diesel train in 1927, it was in September 1931 that the 3ft gauge County Donegal Railways made history by introducing the first successful diesel-powered railcar to operate in the British Isles. This was a diminutive vehicle, but it heralded the dawn of a new era as it chugged steadily through the rugged and beautiful Irish terrain. Two months later the LNER entered the field when they commenced experiments with a bogie diesel railcar, built by Armstrong-Whitworth, and powered by a Sulzer engine; it carried the name *Tyneside Venturer*. In 1933/34 the LNER took into stock three Armstrong-Whitworth diesel-electric railcars which they had operated since 1931/32; the other two were named *Lady Hamilton* and *Northumbrian*.

Development of diesel traction, which proceeded apace on both American and German railways in the early 1930s, attained a degree of reliability which prompted many railway administrations to consider the possibilities of investing in diesel locomotives and railcars. A factor which weighed heavily against the widespread use of diesel traction in Britain was the dependence upon foreign fuel, whereas the steam locomotive was truly indigenous. Nevertheless, the increased availability and efficiency of the diesel engine sufficiently impressed that most conservative of British companies, the GWR, for it to place orders for diesel

railcars. The GWR cars, produced in conjunction with AEC Limited, were of advanced concept, with underfloor engines.

The first batch constructed were single units, with a streamlined driving cab at each end and a central passenger entrance. Some included a small buffet, and toilet facilities, and the saloon seating accommodated between 40 and 70 passengers, according to the amenities provided. To begin with the streamlined railcars were placed in express service between Birmingham and Cardiff and passengers paid a small supplementary fare for the privilege of riding in them. In later days they were chiefly used on branch lines and semi-fast services.

In all, 38 railcars were introduced by the GWR and later examples included some twin-units, gangwayed together at the inner ends. The streamlined bodywork was modified to present a more angular appearance on later cars, and standard buffers and drawgear were fitted in order to permit the attachment of additional loads. The GWR railcars gave many years excellent service and much valuable experience was gained from their operation, which stood BR in good stead when they embarked upon a nationwide scheme for diesel railcars in 1954.

I have already referred to Nigel Gresley's interest in German high-speed diesel railcar development. This had prompted a feasibility study for employing similar trains on the LNER. As already related, Gresley decided against the diesel sets in favour of steam locomotive-hauled carriages, chiefly because of the vastly superior passenger amenities these could provide. Had the pendulum swung the other way it is possible that the LNER diesel sets would have looked something like a cross between the GWR streamlined cars already described, and the LMSR three-car articulated diesel set of 1938. The LMSR design had some pronounced Continental influence in the external styling, following most closely contemporary Dutch and German practice, and in many ways it was a modern design for its time. Six 125hp Leyland diesel engines, mounted underfloor, provided the power, with hydraulic transmission. The three carriages were of saloon layout, with seats for 24 first and 138 third class passengers. The design of seating incorporated a back which could be reversed to allow the passengers to sit facing either direction (a feature of tramcars many years earlier). The passenger doors were air-operated; controlled by the guard. Initial trials were on the St Pancras-Bedford line, following which it went into service on the cross-country route between Oxford and Cambridge via Bletchley. World War II interrupted development of this promising diesel railcar, and it was subsequently withdrawn and converted to a maintenance train for the Engineer's Department.

Returning now to the story of electric train design between the wars; it was the SR which took the lead in converting many of its passenger routes to electrified working, although it was content to leave the freight and mineral traffic to steam traction. The SR adopted the third-rail 650V dc system of the former LSWR as their standard. Despite this an existing scheme to extend the LBSCR overhead electrification (drawn-up before Grouping) was pressed to completion in 1925, only to be demolished and re-electrified on the third-rail principle soon afterwards. It is easy to be wise after the event, but one cannot avoid the feeling that it might have been better for the SR to have persevered with the LBSCR overhead catenary, in view of the perennial icing problems of the third-rail in winter months.

Suburban electrification spread rapidly, fanwise south of the Thames, embracing many of the routes out of London of the SR's pre-Grouping constituents. With the exception of batches of stock built for the Guildford and Orpington schemes, all the electric trains for the suburban electrification were obtained by converting existing steam carriages (in some cases old four or six-wheelers), mounting them upon new underframes and adding electrical equipment. As I have commented earlier in this chapter, the standards of comfort and amenity provided by this retention of the dated non-corridor compartment layout was by no means brilliant.

On the other hand the new electric services were certainly more frequent and reliable, and above all much cleaner. Consequently electrification paid-off handsomely; it created new traffic for the railways, and the speculative builders reaped small fortunes erecting row upon row of new suburban homes where previously cattle had grazed unmoved by the occasional passing steam train. The brilliant blue flashes of the new electrics became almost symbolic as they snaked their way towards Dorking or Guildford, Orpington or Sevenoaks. The SR electrics created the suburban commuters who, in recent years, have taxed the capacity of the rail service almost beyond reason during rush hours.

After considerable further expansion of their electrified suburban services, in 1932 the SR introduced the first main line electrification scheme, from London to Brighton (a plan long cherished by the LBSCR, but never achieved), following this with extensions to Worthing, Eastbourne and Hastings. First of the new

rolling stock to appear was intended for the semi-fast and stopping trains, and was constructed at Eastleigh to R. E. L. Maunsell's design. Designated 4LAV, they were four-car units based very much upon existing steam stock practice. There were three non-corridor compartment carriages, including the two motor coaches, whilst the fourth carriage (an intermediate trailer) was a composite third and first class side-corridor layout with lavatories.

For the express services new six-car multiple-units of rather motley appearance were constructed. The motor coaches, which formed the outer ends of each unit, were all-steel carriages constructed by outside contractors, whereas the intermediate trailer vehicles were of conventional SR steel-panelled teak framed design. Inserted into some sets was a steel-bodied Pullman car of composite third and first class layout with a kitchen. The units were gangwayed within each set, but not at the outer ends. Later sets had an additional first class trailer with a small pantry at one end, instead of a Pullman. The massive motor coaches had a saloon layout with end doors only, whereas the trailer carriages had side corridor compartments with doors to each compartment down one side, and fewer doors spaced down the corridor side. For the 'Southern Belle' service (soon renamed the 'Brighton Belle') three new five-car all-Pullman trains were specially constructed.

A remarkable feature of the new stock proved to be its longevity in service. The express units lasted just over 30 years in regular service, day-in, day-out on the same duties, and a handful were retained longer still for special workings at peak periods. The semi-fast stock lasted even longer without replacement — approximately 35 years in fact — whilst the three all-Pullman sets (which were placed in store for part of the war period) were the last to be withdrawn.

Some observations have been prompted by these extreme examples of the long service life of the typical British railway passenger carriage. First and foremost, it has emphasised the problems of dated appearance and amenity. A carriage constructed in the early 1930s and in continuous service for about 30 years virtually unaltered is obviously going to be considered as something of a museum piece by latter-day travellers. Consider, for example, the enormous progress in aeroplane and motor vehicle design which had taken place during the same period, and then remember that the same people who had witnessed this progress had, perforce, travelled in the same old trains day-in, day-out. Stagnation of design, such as the robust SR electrics created, is

a situation which must at all costs be avoided for the future. Greater flexibility of interior layout, and furnishing which can be altered, or replaced entirely, to meet changing tastes and needs, must nowadays be designed into new rolling stock from the start.

Another feature of the pioneer SR main line electrics which proved troublesome virtually throughout their working life was the poor riding quality of the bogies. Fortunately considerable research has recently been devoted to the problems of multiple-unit bogie design and today's SR electrics offer a far better level of passenger comfort.

The last new emu design for the SR, produced by Maunsell before he retired differed in many ways from the pioneer Brighton line units. Constructed for the Portsmouth electrification schemes of 1937/38, they were of four-car formation, with gangways throughout, including the leading ends, so that up to 12 coaches could be coupled with access to the restaurant or buffet car. Of rather neater external appearance, the Portsmouth express units proved to be speedy and efficient, but still inclined towards rough riding once the newness had worn off. The 1938 batch, for the service from Victoria to Bognor Regis and Portsmouth included some buffet car units (the 1937 Waterloo-Portsmouth batch had a kitchen/dining car layout), and these were of somewhat remarkable design. Delivered after the other carriages had been constructed, the buffet cars were apparently completely redesigned whilst still on the drawing board; hence the delay. The 'Bognor Buffets' as they are generally known, were in fact the first taste of the Bulleid regime in SR coachbuilding.

When Maunsell retired in 1937 and O. V. S. Bulleid (whom we have already met as Gresley's right-hand man in earlier chapters) was appointed to the post of chief mechanical engineer of the SR, he apparently decided that no time should be lost in making his views on design felt; the 'Bognor Buffets' were the outcome! The interior layout comprised a saloon section at one end, a central bar with a long counter and high stools, and a kitchen/pantry at the other end.

The saloon had to seat 16 people around four tables placed adjacent to large windows. Bulleid solved the cramped dimensions this created, by shaping the table edges with four concave curves. The front edge of the long bar counter was similarly treated and the scalloped effect was used on the semi-partitions between saloon and bar, and on ribs let into the walls. There was a noticeable lack of windows in the bar section. But the most striking change from Maunsell's practice was in the interior colour scheme. The traditional wood finishes were replaced by walls, table and ceiling all in a light stone colour edged with black. Upholstery was either brilliant jade green or rich red and gold and a one-piece Wilton carpet was in royal blue with diagonal old gold stripes. The effect was certainly novel, if in somewhat dubious taste. A final touch appeared on the end walls of the saloon — six brass plaques depicting food of various sorts. In later days it was somewhat galling to observe the subject matter of these plaques (which included such delicacies as roast pork and apple sauce, etc), when all that could be purchased was a sandwich or pie!

Bulleid had for many years taken an active interest in the possibilities of welding carriage bodies and underframes, and he was soon involved in some ambitious plans for new all-steel suburban carriages with added seating capacity. But war intervened, and these all-steel ventures must be dealt with in a later chapter. Another Bulleid design which did appear shortly before the outbreak of war, was in some ways his least satisfactory effort for SR electric stock. Known as the 2HAL stock, there were 76 two-coach semi-fast units for the Maidstone and Gillingham services. Based upon Maunsell's 2BIL design, they were close-coupled non-gangwayed sets with a non-corridor compartment third class motor coach and side-corridor composite trailer. Externally they had unusually large radii to the bodyside windows, which appeared almost oval in shape, and they were finished in the brilliant malachite green livery which Bulleid had first applied to

his 'Bognor Buffets'. Internally they were undoubtedly spartan, with a strictly utilitarian finish. Third class passengers had a particularly raw deal with hard, narrow bench-type seating instead of the hammock-slung lift-out cushions of Maunsell's stock; whilst the first class was just about equal to previous thirds in terms of comfort.

Earlier in this chapter I praised the electric rolling stock of the LNWR North London services as splendid examples of coachbuilding. This they undoubtedly were, and in addition they displayed excellent riding qualities. It came therefore as something of a shock to many travellers when the LMSR introduced additional new stock for the services, in 1927, which was in some respects inferior in design and comfort. The new three-car sets were of non-corridor compartment layout, no doubt because of the prevalent belief that this provided quicker loading and unloading at stations. Further stock of this type, of generally similar appearance and arrangement, was introduced in 1931 for the jointly-owned LMSR/LNER Manchester, South Junction & Altrincham line, electrified with 1,500V dc overhead catenary.

A radical change of thought on the subject of electric rolling-stock design came about when W. A. Stanier (later Sir William) took charge of the LMSR Mechanical Engineer's Department. The aim was to reduce the weight of stock without reducing the constructional strength, thereby improving the passenger/tare weight ratio. Careful attention to design and the use of welded

integral steel bodies made possible a remarkable improvement. For example the LNWR saloon electrics already mentioned had a weight ratio of 1,540lb per seat per three-car train whereas Stanier's new electric stock for the Liverpool-Southport line had the ratio reduced to 760lb.

The new Liverpool-Southport stock introduced in the late 1930s to replace life-expired LYR equipment, had open saloon layout and air-operated sliding doors. In many respects it was the most advanced emu stock so far produced for suburban working by a British railway company, rivalled only by the excellent designs of London Transport produced in the late 1930s, and the influence of Stanier's design can be clearly seen in the Glasgow suburban electrics of BR, and in the latest high-density stock. Externally the LMSR stock had a clean modern appearance with flush steel finish large windows, and a well considered front-end treatment.

Finally brief mention should be made of the articulated two-car electric stock produced by Gresley for the Newcastle area in 1937. Built by Metropolitan-Cammell, they had steel sides with closely-grouped large windows and hand-operated sliding doors situated at the ends. The saloon interior had a Rexine finish, and bucket seats (similar to those used in Gresley's 1934 tourist steam stock) provided a good degree of comfort. Externally their neat lines were enhanced by a red and cream livery. When war broke out it was felt that the livery made the trains too conspicuous from the air, and from 1941 they were repainted light and dark blue.

235

236

237

238

239

235   Multiple-unit electric train at Crystal Palace; LBSCR overhead electrification.

236   Third class saloon of LNWR London area electric train, with very spacious layout.

237   Interior of SR third class compartment, multiple-unit electric set. Most sets were formed of existing bodywork from steam-hauled carriages mounted upon new underframes.

238   LNER steam railcar *Flower of Yarrow*, one of over 80 railcars the company operated, of various types, in the late 1920s and 1930s. The names were those formerly carried by road stage coaches, and their livery (after some first appeared in grained teak or red and cream) was apple green and cream.

239   Michelin pneumatic-tyred railcar, at Ascot while on trial on the SR, June 1932. Note the size of the vehicle compared to the man alongside.

240

241

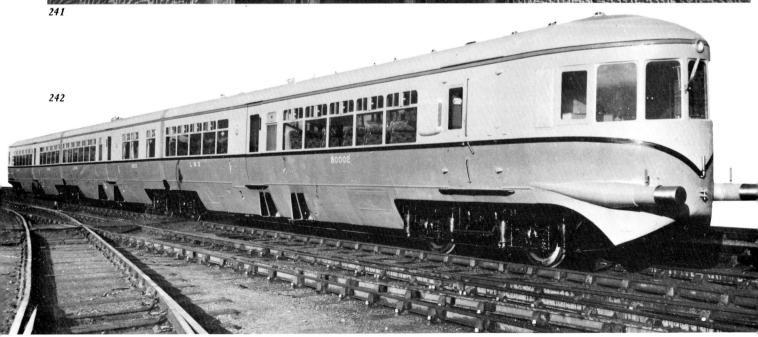

242

240 First widespread application of diesel traction for passenger services in this country was by the GWR, which introduced the first of its fleet of AEC railcars in 1933; No 6 is illustrated.

241 Saloon and buffet area of an AEC/GWR twin-unit cross-country diesel set; late 1930s.

242 In 1938 the LMSR introduced an experimental three-coach articulated diesel train. The unit ran for some time on the Oxford-Bletchley-Cambridge line. Front end design was clearly influenced by contemporary Dutch and German designs.

243 Interior of first class compartment, 4LAV semi-fast emu for the SR Brighton line, 1932.

244 Pullman emu trains were introduced for the 'Brighton Belle' service in 1933. Three five-car sets were built, gangwayed within each set. In traditional Pullman livery, they provided a distinctive contrast to the SR green

electrics. Unit No 3051 is seen leaving the Ouse Valley viaduct just north of Haywards Heath.

245 Interior of Bulleid designed buffet car for the Victoria-Bognor Regis/Portsmouth electrics; introduced 1938. Note the scalloping of tables and counter front, repeated on the ribs let into the walls. Note also the lack of windows in the bar portion.

246 Motorcoach saloon of a 1937/38 Waterloo-Portsmouth main line electric, SR. This photograph was taken to show the blackout precautions introduced in November 1939, with reduced lighting, to reduce the risk of air attacks. (The newspaper headline reads 'Winston Dooms Sea Raiders'.)

243

244

245

246

247

247   Among the least-inspired suburban electric train designs produced between the wars were these 1931 compartment, non-corridor sets for the jointly owned LNER/LMS Manchester, South Junction and Altrincham line.

248   Exterior of the LMSR Liverpool-Southport electric stock, with air-operated sliding doors. Some similar but slight smaller stock had been built the previous year, 1938, for the Wirral line.

249   Interior of third class saloon LMSR Liverpool-Southport electric stock, introduced 1939.

250   Gresley articulated twin-set electric multiple-units for the Newcastle area, 1937. Livery when new was red and cream later changed to two shades of blue.

249

248
250

15 Architecture in the Doldrums

When compared to the mechanical developments described in previous chapters, the railway architecture of the period 1914-1939 does not provide much of a story, either in terms of progress of aesthetics. Reduced standards of maintenance were unavoidable during World War I, and the results of this later became apparent in the rapid physical deterioration of many of the older structures still in use. Allied to this there was a plethora of ill-conceived additions, mainly to cope with extra traffic, which were grafted on to existing buildings, sometimes with disastrous effects upon their apearance.

The Big Four railway companies inherited numerous long-term agreements which their pre-Grouping constituents had entered into, for the supply of gas for station lighting. Consequently many stations retained gas-lighting throughout the period under review; in some cases even when they were completely rebuilt. Thus one had such curious anomolies as Horsham and Haywards Heath, where gas-lighting remained when the stations were reconstructed to serve the new electric trains operated by the SR. Other eyesores, common to many railway stations, included the erection of ugly self-contained kiosks for booksellers or confectioners under the platform canopies (a sort of house within a house) and galaxies of poster displays which were scarcely ever sited with any consideration for the architectural merits of the building.

Opportunities for the design and construction of new large stations were very few and far between; notable examples completed within the period being Aberdeen Joint (1915) and Waterloo (1922). Of these, Aberdeen was a stolid granite-faced building of some merit, with a spacious covered circulating area. Today, with steam replaced by diesel, it seems cold and empty, particularly in the winter months; steam added a vital quality to such architecture.

Waterloo, despite the aesthetic weaknesses of its war memorial facade and its impersonal grandeur of style, must be regarded as one of the best examples of major railway station architecture produced in this country since Victorian times. It had a well planned layout with an admirable concourse which provided a fine sense of space and efficiency. The overall roof, of steel and glass to the design of Alfred Szlumper is in many ways the most satisfactory feature of the building; particularly good is the complete absence of supporting pillars in the circulating area.

A scheme to rebuild Euston, which was announced in 1935, would have involved the demolition of all the existing buildings, including the Great Hall and the Doric Arch, in order to extend the inner ends of the platforms nearer to the Euston Road. The frontage, which would have come practically up to the line of the present Euston Road, incorporated a large central hall flanked by two massive blocks which were intended to house a hotel and offices. Due to the worsening financial position of the company the project was shelved before World War II, but an artists impression has survived (now housed in the National Railway Museum) which shows that the new station would have been on an imposing scale. The architectural style proposed was typical of many late 1930s buildings, being of the monumental 'cinema' concept epitomised in the Shell-Mex building on the Charing Cross embankment of the Thames.

The design of smaller stations constructed during this period makes an interesting study, as they reflected more clearly the influences of social change. Most of the new stations were constructed to meet the needs of suburban communities, which in many cases had been encouraged to develop by the railway electrification schemes. An opportunity to rebuild some wayside country stations in the north-east area occurred when the LNER widened the York to Northallerton section of its East Coast main line; but for the most part it was suburban development that encouraged new station design. In the early 1930s, new station architecture tended to reflect both the changing social environment and the general reaction against Victorian fussiness which was a characteristic of most artistic endeavours at this time.

For example, in connection with the electrification of the Barking-Upminster section of the LMSR Southend line (operated by London Transport electric stock), two new stations were constructed in 1932, and a number of others modernised. Typical was the style of the new station at Upney (photo 252) which echoed the plebeian design of the nearby houses and shopping parades, with brickwork of uninteresting hue used to create characterless blocks, indecisively punctuated by metal-framed windows. The platform awning was fabricated from steel girders and sections of standardised dimensions and the platform itself was composed of pre-cast concrete segments covered with asphalt. The result was functional and above all 'safe'; it was certainly not inspired.

The rebuilt country stations on the LNER York-Northallerton section also featured much standardisation of units, such as platforms, lamp standards and fences, all of which were produced in pre-cast concrete and delivered to the site for erection. The architectural style adopted was restrained, although an attempt to imbue an element of traditional railway granduer resulted in a ponderous use of stonework for the main entrances. Considerably more praiseworthy, as an honest solution to the problem of providing economical passenger amenities at a small wayside station, was the wooden structure erected by the LNER at West Monkseaton, served by the Tyneside electric trains.

From the mid-1930s onwards some masterly new stations were constructed by the London Passenger Transport Board to serve their electric railway system, as it was extended to new Outer London suburbs. As already observed, this was the age of streamlining; speed was a craze which manifested itself in all manner of exaggerated architectural feats along our highways. Streamlining — a scientific art developed in the quest for greater efficiency at speed for land and air transport — became a debased mode of applied decoration. Small semi-detached houses had streamlined frontages and motifs, whilst the interior decor of the super cinemas stretched imagination to the limit; even fish-and-chip parlours took on a new and entirely phoney magnificence. Viewed against this prevailing taste for sham opulence, the stations erected by London Transport were all the more remarkable for their good looks and sanity. To a large extent this achievement can be credited to one man, Frank Pick, who, although not an architect himself, fully realised the responsibility of a large industrial concern as a patron of the arts.

Compared to the near-classics of London Transport, the new suburban station constructed by the SR in the late 1930s appear less successful. Nevertheless, they did not concede much to the vulgarities of the period, and in many ways they were a considerable improvement upon the earlier new railway architecture, described in this chapter. Stations such as Surbiton, Woking, Horsham, Chessington North and Chessington South, were all characterised by plain surfaces — sometimes of brick, sometimes of cement — with the visual emphasis upon long horizontal lines and radiused corners. Their chief fault was lack of attractive texture, which became even more apparent as the newness wore off and the inevitable rust staining appeared on the concrete. One enterprising feature of the new stations on the Motspur Park to Chessington branch was the design of the platform awnings, in pre-cast concrete, with well planned strip lighting giving excellent illumination at night.

With the excellent examples of London Transport, and signs of a new awareness on the Southern, we might have seen some splendid railway architecture of harmonious functional and aesthetic concept produced in the 1940s. But fate decreed otherwise; before long our stations were to be prize catches for the bomb-aimers of enemy aircraft.

251
253

251 **The great covered area of Waterloo station, seen while in course of completion (note unfinished portion in the lefthand background), with a double-headed suburban train about to depart.**

252 **Platform view of Upney station on the newly electrified Barking-Upminster line; August 1932. Practical ugliness and generally uninteresting surface treatments.**

253 **West Monkseaton station for the LNER Newcastle suburban electrification scheme, showing a praiseworthy attempt to meet the functional needs of a lineside stopping place.**

254 **Municipal pomp for a wayside station. Otterington LNER, 1933.**

252

254

255
256   *257*

255 Classic example of the new wave of
suburban station building in the late 1930s.
Tolworth station, SR. Extensive use was made
of concrete and similar finishes. Photograph
taken on day of official opening in 1938.

256 The design of the platform awnings was
particularly interesting; with adventurous use
of concrete. Malden Manor, SR.

257 Waiting room, Surbiton station, 1938
with furniture design integrated with
architectural style.

16 Graphic Design and Liveries, 1923-1939

Although it was, without doubt, the major elements of the steam railway system — its locomotives, rolling stock and architecture — which most readily created its visual character, the smaller details also played their part. Graphic design, whether it be printed, painted or applied in some three dimensional form, constituted a method of visual communication. It was by the intelligent use of lettering, symbols, colours and pictorial images, that this large industry established a visual public image of its many activities.

Posters advertising the services offered, timetables giving details of them, symbols identifying their trains, nameplates for their locomotives, all these and many more examples constituted the graphic image of the railway system.

An excellent example of a considered graphic image was that achieved in the mid-1930s by the London Passenger Transport Board, under the direction of Frank Pick. Strict standards were drawn up, and rigidly adhered to, for the typeface of printed matter and signs, for the liveries of trains and buses and for numerous other manifestations of the Board's activities. The results, including the excellent 'bullseye' totem, have now achieved world-wide recognition as an outstanding artistic achievement by an industrial concern.

Control of their graphic image by the Big Four companies was unfortunately nowhere near as effective as that of London Transport. This was largely due to the complexity of their organisations and the lingering influences of pre-Grouping traditions. The choice of liveries for rolling stock was based on the personal preferences of the Board of Directors rather than on a logical desire to create a new identity. Thus three of the companies chose shades of green for their locomotives, and the fourth adopted crimson, all based upon practices of pre-Grouping days. For carriages there was a similar lack of real appreciation of the need for a clear identity, although it must be conceded that it was easier to differentiate the four companies' coaching

stock by means of their livery, than was the case with their locomotives.

The choice of lettering for rolling stock likewise echoed pre-Grouping practice to some degree and heraldry remained in favour for added identification. The SR showed signs of a break with tradition, by using the single word 'Southern' as a slogan on the tenders of steam locomotives, but their carriages still bore the full legend. By the mid-1930s, however, there was less insistence on the heraldry, and an increasing use of the initials of the companies as a means of identification, particularly by the LMSR and LNER. Two companies, the GWR and the LNER, produced monogram versions of their initials which were widely used for publicity purposes. The GWR monogram was also applied to locomotives and rolling stock for some years prior to World War II, but the LNER example was only used for a few such applications.

A notable move towards a modern and efficient graphic image was made by the LNER in 1933 when it standardised upon Gill Sans typeface for all printed matter and signs, at the behest of its advertising department. Some idea of the printed matter produced by this department can be gained from the fact that in a typical year some 90 printers were contracted to produce no less than 40 million copies of handbills, leaflets and pamphlets. Viewed against this, the merits of standardising upon one clear, legible and attractively modern typeface become obvious. Everything, from the large timetable sheets to smaller items such as dining car menus, and company reports were redesigned, and layout artists and signwriters were educated in the subtleties of the new lettering. The initial step was taken when Eric Gill himself was commissioned to paint the headboard for the 'Flying Scotsman', for which he stipulated that his fee should include a trip on the footplate non-stop to Edinburgh!

The pictorial poster printed in lithographed colour reached its highest achievements as a work of art in the period between the two wars, and the

railway companies ranked amongst its foremost patrons. Some superb posters were produced by leading artists of the day, which did much to brighten the everyday lot of the traveller. Seaside holidays, country rambles, special events, zoos, fairgrounds and naval reviews, these and many other attractions, were advertised with the added inducement to travel by rail. Another series of posters — described as 'prestige' — illustrated the motive power and operations of the railway companies. A regrettable feature of railway advertising was a tendency to preach to the converted by advertising railway services to railway users, on station platforms, rather than striking out at the new motorcar-conscious generation that had forsaken the trains.

The naming of express passenger locomotives was perpetuated by the Big Four companies. It was on the SR, which had come in for a lot of adverse public comment and criticism from the national newspapers in the latter part of 1924, that a new awareness of the publicity value of locomotive names arose, although it must be stressed that both the GWR and the LNER pursued an unbroken policy of naming their express passenger engines. The SR created a new post in business management in a bid to improve public opinion, when early in 1925 a certain Mr John Elliot was appointed to the new role of Public Relations & Advertising Assistant — and the now indispensable PRO was born! One of Elliot's suggestions was the naming of Maunsell's new 4-6-0 class express engines after the Arthurian legend. The 'King Arthur' class captured popular imagination, although there is a story that when Maunsell was told of the decision to name his engines (and to include the earlier Urie 4-6-0s in the class) he stated that although he had no objection to the scheme he wished to inform the General Manager that '. . . it won't make any difference to the performance of the engines!'

Generally speaking, the design of steam locomotive nameplates followed traditional practice. Although there was a marked tendency towards simplification, with sans-serif letterforms, the GWR perpetuated the heavy slab-serif alphabet in use since Brunel's day with cast numberplates of similar style affixed to cab sides. On the LNER, after the adoption of Gill Sans, already mentioned, some of the streamlined A4 Pacifics and the special rolling stock, had stainless steel lettering and numerals applied to them, but for the most part shaded transfers were still favoured for these applications.

I made brief mention at the beginning of this chapter of the choice of liveries by the Big Four. To begin with, locomotive cleanliness was of a good overall standard and many classes looked undeniably attractive in their new coats of unfamiliar hue, although much has been written about the dislike of ex-LNWR men on seeing their engines in the red of the former Midland company, and so on. But in due course such prejudices waned as the new liveries became familiar, and by 1928 the transformation was virtually complete. By this time, however, cleaning was becoming a problem, and both the LMSR and the LNER announced their intention of painting all but the main line express engines black. The great industrial depression of 1931 had even worse effects upon standards of cleaning and maintenance in that and following years. I am convinced that the previous decision to paint so much of the stock black was retrograde, as it provided still less incentive to cleaners, and had virtually no publicity value, even when cleaned.

Throughout the period up to the outbreak of World War II, the standard of cleaning bestowed on main line express engines remained commendably good; it was the secondary and freight types which generally suffered. Of course the situation varied somewhat in different areas of the country, and many humble tank engines at small sub-depots still shone like bright new pennies!

Coaching stock liveries were simplified in the 1930s as more and more steel-panelled carriages entered service, although there was a transitional phase when elaborate panelling was painted on to the steel sides. In 1938 Bulleid introduced a new livery for the SR which was entirely devoid of lining or panelling and depended on the brilliance of a single colour for its effect. The colour chosen, known as malachite green, weathered extremely well in traffic conditions, whereas the previous sage green had tended to fade badly and take on a blue appearance.

For the streamlined high-speed trains new and brighter liveries were adopted by the LNER and LMSR, as described in earlier chapters, and special attention was paid to cleaning this stock. The publicity value of attractive liveries was a proven

fact, and it is interesting to speculate upon what developments might have taken place in this field, if war had not intervened. In the grim years 1939-45 a coating of grime effectively hid the liveries of our trains, and black paint was applied to many of the largest express engines as they became due for overhaul and repainting.

258   LMSR ticket of the early 1930s, on green card, with a slotted pocket holding an advertisement for China Tea.

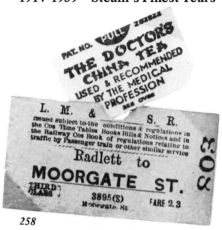

258

259

SCOT PASSES SCOT

By Bryan de Grineau.

LMS   10·0 A.M. EUSTON TO GLASGOW AND EDINBURGH
10·0 A.M. GLASGOW AND EDINBURGH TO EUSTON

260
262

261
263

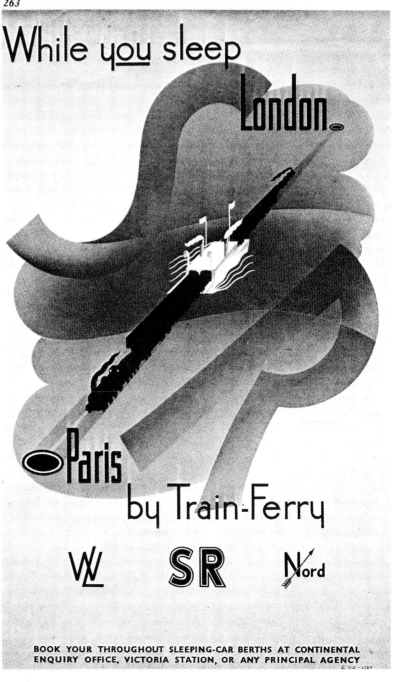

While you sleep
London.

Paris
by Train-Ferry

WL   SR   Nord

BOOK YOUR THROUGHOUT SLEEPING-CAR BERTHS AT CONTINENTAL
ENQUIRY OFFICE, VICTORIA STATION, OR ANY PRINCIPAL AGENCY

259 The famous Skegness poster by Hassall, first produced by the GNR, and perpetuated by the LNER.

260 SR posters promoting a move to areas served by the new electric trains, on a hoarding alongside the barrier at Waterloo.

261 Dramatised artist's impression of a 'Royal Scot' 4-6-0; poster for the LMSR by Bryan de Grineau.

262 Monogram devised by the GWR in the 1930s and applied to rolling stock, architecture and publicity material.

263 Imaginative treatment for the cross- Channel 'Night Ferry' service, produced by the SR in conjunction with the Wagons-Lits Company.

264

265

264   Stainless steel Gill Sans numerals on the cabside of a Gresley A4 Pacific.

265   Original nameplate of Fowler 'Royal Scot' class 4-6-0 No 6135 *Samson*, with small oval brass plaque depicting the original L&MR engine of the same name. (No 6135 was later renamed after *The East Lancashire Regiment*.)

266   Nameplate of NER Raven Pacific *City of Newcastle* with rather poor serif letters.

267   Nameplate of SR Maunsell 'Schools' class 4-4-0 No 913 *Christ's Hospital*.

268   Black wartime paint for the once proud streamliners. Note that the valance over the driving wheels has been removed to facilitate routine maintenance. LNER Class A4 Pacific No 4466 *Sir Ralph Wedgewood*.

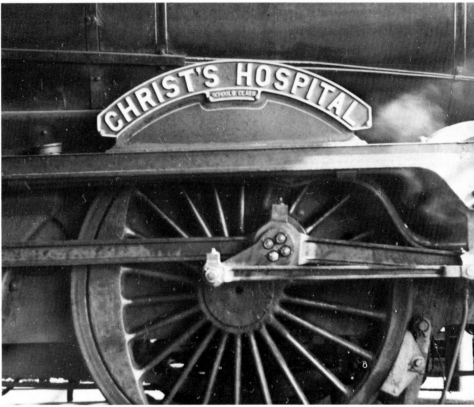

266

267

268

1939-1960
War and
Aftermath

EVENING STAR

92220

17 Utilitarian Steam Design

Some promising locomotive designs were nipped in the bud by the outbreak of World War II, in particular on the LMSR and LNER. On the LMSR, William Stanier had started to plan a 4-6-4 Hudson type locomotive for express passenger duties, which would have been considerably more powerful at speed than his splendid Pacific design of 1937. Increasing air competition made an acceleration of the daytime Anglo-Scottish expresses seem most desirable; with heavier loads than the 300 ton limit of the high speed 'Coronation Scot' train. The Hudson design, as outlined, had a streamlined casing similar to the 1937 engines, with an eight-wheeled tender and mechanical stoker. It would certainly have been an impressive addition to the Stanier stud. On the LNER, Sir Nigel Gresley was planning an even larger engine, with a 4-8-2 wheel arrangement, intended for heavy passenger work, but this proposal was also killed by the outbreak of war.

However, two new designs drawn-up during the final days of peace and early days of war were carried through to completion, despite the problems of workshop capacity and the priorities of metal for armaments. These two designs might be taken to represent, in the one instance, the final example of the classic British steam locomotive as it had been developed during the preceding 20 or so years, and in the other, the foretaste of postwar locomotive design.

Early in 1939 a new design for a locomotive to perform secondary and branch-line duties was prepared at Doncaster to Gresley's instructions. At this time, all four railway companies were still relying on locomotives of pre-Grouping concept for many of these lesser duties, and obsolescence was making its mark on their performance. New designs of medium-size locomotives were a top priority which was nevertheless to be shelved for the duration of the war, when the emphasis was on heavy and powerful freight engines to assist in the war effort. Gresley's 1939 design took the form of a small three-cylinder 2-6-2 tender engine, with a typical, but scaled down, handsome

Gresley outline. A prototype, No 3401 *Bantam Cock*, was completed in February 1941, with the classification V4; a second example, No 3402 (unnamed, but nicknamed by engine crews *Bantam Hen*), appeared the following month. The V4s proved very powerful and efficient for their size, but in the prevailing era of wartime austerity they were too expensive to construct and maintain. They were, as one authority aptly put it, 'Rolls-Royce engines for a Ford car job'. No further examples were constructed, and the design was to prove the last produced by Sir Nigel Gresley, who died in April, 1941.

The other design, which also took the rails in the grim year 1941, was by O. V. S. Bulleid, who had been Sir Nigel Gresley's assistant for many years before his appointment as Chief Mechanical Engineer of the SR, on the retirement of R. E. L. Maunsell in 1937. Bulleid's new locomotive, a powerful Pacific was in many ways a revolutionary design. No 21C1 *Channel Packet*, the prototype of the 'Merchant Navy' class was unveiled to the press at a naming ceremony at Eastleigh works in March, 1941. The ceremony was performed by the Minister of Transport, but the Press, much concerned with immediate issues of war found little space to describe the new machine. For the time being, therefore, the new Pacific did not make much impact on the public mind, the more so because early duties were on freight trains whilst teething troubles were being eliminated.

Channel Packet and a sister engine, No 21C2 *Union Castle*, were followed by four more examples by the end of 1941, in which many of the early lessons learned were incorporated from the start. The locomotives then began to establish a favourable reputation with their crews, despite their many novel features, and the stringent wartime conditions affecting everyday running and maintenance.

The 'Merchant Navy' class had an air-smoothed outer casing somewhat reminiscent of Gresley's *Cock o' the North* 2-8-2 design (on which Bulleid had worked), and there were numerous novel features, including a chain-driven valve

gear encased in an oil bath, electric lighting, patent Boxpok wheels, and a vastly improved cab layout. The exterior finish was in malachite green with three horizontal yellow stripes, and on the prototype large cast gunmetal name and numberplates were applied, but later engines did not perpetuate this feature. Space does not permit me to expound at any great length upon this remarkable design, but it will be referred to again later in this chapter.

I have already mentioned, in chapter 12, the Stanier class 8F 2-8-0 goods locomotive of the LMSR, which was adopted as a war locomotive at the commencement of hostilities. This design, produced to the standards of a peacetime railway, was entirely satisfactory in terms of power and performance, but under the stress of war there was a need to economise in every possible way in the construction of new locomotives without in any way sacrificing their reliability. A rugged simplicity was the order of the day, and the outcome was a new design of 'Austerity' freight locomotive, based on the Stanier 8F, but with a strictly utilitarian approach to every feature of its design. Cast iron replaced precious steel for a number of features, and fabrication of parts was adopted to avoid the need to compromise urgent war demands for steel castings. The overall concept was for a locomotive capable of operating under far from ideal conditions, with a minimum of maintenance. The design was produced by R. A. Riddles, formerly of the LMSR, who was now Deputy Director General of Royal Engineers' Equipment. The first 2-8-0s appeared in service in this country in 1943. Many were later shipped across to the Continent after the D Day landings, and they proved very successful engines in war service. Examples survived in service on British Railways for more than 20 years after the end of the war. A 2-10-0 version was produced in 1944; it had a considerably larger boiler but basically similar appearance.

Features of the Riddles 'Austerities' were the basically simple outline, with a cast-iron chimney with slightly flared lip, a tender with narrow bunker to give a good lookout when working tender first, and a complete absence of any decorative elements.

So urgent was the need for heavy freight power in the months preceding the Allied invasion of France, that orders were also placed with American builders for a quantity of 2-8-0 locomotives which would be capable of operating both within the limitations of the British loading gauge and subsequently on railways overseas. Although the detail design was entrusted to the American manufacturers, these locomotives followed the same utilitarian concept that characterised the Riddles locomotives, but many typically American labour saving features were incorporated, such as rocking grates and self-cleaning smokeboxes.

Approximately 400 of these USA 2-8-0s were shipped across to this country; long lines of them stood idle under armed guard in remote sidings in Britain, awaiting the D Day call to duty. Others were steamed-up and used on our railways to help relieve the chronic motive power situation. Once the engine crews had grown accustomed to their unfamiliar features the 'USAs' gained a good reputation for hard work.

A small 0-6-0T engine design was also imported from America to assist in the war effort. This had outside Walschaerts valve gear and a simple, rugged construction similar to the larger freight engines. Intended primarily for shunting work, this modern tank design proved both powerful and economical to maintain. Despite its somewhat blatantly American appearance, with sandboxes mounted upon the boiler in small domes, the 'USA' 0-6-0T was soon accepted as a most useful engine. A number operated at ordnance depots and in marshalling yards in this country, and after the war some were purchased by the SR for shunting in Southampton Docks. Some of the SR examples survived until the demise of steam, and several have since been preserved in working order. I have mentioned these American locomotives in some detail, as they were to have a certain amount of influence upon postwar locomotive design in Britain, as we shall see presently.

After the death of Sir Nigel Gresley, in 1941, the locomotive policy of the LNER underwent a considerable change. Gresley's successor, Edward Thompson, produced a new mixed-traffic 4-6-0 design in 1942. Classified B1, the new locomotive was in fact produced from a synthesis of existing standard parts, but it had a simple two-cylinder layout instead of the three-cylinder arrangement favoured by Gresley. It was a compact and neat design to look at, with considerably fewer

concessions to wartime utility than the Riddles and American designs just described.

Another class which first appeared in 1942 created an uproar because of the unconventional — and undeniably ugly — appearance it presented to British eyes as yet unaccustomed to strict funtionalism. I refer of course to Bulleid's Q1 class 0-6-0 locomotive, of which 40 examples were constructed at Brighton Works. The most powerful 0-6-0 goods locomotive ever built in this country. the Q1 class were capable of operating over most of the SR system. The design was produced with the problems of weight reduction very much in mind, and also with a keen regard for the current shortage of raw materials. Accordingly, the locomotive was, to put in bluntly, *left undressed*! There were no frills of any description; splashers and footplating were abandoned as relics of past practice, and the smokebox, boiler and cab were all finished in a thin sheet-metal casing. The chimney and dome were in the same austere style, completely devoid of ornamentation.

It was not long before the traditionalists raised loud voices in protest at this apparition, but Bulleid was unmoved; he had followed his principles, and the external appearance of the Q1 was determined by practical considerations of everyday function. Ironically, the utilitarian British steam locomotive was born in its most extreme form at the same locomotive works that some 60 or more years previously had constructed the artistic classics of Stroudley's regime. The last word on the subject of the Bulleid Q1 class should be that of the designer himself, who on one occasion pointed out that the design worked out at about 14ton lighter than a conventional locomotive of comparable capacity. This was equal to about 700ton of raw materials, enough to build nine more engines and tenders. Artistic disputes or not, this was a remarkable contribution to the war effort.

The streamlined outer casings of the LMSR and LNER prewar Pacific designs were of no functional value during the war years. Speeds had been drastically reduced, while loads were sometimes of formidable size. Prodigious exploits were recorded with the Pacifics hauling 20 coaches or more, packed to capacity on the Anglo-Scottish services. In wartime conditions the streamlining was useless deadweight, which proved a hindrance to rapid maintenance in running sheds where conditions were very far from ideal. It was not long before the valances were removed from Gresley's A4 Pacifics to expose the driving wheels and valve motion. On the Stanier engines a more drastic decision was taken after the war, when existing

streamliners were 'de-frocked' as they passed through works for major overhaul, while new examples of the class were constructed in non-streamlined form.

Stanier transformed the appearance of the Fowler 'Royal Scot' class three-cylinder 4-6-0s, when he decided to convert them to taper-boilered engines with double chimneys. Authority was given in 1943 for 20 'Royal Scot' conversions to be undertaken at Crewe, as examples of the class became due for new boilers and cylinders. Early in 1943 two 'Jubilee' class 4-6-0s, *Phoenix* and *Comet*, were rebuilt with new taper boilers and double chimneys, and the announcement was made that all engines of the 'Jubilee' class would be similarly converted. In fact this plan to rebuild all 183 engines of the two classes as 'Converted Scots', did not materialise. The entire 'Royal Scot' class was converted over a period of years as planned, but the 'Jubilees' remained unaltered. The transformation of the 'Royal Scots' produced an undeniably handsome machine, and they proved to be most capable performers. After the war rather ugly smoke deflectors were added to combat the problem of exhaust obscuring the driver's vision, a problem with many large-boilered steam locomotives.

Another locomotive might-have-been was a GWR plan for a 'super-Pacific' drawn up at Swindon in later war years as a proposed replacement for the ageing 'King' class 4-6-0s. F. W. Hawksworth, who had succeeded C. B. Collett as CME in 1941, had worked on the drawings for Churchward's *Great Bear* in his youth, and it would have been very interesting to see what his own Pacific proposal would have looked like, had circumstances permitted the project to proceed. In the event, the 'King' class remained in service on top-line duties for nearly 20 more years, with some notable mechanical improvements incorporated in the last years of their existence.

Sir William Stanier retired from his post on the LMSR in 1944, in order to devote himself to his duties as Scientific Adviser to the Ministry of Production, and C. E. Fairburn (who had been, in fact, acting CME of the LMSR since 1942) was duly appointed in his place. The sudden death of Fairburn, late in 1945, resulted in the appointment of H. G. Ivatt, son of H. A. Ivatt of GNR Atlantic fame.

By 1944-45 there was a gradual change of emphasis from the urgency of wartime production towards planning for the railways' needs once peace was restored, though much of this was mere doodling. The rigours of wartime railway operation had emphasised the importance of fully considering the servicing and maintenance aspects of any new locomotive designs.

Staff shortages had to be allowed for, and mechanical means of performing many tasks hitherto the lot of manual labour, were now of considerable importance. I have already referred to the American 2-8-0 locomotives which had incorporated a number of labour-saving devices (such as had been a feature of prewar American practice), including self-cleaning smokeboxes and rocking firegrates. On the LMSR, H. G. Ivatt introduced and perfected such devices for postwar construction.

The design of locomotives to perform secondary and branch-line duties now took on new importance, as the existing stock of such engines, including many examples dating back to the days of Johnson, Stroudley, Stirling and others, had much of the final wind knocked out of them by wartime service. Ivatt on the LMSR realised the need to produce thoroughly modern small designs for such duties, and he carried through to completion proposals of the Fairburn era for lightweight 2-6-0 and 2-6-2T designs. Fairburn had actually gone to the length of producing a full-size wooden mock-up of the 2-6-2T design, constructed by craftsmen carpenters of Derby Carriage Works. This idea was received with very mixed feelings at the time, but construction of mock-ups has since become an accepted stage of new design development on BR. Fairburn's object was to finalise design details before commencing actual construction, by showing the proposals in mock-up form to the various shed staff, fitters and drivers who would be called upon to operate and service the new engines. As constructed by Ivatt the two lightweight designs had an acceptable straightforward appearance with an air of businesslike modernity. Many details were of obvious Stanier origin, but a number of concessions were made to the new emphasis upon servicing and maintenance. These small and essentially functional engines soon proved most acceptable replacements for the various elderly classes, on a variety of duties.

On the GWR F. W. Hawksworth introduced an 'Improved Hall' class mixed-traffic 4-6-0 in 1944 with certain constructional changes, in particular to the main frames, which gave the design a somewhat crisper appearance at the front end. Outwardly the final years of GWR practice seemed to differ little from the noble traditions of Churchward and Collett, but a design produced by Hawksworth, which was authorised towards the end of the war, indicated the likely trend of future GWR locomotive design. This was a two-cylinder mixed-traffic 4-6-0, the 'County' class of 1945, which had a number of breakaway

features from established Swindon practice. Visually, the most noticeable change was the single continuous splasher above the running board and the flush-sided tender. The first locomotive of the class, No 1000 *County of Middlesex*, was constructed with a large copper-capped double chimney but the remainder were delivered with a typical GWR single chimney. In later days, under BR, the class were fitted with another design of double chimney of curiously squat dimensions, which gave the engine a most odd appearance when viewed from certain angles.

On the LNER, Edward Thompson rebuilt Gresley's 'Cock o' the North' class P2 2-8-2s as Pacifics producing a locomotive of curiously hybrid and clumsy appearance. In 1946 further examples were built new to much the same design. Considerations of performance aside, these Thompson engines were a sad departure from the Pacifics of Gresley's regime at Doncaster. In 1947 a revised version was produced by A. H. Peppercorn, who had succeeded Thompson as CME, and in these engines of Class A2, which were of more orthodox proportions, the overall appearance was greatly improved.

I have already commented upon the remarkable originality of design displayed by the Bulleid 'Merchant Navy' class Pacific of 1941. Quite severe teething troubles were inevitable with a design incorporating so many novel features, but once these snags had been remedied the true merits of the design became apparent. Various changes were made in the external appearance of the front end in attempts to improve smoke-deflection, but otherwise the air-smoothed casing and welded flush-sided tender remained intact; unlike the LMSR and LNER streamliners. One idea behind the casing was that the locomotive could be easily cleaned by passing it through a carriage washing plant, but I have no personal memory of seeing this feat performed.

Bulleid's second Pacific design was a lightweight version intended to have wide route availability over secondary lines, where previously the largest locomotives available had often been the Maunsell Moguls. The new class was appropriately named 'West Country', in view of the decision to allocate the first examples to work traffic on the lines west of Exeter. A later series of engines, allocated mainly to depots in south-east England, were named the 'Battle of Britain' class to commemorate the defeat of the Luftwaffe. The first lightweight Pacific appeared in June, 1945, and externally it bore a strong family resemblance to the 1941 design. The success of the Lightweights, as they were often named, was acclaimed as even

greater than the larger 'Merchant Navy' design.

Paradoxically, Bulleid's Pacific designs made a feature of enclosing the 'works', whereas his wartime Q1 class 0-6-0, already described, had them virtually naked. On the Pacifics the valve gear enclosed in an oil bath, and the air-smoothed casing, proved something of an embarrassment to enginemen, who were unable to detect easily the source of suspected troubles. Shed staff were critical of the lack of accessibility which prolonged maintenance and added to repair bills. But despite these criticisms all concerned were loud in their praise of the performance of the engines in everyday service, and there were many small details which were greatly appreciated for their careful design.

For the duration of the war the railways had been under State control, and with a Labour Government elected in 1945 Nationalisation was regarded by many people as inevitable. The bells that heralded in the New Year for 1948 also sounded the death knell for the Big Four railway companies. The new State-owned railway system with the Railway Executive situated in London and six Regional areas under the management of Chief Regional Officers, was given a remit which included the behest that it should weld four Groups into one and replace the existing variations in techniques and traditions by a new policy of standardisation based on analysis of the differing company techniques and procedures. The operative word being *standardise*.

R. A. Riddles, designer of the wartime 'Austerity' 2-8-0 and 2-10-0 locomotives, was appointed Member of the Railway Executive responsible for mechanical and electrical engineering. He and his chosen team represented a strong ex-LMSR influence, but in fairness it must be observed that they embarked upon a comprehensive evaluation of the existing practices of the four former companies, as their remit required of them. As E. S. Cox has observed, in his excellent book *British Railways Standard Steam Locomotives*, the time was hardly ripe for large-scale investment in diesel or electric traction. So steam was chosen for new construction; but what form was it to follow?

To help decide this, a large-scale series of interchange trials was organised, with representative locomotives of the former companies operating over the main lines of all Regions. It is beyond the scope of my present story to mention the various findings of these trials, which have in any case been exhaustively chronicled. Whilst the trials proceeded much investigation work went on to decide the nature of the proposed new standard British locomotives. Meanwhile an initial step was taken by the selection of certain existing designs for immediate construction until such time as the new standard designs were ready. The choice of these existing designs was significant indeed, demonstrating that the functional school of thought, as developed by Ivatt on the LMSR, could be expected to exert strong influence upon the future trend.

The passing of the Big Four railway companies also marked the demise of the autocratic CME. Although the last generation of these men remained *in situ* they lost much of their design responsibility and were directly answerable to Riddles at the Railway Executive headquarters. Such a situation could not have been easy, particularly in the case of Bulleid, who held firm views on the subject of locomotive design, in many instances diametrically opposed to those of Riddles and his colleagues. Nevertheless the drawing offices of the former companies began to work well together on the design stages of the new standard engines.

Before going on to examine the new Standard designs for BR, mention must be made of Bulleid's revolutionary 'Leader' class design, as it differed so completely from the prevailing postwar trends. The design stages of the 'Leader' appear to have been clouded with apprehension. Bulleid was well aware that plans for a locomotive of such completely new concept might not survive the review of current motive power, when the Railway Executive embarked on its new policy of standardisation. So he pressed forward with the design as quickly as possible during the last months of the SR existence. In the event he just scraped through, with authority to proceed with construction of five experimental prototypes (his original scheme envisaged a further 30 engines).

The design was for a mixed-traffic 0-6-6-0T engine with 100% adhesion, achieved by two six-wheel powered bogies

with three-cylinder sleeve-valve engines. The superstructure was an overall casing with two driving cabs, one each end, and a central compartment for the fireman. This central compartment proved in practice to be unbearably hot, but this could have been avoided by conversion to oil firing instead of coal.

Prepared with such haste, and with so many innovations, prolonged teething troubles were inevitable. But the prevailing political climate definitely did not favour such novelties, however much long-term potential they might offer, and development work was halted when only one example had been completed and put on test. In retrospect one cannot avoid a certain sadness that this considerable attempt to improve upon the conventional Stephensonian steam locomotive was dismissed so readily in favour of the utilitarian trend of postwar days.

A range of new standard designs was drawn-up, to embrace the whole sphere of railway operations from express passenger to heavy freight; some types were to be completely new, others would be based upon existing engines. The trend was to be towards simplification, good accessibility of all parts requiring attention, and reduction in time required for repairs and servicing. Clearly the postwar LMSR engines produced by H. G. Ivatt were likely to satisfy these requirements.

Ivatt had concentrated upon just such features of steam locomotive design, and, in addition to the light 2-6-0 and 2-6-2T designs already mentioned, he had produced a larger mixed-traffic 2-6-0, and modernised versions of Stanier's famous Class 5 and Pacific designs. Consequently it came as no surprise when the standard versions of the two 2-6-0s, the 2-6-2T and

the Class 5 4-6-0, bore very striking similarity to LMSR practice.

A high degree of standardisation was insisted on for the new designs, and to achieve this the work was distributed to the various drawing offices, each of which became responsible for certain features and components; whilst each office was also parent to particular types, for which it had to assemble the completed production drawings. Thus a cross-fertilisation of ideas was allowed without Regional discrepancies such as would otherwise have been rife!

On 2 January 1951 the pioneer standard BR class 7 Pacific was steamed for the first time at Crewe. At the end of the month a naming ceremony took place at Marylebone station, when No 70000 was christened *Britannia* by the Minister of Transport. With a two-cylinder layout, Walschaerts valve gear, taper-boiler and wide Belpaire firebox, *plus* a high running plate which exposed the driving wheels, the new locomotive clearly belonged to the modern functional school of thought. But there were significant signs of an attempt to produce harmonious lines for the external appearance, and the sum total was considerably less austere than either Ivatt or Riddles himself would previously have allowed. For instance the high running board was of deep section, and it sloped down to the buffer beam at the front end in a neat manner. And the chimney was immediately recognised as being pure Horwich in style! The design of cab and tender had been carefully considered (another full-size mock-up was constructed for this), and generally speaking the corners had been rounded-off the utilitarian concept.

269 Sir Nigel Gresley's final locomotive design, which made its debut in the midst of wartime struggle; the first Class V4 2-6-2 No 1700 completed, *Bantam Cock*. Only two of the type were completed as they were too expensive to build during the austere conditions of the time.

It is not my intention to embark on an evaluation of the standard BR locomotives in service; suffice to say that they won greater acceptance on some Regions than on others. But all told they were a tough breed, born of difficult times and blessed with modestly handsome outline. As to what might have emerged as a range of standard locomotives had someone like Bulleid been in charge, that remains for the imagination. But the standard Riddles engines, derived from postwar LMSR practice and incorporating certain excellent features from the practice of the other three railway companies, must be taken to represent the final essay in utilitarian steam design. As such they deserve much praise for the reasonable compromise they achieved between the stark wartime trend of the 'Austerity' locomotives, and the classic conventions of British steam locomotion, as it had developed over the preceding 120 years.

A final episode in the story of postwar steam concerns the two Bulleid Pacific designs already discussed. Clearly their

design did not comply with the BR ideals of simplicity and serviceability, although their performance was undoubtedly excellent. After Bulleid's retirement from BR affairs, the decision was taken to convert the engines to more orthodox layout. The air-smoothed casings were removed and Walschaerts valve gear replaced the original oil-bath and chain-drive layout. The resulting locomotive, with certain stylistic features in common with the BR standard engines, was in many respects the most handsome product of the final decade of steam.

When the inevitable ceremony to mark completion of the last steam locomotive to be constructed for British Railways was performed at Swindon in 1960, the locomotive concerned — a Riddles Class 9 2-10-0 No 92220 — was appropriately named *Evening Star*. No one present failed to notice that the nameplate had typical GWR lettering, whilst the chimney sported a polished copper cap; Swindon had the very last word in BR steam design!

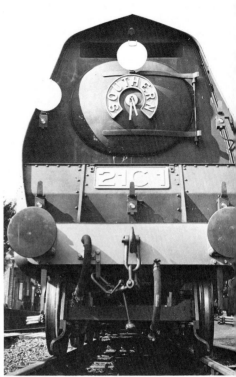

270

272

271

270 Front end of Bulleid's first Pacific locomotive, No 21C1 *Channel Packet*, as originally designed and built in 1941. This unorthodox locomotive design concept had many modifications in the cause of time.

271 A later picture of one of Bulleid's 'airsmoothed' 4-6-2s; No 35007 *Aberdeen Commonwealth* in early BR blue livery, taken as it drifted downhill into Salisbury at the head of an Exeter-London express on Easter Monday 1954. This angle clearly shows how the profile of Bulleid's carriages and Pacifics was carefully matched.

272 Bulleid's powerful but extraordinarily ugly wartime goods locomotive, Class Q1 introduced 1942. No 33027 is shown in BR days.

273 The British 'Austerity' 2-8-0 goods locomotive. A simplified version of the Stanier 8F, designed by R. A. Riddles in 1943. No 90294 is illustrated working freight towards London from March, at Great Chesterfield in May 1951.

273

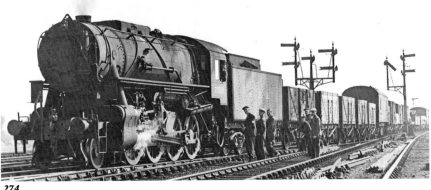

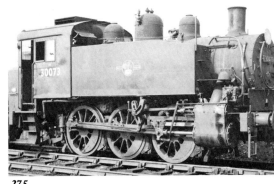

274

275

6103

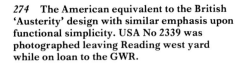

274 The American equivalent to the British 'Austerity' design with similar emphasis upon functional simplicity. USA No 2339 was photographed leaving Reading west yard while on loan to the GWR.

275 The American built wartime 0-6-0T. A design which had the emphasis placed upon accessibility for repair and maintenance. Some examples were purchased by the SR after the war, as seen here in this picture of No 30073, taken in 1961.

276 Sir William Stanier's rebuilt 'Royal Scot' was a handsome transformation prior to the addition of ugly smoke deflectors. No 6103 *Seaforth Highlander* is illustrated in postwar LMSR black livery.

277 Thompson's rebuild of the original Gresley Class A1 Pacific, No 4470 *Great Northern*, was intended to simplify the basic design and reduce maintenance and running costs. It met with a very mixed reception from

276
278

L N E R
9000

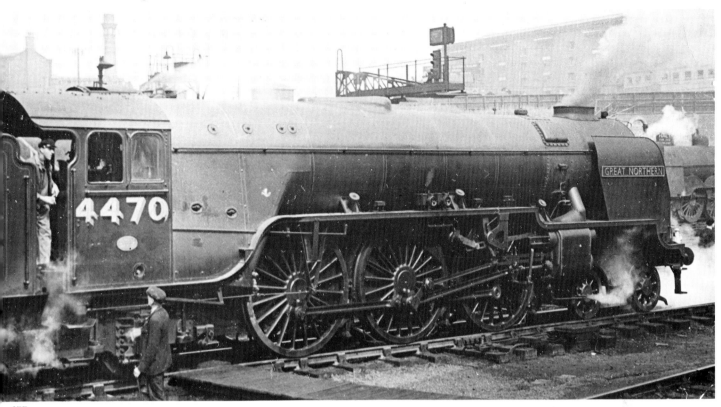

277

both enginemen and enthusiasts. Here it is seen after the addition of smoke deflectors, and with an improved cab design, but still retaining the stovepipe double chimney and experimental dark blue livery first carried; pictured at Kings Cross, on the 'Flying Scotsman' in June 1946.

278 Thompson's ideal was basically sound; ie to simplify the layout of LNER locomotives in order to meet the harsh demands of the late wartime and postwar operating. The sophisticated designs of Sir Nigel Gresley did not respond too well to such lack of care and maintenance; whereas Thompson's engines were more able to take such rough useage. His L1 class 2-6-4T was a neat and useful design, seen here in the prototype No 9000, which was however soon displaced by electrification schemes on the routes for which it was most suited. The engine is in postwar apple green livery.

279 On the LMSR a simplified version of the excellent two-cylinder Stanier 2-6-4T was introduced by his successor, C. E. Fairburn. Examples were built after Nationalisation for use on the Southern, Eastern and North Eastern Regions. Illustrated is SR-based No 42096 working a Ramsgate-Ashford train, with a Maunsell N class 2-6-0 passing on a train of coal empties.

280 H. G. Ivatt's lightweight 2-6-2T design for branch line and local duties. A simple layout with the emphasis upon operating and maintenance requirements. No 41220 is illustrated working a Stanmore branch push-pull set.

281 The 2-6-0 tender engine version of Ivatt's lightweight design; basically similar to the 2-6-2T. No 46488 was photographed at Keswick in April 1964.

282 Hawksworth's postwar mixed traffic 4-6-0 'County' class, GWR No 1009 *County of Carmarthen*, was photographed leaving Parsons Rock Tunnel with the 7.30am Paddington-Plymouth train, in April 1957, with later design of squat double chimney.

283 Bulleid improved the front end and draughting on some of Maunsell's engines, adding rather an ugly multiple jet blastpipe and wide chimney, as seen here on 'Schools' class 4-4-0 No 30939 *Leatherhead*, photographed (in early BR lined black livery) as it worked that 9.15am Charing Cross-Dover express near Grove Park, in May 1952.

279

280
281

282

283

284 Final version of the Stanier Pacific, with modifications by H. G. Ivatt. Introduced 1947, this might justifiably be described as the finest development of the heaviest express steam power in Britain. No 46257 *City of Salford* is illustrated.

285

288

286

287

285 H. G. Ivatt's Class 4 mixed traffic 2-6-0 for the LMSR had a number of features directly taken from contemporary American practice. The front end of prototype No 3000 is illustrated, showing the high running boards above the cylinders.

286 An example of the postwar lightweight versions of the Bulleid Pacific — the 'Battle of Britain' and 'West Country' classes — seen here in strange company. No 34059 *Sir Archibald Sinclair* was photographed at Norwich shed on 18 May 1949 after working the down 'Norfolkman'; whilst on loan to the Eastern Region with a GER J15 0-6-0 alongside.

287 Ivatt applied his ideas to the final examples of the Stanier 'Black Five' 4-6-0; also adding Caprotti valve gear and a double blastpipe and chimney, as seen here on No 44687, on the turntable of Patricroft shed.

288 Resplendent in BR blue livery, Class A1 Pacific No 60154 *Bon Accord* designed by A. H. Peppercorn showing original stovepipe double chimney, and the electric lighting fitted.

289 Standard BR Pacific design. 'Britannia' class No 70028 *Royal Star* hauling a Newport-Paddington train near Twyford. A creditable attempt to produce a functional but neat appearance.

289

290

291

290 The remarkable 'Leader' class 0-6-6-0T by O. V. S. Bulleid; first steamed in June 1949. A bold attempt to advance the design of steam locomotive a stage further. No 36001 is seen on one of its final runs (before the project was abandoned by BR), near Eastleigh, with the ex-LNER dynamometer car attatched, in August 1950.

291 Emphasis upon ease of maintenance was the underlying requirement of all of the BR

Standard steam designs. Here Class 5 No 73171 receives some attention from fitters at Nine Elms shed, in July 1966.

292 Standard BR mixed traffic Class 5 4-6-0 with Caprotti valve gear. No 73154 was photographed at Derby in June 1957, just after completion.

293 Brand new and with nameplates covered-over, the sole express passenger

Standard BR Pacific of Class 8 No 71000 (later *Duke of Gloucester*) was photographed at Shrewsbury, on a running-in turn from Crewe Works. Further development was halted by the decision to abandon steam in favour of electric and diesel traction.

294 Standard Class 4 2-6-4T, largely based upon former LMSR practice. No 80028 (with small snowplough fitted) shows-off their rakish appearance.

292

293

295 Trials with some 2-10-0s fitted with Franco-Crosti boilers did not produce the hoped-for extension of steam locomotive development. No 92028 was photographed at Preston Park, SR, after a visit to Brighton Works for official inspection in September 1955. The unusual location of the final 'chimney', on the side of the boiler gave an odd aspect to these engines.

294
295

296

300

296 Latter-day modifications gave an extended lease of top-link life to a number of prewar designs. Gresley A4 Pacific No 60028 *Walter K. Whigham* is seen here in final form, with large double chimney, at Kings Cross shed.

297 The BR rebuilding of Bulleid's airsmoothed Pacifics produced a most handsome transformation. No 35027 *Port Line* displays its powerful forms in this striking night scene taken at Banbury in March 1966.

298 Modernised front-end layout, with improved superheating and double chimney, gave the Collett 'King' class 4-6-0s an impressive new look in their final years on BR. No 6000 *King George V* was photographed at Old Oak Common in April 1961.

299 Particularly striking was the visual change brought about by fitting some of Gresley's A3 Pacifics with German-type smoke deflectors and double chimneys. No 60056 *Centenary* was photographed at Copley Hill shed.

300 No 92220 *Evening Star*, the last steam locomotive constructed for service on British Railways. Built at Swindon in 1960, the locomotive is seen when new, posed alongside an ex-GWR 5700 0-6-0, No 8773, at Old Oak Common shed. *Evening Star* displays the handsome appearance of the Riddles' Standard 9F 2-10-0; in this case embellished by lined green livery and copper-capped double chimney.

297

298

299

18 Postwar Carriages

Plans for postwar carriage construction began to take shape in the later months of 1944, as the end of World War II became apparent. By this time the existing carriage fleet had suffered considerable loss and damage, and its general condition was decidedly shabby. The railway companies were faced with a formidable programme of repair and renovation, besides urgent new construction. Nevertheless there was evidently a keen desire to improve on existing designs for the new carriages to be built, and optimistic announcements began to reveal future trends. For example, during 1944 the GWR made plans for a new main line corridor carriage design, and by late 1945 it had announced that 260 new fluorescently-lit coaches would be constructed during 1946, at the rate of one a week. In addition to the fluorescent lighting other new features were to include special interior finishes, and experiments with the use of aluminium alloy for both construction and detail fittings.

In the event this announcement proved unduly optimistic and shortage of both men and materials prevented the construction schedule from being attained, whilst the special interior finishes were abandoned after only a few prototypes had displayed them. The fluorescent lighting was also abandoned after only half-a-dozen carriages had been fitted-out and normal filament lighting was substituted for the production batch. Nevertheless this was a bold experiment for the time; the only carriages with fluorescent lighting, previously operated by a British railway, had been some District Line emu stock of the London Passenger Transport Board introduced in 1944.

On the GWR locomotive-hauled, fluorescently-lit carriages trouble was experienced when the batteries were not fully charged, and the hot cathode tubes employed gave a rather unpleasant reddish light effect. The employment of special plastic interior finishes was dropped for economy reasons, and new production had either oak veneer or Holoplast enamelled hardboard.

These postwar GWR carriages, of Hawksworth design, introduced a new look to the rolling stock of that company. They were of dimensions suitable for operation over the majority of routes, with a slab-sided body profile, and had bow-ended roofs similar to prewar LNER carriages. A more speedy method of construction was employed, with direct assembly of the body on to the underframe, and (as already mentioned) a number of experiments were made with the use of aluminium alloy. These included a batch of 25 carriages with aluminium body panelling, and one carriage with a complete aluminium underframe. For normal production ordinary mild-steel panelling was employed, screwed to timber framing.

No new dining cars were built by the GWR after the war, but it announced in 1945 that 90 prewar restaurant cars would be refurbished, also some sleeping cars. For the restaurant cars the company commissioned schemes from specialist interior decorators and the results were decidedly *à la mode*! For the first class cars such features as recessed ceiling lights, revolving pedestal-mounted armchairs, pink-tinted mirrors with etched floral motifs, and wood veneer finishes, were proposed. The scheme for third class renovations included tip-up seating, recessed lighting, ash panelling and furnishings in pastel shades. Perhaps it was just as well that only a few of these carriages actually appeared and a less exotic decor substituted, with leather bench seats and glass partitions. The sleeping car refurbishing was more restrained, with the emphasis on plastic wall surfaces and improved fittings.

An exhibition was staged at Paddington station in November 1946 to publicise the proposals for future GWR rolling stock. This included examples of the refurbished dining and sleeping cars as well as fluorescently-lit corridor carriages. But deliveries of new stock lagged badly behind schedule, and with the impending nationalisation of the railways, much of the promise for the future was destined to remain unfulfilled.

On the LMSR, where a programme for 800 new passenger carriages was announced, the general layout of postwar construction followed their standard practice of the late 1930s, although further carriages of all-steel construction were introduced. These differed from their steel and timber brethren in having circular porthole windows for the toilet compartment and corridor wall opposite. Like the GWR, the LMSR also consulted interior decorating specialists for refurbishing schemes for their dining cars, with somewhat happier results. As an experiment, two refurbished prewar dining cars were placed in regular operation in May 1947. They featured an interior decor of pleasantly restrained style, with increased floor and table space to facilitate serving by waiters. Other features were double-glazed windows, separate chairs, and improved heating, lighting and ventilation. The LMSR also experimented with fluorescent lighting, on a first class carriage which operated on the St Pancras-Bedford service during 1947.

Postwar main line stock for the LNER, designed by Thompson, broke almost completely away from the long-standing Gresley traditions. Articulation of carriages was abandoned and construction was of composite wood and steel panelling. The flush steel sides were painted in imitation varnished teak livery to match the existing teak carriages. The windows had a rather severe angular appearance (later a small radius was introduced to reduce corrosion of the steel panels), except the toilet windows, which were of oval-shaped opaque white glass. A notable experiment was made with the design of six prototype third class sleeping cars, which had single- as well as double-berth compartments with full bedding and individual wash basins.

O. V. S Bulleid, who had gained considerable experience in coaching stock design during his days on the LNER with Gresley, introduced some striking changes in SR design policy. Even before the outbreak of World War II suburban rush-hour traffic had grown to the extent that it taxed the existing electric rolling stock to the limits of capacity. In 1939 Bulleid proposed a new design of suburban carriage with the use of curved and welded-steel bodysides, 9ft wide, to allow six-a-side seating; thereby increasing the capacity without adding extra carriages. It was not until 1941 that the prototypes appeared, and further construction was postponed until the emergency was over. The prototypes had a distinctive appearance with curved steel bodysides and a domed roof over the driving cabs, at each end of the four-car set. Roof construction was of traditional wood and canvas. Seating was rather cramped due to the narrowness of some compartments; in fact some trailer vehicles had 11 compartments seating no less than 132 passengers.

Later Bulleid suburban electric sets built from 1946 onwards, were rather less austere and uncomfortable. They had one compartment less in the same overall length per carriage and a saloon layout with five-a-side seating also was introduced (arranged two and three each side of an off-centre passageway). Externally the 1946 stock was different from the prototypes, with all-steel construction and a full front end without the domed roof over the driver's cab. The curved steel bodysides, with doors to every compartment, or saloon bay, had round-cornered windows and toplights in the doors. The design was constructed in batches, with only slight variations, for four years after nationalisation, using for the most part underframes and bogies from withdrawn sets.

For main line locomotive-hauled stock Bulleid produced a prototype composite coach, which was displayed to the public at Victoria, Waterloo, Charing Cross and elsewhere in the early autumn of 1945. The public was requested to comment on the various new features proposed and to state whether it preferred compartments or saloons. The first examples of postwar main line stock had a side-door arrangement very similar to the new suburban carriages, but after assessment of public reaction to the prototype just mentioned, the side doors were eliminated and large compartment windows allowed passengers a fine view, while giving a spacious feeling to the interior. End doors were provided with, as a rule, intermediate doors and transverse vestibules in the middle of the coach.

Despite a three-to-one public vote in favour of compartments some open saloon carriages were built, whilst some brake thirds had a saloon and compartment layout.

Externally the new Bulleid corridor stock was of handsome modern appearance with curved steel sides and neat detailing. The livery was an overall malachite green to match the locomotives,

and the effect was enhanced because the new carriages were marshalled in set formations.

Public opinion, after inspection of the 1945 prototype, compelled provision of corridor heaters and individually-switched reading lamps in addition to the normal ceiling lights. New restaurant cars were constructed, of straightforward design and layout with a noticeable lack of gimmicks, although recessed fluorescent lighting was employed in the first class saloons.

Before proceeding with an account of the effects that the railway nationalisation of 1948 had upon carriage design, mention should be made of some attempts to break away from established design concepts for British railway carriages, produced between 1947 and 1949.

To increase the capacity of a railway carriage without fouling the severe restrictions of the loading gauge, two designs for forms of double-deck layout were produced, although only one was proceeded with. In 1947 a Britain Can Make It exhibition included a scale model of a double-deck third class sleeping car, produced by Design Research Unit. As shown in the sectional illustration (photo 307), the design incorporated a well construction for the central portion of the coach. There were 14 two-berth and six single-berth compartments. Externally the design somewhat resembled Bulleid's new corridor stock, but Gresley bogies were used.

Although this interesting proposal never proceeded beyond the design stage, it is of particular interest to our present story as it was an early example of the work of an industrial design team for railway stock. One member of the team was George Williams, who later became Design Officer on British Railways.*

The second attempt to produce a satisfactory double-deck carriage was by O. V. S. Bulleid for the SR, and construction of prototypes was in this case authorised. These actually entered service in November 1949 after Bulleid had retired from BR to take up a new appointment in Ireland with Coras Iompair Eireann. Produced as a solution to the sharp increase in rush-hour loadings on the south-east suburban routes, the double-deck electric trains had a dovetailed arrangement of compartments, with the lower ones connected to the higher ones by a short staircase. The capacity of an eight-car train was increased by 31% without altering the overall length or height or adding to the tare weight.

Unfortunately, the public did not take very kindly to being penned in this fashion; there were complaints about poor ventilation in the upper-deck compartments and about limited head

room and uncomfortable seats. From the operating point of view a more serious defect revealed itself when the time taken to load and unload passengers made the trains run late.

Perhaps the idea could have been pursued and the snags ironed out but the decision was taken to embark on an alternative scheme for lengthening trains to 10 coaches, with all the added expense of extra new carriages, lengthened platforms and new signalling. The prototype double-deckers continued in service and objections to them largely subsided as passengers grew accustomed to their layout. Certainly the overcrowding in the 10-coach trains of conventional SR electric stock later reached proportions every bit as unpleasant as the restricted confines of the double-deckers.

In 1947 a carriage built by the Budd Company of America was loaded at Philadelphia for shipment to Britain. This was an adaptation, for the British loading gauge, of a typical American streamlined stainless steel railway carriage. Named *Silver Princess,* the carriage had an unpainted stainless steel exterior, with horizontal corrugated side and roof panels. It ran on the LNER and LMSR, and also in Ireland for a while (mounted on broad gauge bogies). Sponsored by the Pressed Steel Company, the carriage was demonstrated in an effort to procure orders for similar carriages to be built in Britain; but the Nationalisation of the railways in 1948 appears to have killed interest in this enterprise. No further examples have ever been built for BR but the French Railways today operate a considerable fleet of stainless steel carriages of advanced design; this was indeed an opportunity missed on our part.

Internally the *Silver Princess* carriage had a first class compartment section, based on British practice, with fluorescent ceiling lights, and luggage rack mounted reading lights, ashtrays in the padded armrests and overall decor of American fashion completely devoid of pattern. The third class section of the carriage was based upon American practice, with a saloon seating 30 passengers in individual reclining, rotating armchairs. A central fluorescent light fitting, situated at ceiling height, was augmented by individual reading lights recessed into the luggage rack supports.

In later years the *Silver Princess* was purchased by BR, the name was removed and it was upgraded to full first class. Later still a lounge bar replaced the compartment section, the distinctive corrugated sides were panelled over, and standard paint livery applied. It was allocated to the London Midland Region

---

* See *British Rail 1948-78, A Journey by Design* by the same author.

and was often included in the Ulster Express.

In matters of design for both locomotives and carriages, O. V. S. Bulleid had often pronounced his belief that Form follows function and function creates form. Viewed against this, the design of the 'Tavern cars' he produced in 1949 seems the more incredible. The basic idea was to create a public house atmosphere for a railway buffet car, which would encourage passengers to partake of a quick one during the journey and then return to their seats. A problem in existing SR buffet cars had been the bar lizards who snatched a seat before the train departed and then lingered over a single glass of beer or a snack of some sort for the entire journey, thereby preventing further customers from enjoying the amenities. In this respect it appears that the 'Tavern cars' were successful; sales of beer reached record heights.

But aesthetically the 'Tavern cars' were disastrous and protests soon appeared in the newspapers, sometimes ridiculing BR for allowing such a design to be constructed. The interior of the tavern portion had a pseudo-antique decor based on the interior of an English pub (actually it was the *Chequers Inn* at Pulborough). The small, high windows had imitation leaded lights and the furniture was of stained wood, including the seats. Mock-Tudor dark-oak beams were set into roughcast wall and ceiling finishes and little square metal lanterns completed the impression. In remarkable contrast to this mobile stage set the cocktail bar itself was constructed in plastic and stainless steel to modern design.

A restaurant car was attached to the kitchen end of the 'Tavern Car', with both first and third class accommodation. The first class section had inward-facing seats arranged down the two walls of the carriage, with separate tables to each pair of seats, while the third class section was of conventional layout with movable chairs. The interior decor echoed the timbered effect of the 'Tavern car', but light oak beams were used, with shiny plastic panelling and recessed fluorescent lighting. The windows in both the 'Tavern cars' and the restaurant cars were confined to small toplights, which prevented passengers from enjoying the passing scene. This feature alone aroused such wrath that the cars were withdrawn and converted to conventional buffet and restaurant vehicles.

The exterior of the 'Tavern cars' was no less remarkable than the interior, with imitation oak beams painted in black upon the cream upper panels of the steel bodysides, and a brickwork effect painted upon the crimson lower panels. Each 'Tavern car' was given a name — *The*

Green Man, The Crown, Jolly Tar, Dolphin, and so on — and an inn sign was painted on the sides. Some of the carriages were allocated to the Eastern Region as well as to the Southern.

The design of Pullman stock remained very much on traditional lines. A number of prewar cars was extensively refurbished with modern materials, but new cars constructed for the Golden Arrow train in Festival of Britain year, 1951, had dated interiors which did not compare well with comtemporary developments in competitive spheres of transport. Their exterior differed in having flush steel sides, and Gresley bodies were used, but the livery remained strictly traditional, with names allocated to first class cars.

There was a noticeable increase in the use of buffet cars in the late 1940s, to cope with demands for quick meal service, especially on excursion trains. Soon after Nationalisation a number of existing catering vehicles was gutted and rebuilt as cafeteria or buffet cars. Some had a self-service layout, while others had a long counter with stools and an attendant serving up to 20 people. Some of the features incorporated were used in the design of new standard catering vehicles for BR, but the converted cars had a short life; which was perhaps just as well, as they had very utilitarian decor and fittings.

I have already discussed the remit of standardisation given to the new Railway Executive, when the railways were Nationalised in January 1948 in my pervious chapter on final steam designs. This remit applied equally to the production of new passenger carriages.

To the newly-created design team at the Marylebone Road headquarters, there fell the task of evaluating the existing carriage designs and practices of the four former railway companies, and of producing a new standard carriage concept incorporating the best of these existing features. This was to prove no easy task, as the new stock would be required to operate over virtually the entire British Railways network of routes. In the event it took them three years to finalise the design and construct the first examples. Meanwhile construction of existing pre-Nationalisation designs was allowed to proceed unhindered.

The first standard carriages were delivered for service in 1951 and the opportunity was taken to place them in the public eye by allocating them to special express duties, in some cases hauled by the new standard 'Britannia' class Pacific locomotives.

Construction of the standard carriages was all-steel, with the body shell welded to the underframe, which was 63ft 5in long for main line stock. The body profile was

curved, similar to that employed by Bulleid for his SR designs, and allowed slightly greater width at shoulder height. Buckeye automatic couplers and Pullman type gangways at last became standard equipment, except for suburban carriages, which retained conventional screw couplings and buffers.

The general concept of the new standard stock was undoubtedly influenced by the prevailing emphasis on economy. The design was essentially utilitarian, with rather spartan appointments and simple details, which in many instances fell short of the best standards of the former railway companies. The exterior finish was simple, with a rather heavy roof line and deep guttering, but not altogether unpleasing to the eye. There were no refinements such as double-glazing, air-conditioning or fluorescent lighting, while sound insulation was poor — a feature emphasised by the higher noise level which is a characteristic of all-steel bodies.

The real Achilles heel of the new stock turned out to be the bogie design, which did not come up to expectations in service. Although it gave a reasonably smooth ride when new, or recently overhauled, it developed quite rough characteristics once wear set in; these could prove particularly uncomfortable for the occupants of sleeping or dining cars. Worst of all were the bogies of new standard emu stock, of which more anon.

A range of new standard catering vehicles was introduced, including a variety of buffet cars and full restaurant cars. For the earliest examples a spartan interior treatment was adopted, with some resemblance to the refurbished LMSR dining cars referred to earlier in this chapter; later vehicles had rather jazzy interiors with plastic patterned wall surfaces and furnishings of gaudy hues. New designs for standard sleeping cars did not appear until 1957, and before this further examples of pre-Nationalisation types were constructed. One improvement introduced soon after Nationalisation was the general introduction of third class sleeping cars with two-berth compartments, each containing one lower and one upper bed, with full bedding. The interiors of the 1957 standard sleeping cars remained in the functional tradition created by Bulleid for the LNER some 30 years earlier, with neat but uninspired decor.

For suburban and stopping services a retrograde decision was taken to build new standard non-corridor carriages, thus perpetuating an unbroken tradition dating back to the earliest days of rail travel. The non-corridor coaches were mostly on 56ft 11in underframes, with the same body profile as the main line stock. Side doors were of conventional pattern, and toilet facilities were restricted to some examples with saloon layout. It would not be unfair to say that this stock was obsolete whilst still on the drawing board.

The designs for standard emu stock were in reality a combination of existing SR practice and new standard constructional features. This was perhaps understandable in view of the predominance of the SR in electric traction affairs at this time, but it was unfortunate, because in many respects the SR stock was not the best available. The prewar Liverpool-Soutport stock of the LMSR, the surface line stock of London Transport, and the Liverpool Street to Shenfield stock of the LNER (actually completed after Nationalisation) all were more sophisticated answers to the problem of suburban electric trains. But it was the non-corridor layout with slam doors to every compartment or bay that BR adopted for new standard construction; and suburban electric trains of basically Southern design were delivered to the Eastern Region, for their new services to Southend, etc; to the North Eastern Region, for use on Tyneside; and to the London Midland Region for the Euston-Watford and North London line services (where they were widely regarded as inferior to both the original LNWR sets and the LMSR compartment stock).

The riding qualities of the standard bogies designed for these electric trains were particularly bad, and many complaints were voiced by passengers, with the ultimate result that modifications were made to their design. As a temporary measure Gresley bogies were fitted to new stock for the London Midland and the Eastern Regions, and Commonwealth bogies were used for new Southern Region main line electrics. Commonwealth bogies were also employed as a stop-gap for new locomotive-hauled main line carriages, pending the completion of development work on an entirely new standard BR bogie design, for carriages destined to operate at speeds of up to 100mph in regular service.

Lighting for the 1951 design of standard carriages was by normal filament bulbs, and heating for locomotive-hauled stock was by steam from the locomotive. In 1956 the existing third class accommodation was upgraded to second, as a result of a decision taken by the International Union of Railways to abolish three-class travel on most European railways. In fact, in recent years the only second class accommodation provided by British railways had been in special boat train carriages, to meet the needs of European travellers with through second class tickets.

Although, strictly speaking, not within the period dealt with in this book, mention should be made of some prototype main line passenger carriages which were first exhibited to the public at a Modern Rail Travel exhibition at Battersea in 1957. These prototypes were introduced in an attempt to improve on the general standards of comfort and amenity of the 1951 stock (of which, by then, several hundred were in operation), whilst retaining the standardised construction features. They were of varied layout and design, some produced by BR workshops and some by outside contractors. A relatively free hand was given to the introduction of new ideas and in some cases novelty ran riot at the expense of practicability.

Generally acclaimed as the most impressive vehicles, were the two open saloon carriages designed by Cravens Limited, one first, and one second class. These had extra-wide double-glazed windows, fluorescent lighting, improved insulation and very pleasant decor, with comfortable reclining seats. Other carriages of note were produced by the Birmingham Railway Carriage & Wagon Company, whose two saloon carriages had a refined appearance; and by Doncaster Works, which produced an open carriage with airline style reclining seats, amongst other variations.

Decidely less successful were some of the compartment-style carriages, which relied for the most part on colourful surface treatments for novelty and included some very brassy detail finishes.

Although placed in regular service on selected trains, with passengers subjected to market research questionnaires, none of the Battersea prototypes were subsequently adopted as standards, although many of their features undoubtedly influenced later designs.

The significant point about the Battersea prototypes was that they represented the first real attempt to break away from established design concepts for British railway carriages, many of which dated back to the 1930s and had subsequently suffered during enforced periods of austerity and economy. Significantly, the previous year had witnessed the setting up of the BR Design Panel, to advise on aesthetic and amenity aspects for the new equipment to be produced under the modernisation plan. Their achievements in this field are fully described in the companion volume to this book, entitled *British Rail 1948-78, A Journey by Design* (Ian Allan Ltd 1979). The Battersea prototypes were not the work of the Design Panel but they displayed the same new awareness that had grown within BR, of the pressing need for improved carriage designs, if the railways were to remain in the passenger business at a time when competition from road and air was of unprecedented intensity.

301 **Compartment of postwar (1946) third class main line carriage by F. W. Hawksworth for the GWR, with restrained styling and finishes.**

301

302

303

304

305

306

302 First class dining car for the LMSR, with renovated interior and new seating; 1947. The spacious layout was achieved using some loose and some fixed seats, with low backs and octagonal tables for the layouts for four.

303 Thompson corridor carriage for the LNER, with steel panelling finished in imitation teak livery; 1945. The sole concession to style was the elliptical lavatory window in an otherwise very austere-looking vehicle.

304 Bulleid's all-steel suburban non-corridor electric trains for the SR the 4SUB type; many of which have survived into the 1980s. In early BR livery, set S4367 is seen approaching Clapham Junction on a West Croydon train, when newly-built in November 1949.

305 The LNER favoured the saloon layout with sliding doors for its new suburban stock. Actually delivered after Nationalisation in 1949, the Liverpool Street-Shenfield units started service in November of that year.

307

308
309

306 Interior of third class compartment, postwar prototype main line stock for the SR by O. V. S. Bulleid; photographed September 1945. Note the central table then proposed, and the chromium plated luggage racks and fittings.

307 Model of third class double-deck sleeping car, exhibited at the 'Britain Can Make It' Exhibition in 1947. The 'well' contruction between the bogies allowed for the double-deck arrangement within the loading gauge. Exterior appearance was a combination of contemporary LNER and SR practice.

308 The Silver Princess built 1947 by Budd of America and demonstrated in England and Ireland by the Pressed Steel Company. It later became the property of BR. The many novel features included the corrugated stainless steel bodysides.

309 In 1949, Bulleid introduced his highly controversial Tavern Cars which were intended to portray the atmosphere of an old English pub. The interior of the 'Tavern' and the interior of the restaurant both had very small window areas, thus depriving passengers of the usual view from a train.

310

310 Third class saloon of a Bulleid 'Tavern' trailer, as built, with small bodyside windows and fluorescent lighting.

311 Pullman car for the 1951 'Golden Arrow' service; illustrated is a first class parlour car. These cars retained traditional prewar decor to a large degree.

312 Profile adopted for new BR standard carriages, 1951.

313 Standard BR all-steel main line corridor carriage, a Brake Second Mark I, with original bogies. The livery is SR green, which replaced the original carmine red and cream for selected named trains on the Region in 1956.

314 The interior design of all the Standard BR stock in the period 1951-57 remained to the original utilitarian and basic concept, with a minimum of decorative finishes. The third open saloon was the prototype for the SR Kent Coast main line electrics, introduced in 1956 and operated on the London-South Coast services. Note the naked lamp bulbs in the ceiling — a feature peculiar to SR practice.

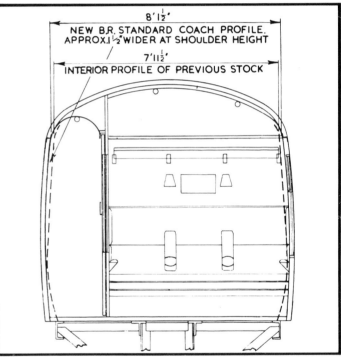

311

312

313

314

315

315   The retrograde decision was the continued production of non-corridor compartment carriages to new BR all-steel specification — thereby perpetuating a Victorian concept of surburban rail travel. Illustrated is the somewhat cramped compartment of a Swindon-built Standard third.

316   Battersea prototype open-plan first class carriage, with fluorescent lighting, designed and built at Doncaster in 1957. The seats in this experimental carriage were clearly based upon Gresley's prewar 'bucket' seats (see photo 224). Another Doncaster design had airline type reclining seats.

317   Plastic laminate wall surfaces, modified fittings and brighter moquettes were features of the Gloucester Railway Carriage & Wagon Co Battersea prototype first class main line carriage. All the prototypes utilised the basic Standard Mark 1 underframe and bodyshell, but interiors varied considerably.

316

317

19 Postwar Miscellany

The immediate postwar years witnessed an attempt to restore some colour to the scene, except on the LMSR. The other three main line companies all announced their intention of reintroducing the prewar liveries, and engines began to return from overhaul looking unbelievably smart to eyes accustomed to wartime drabness. On the LMSR, however, a more pessimistic view prevailed and the decision was taken to retain black for locomotive liveries, with straw and maroon lining; the carriages would remain in maroon livery but with simplified straw and black lining, and sanserif lettering and numerals would be standardised for rolling stock generally. In the event , Nationalisation prevented much progress being made with the postwar liveries of the Big Four companies, and inevitably attention was switched to producing new standard liveries for the new State-owned concern.

A period of experimental liveries in 1948, intended to provoke public interest and response, resulted in a series of compromise decisions which produced a motley array of new colours for rolling stock. The experiments included locomotives in the various shades of green favoured by three of the Big Four companies, in blue reminiscent of the CR and GER, in black lined out LNWR style; with carriages in GWR chocolate and cream, LNWR plum and spilt milk and LMSR crimson lake. Finally, a medium blue was chosen for the largest express engines, lined out in black and white, and a shade of green based on the GWR brunswick green was chosen for medium-power express engines, with orange and black lining. Black lined out LNWR style was chosen for mixed-traffic engines, and plain black for freight engines. Corridor carriages were painted a sickly red and cream; non-corridor carriages plain carmine red and emu stock SR malachite green.

Before long the blue was abandoned on the grounds that it did not wear well, and green became the livery for all express engines. At a later date the LMR Pacifics began to emerge in maroon livery, whilst both the SR and WR reverted to the colours of the pre-Nationalisation era for their carriages. At the same time the red and cream gave way to lined maroon for locomotive hauled stock on the London Midland, Eastern and North Eastern, and Scottish Regions. By 1955 the liveries in current usage on BR were a perplexing assortment of hues, based upon outdated loyalties and with a lack of understanding of the need for a consistent and modern visual image.

Besides new colours, a new emblem was required for the Nationalised concern, and several experimental versions were given an airing. One particularly unsuitable design was splashed right across the tender of SR 'Schools' class No 926 *Repton* which arrived at Waterloo one day in March 1948 for official inspection. Happily it was not adopted for rolling stock, but it did become the symbol used for station signs and publicity material. Unofficially it was nicknamed the BR 'Hot Dog'. A highly stylised totem of a Lion surmounting a railway wheel was adopted for rolling stock. This piece of mock heraldry came in for considerable public criticism, in particular the Lion itself, which looked half-starved. Hardly a suitable state of health to symbolise the new Nationalised rail system!

In 1956 two revised versions were produced for rolling stock, with a far more naturalistic Lion, who unfortunately had serious anatomical deficiencies. The version applied to locomotives was a weak affair with poor lettering, whilst the carriage version had obvious affinities to the crest of the LMSR, in its overall design. Neither could be classed as modern representations of an efficient rail system.

For signposting and publicity applications the new Nationalised concern adopted the Gill Sans alphabet that the LNER had introduced in the 1930s. Six Regional colours — maroon, orange, green, chocolate brown, dark blue and light blue — were used as background colours to station name signs, and as Regional identification on timetable covers, etc. Much of the potential publicity value of these colours was lost because the trains themselves did not comply. For example, in the North Eastern Region (where orange was the Regional colour) the electric trains operating in the Newcastle area were painted SR green. Likewise the locomotives were finished in GWR green or LNWR black, the carriages in the carmine-red and cream, which clashed badly; and so on. Another aspect of the Regional colours was the drab effect that indiscriminate applications to architecture created. Many potentially attractive stations were submerged beneath institutional coats of green and cream, crimson and cream and brown and cream etc.

The standardisation of Gill Sans for publicity and signposting also applied for the lettering and numerals on locomotives and carriages. Before Nationalisation some attractive nameplates had been produced by the SR for the Bulleid Pacifics, while the GWR continued to use the slab-serif Egyptian dating from Brunel's day. On the SR, Bulleid's nameplates were most elaborate, even after Nationalisation but the nameplates for the Standard BR engines were of very simple Gill Sans design, exceptions being the Class 5 4-6-0s of the Southern Region, some of which carried replicas of the 'King Arthur' class nameplates, and the final BR locomotive, *Evening Star,* which had great Western style lettering.

Poster designs alas, did not respond to the changing times and moods and many of them appeared to be repetitive versions of the 1930s classics — a sad reflection of rather better times — sometimes even the locomotives depicted were the prewar streamliners (now in actuality rather timeworn). Worse still were the attempts to revive the holiday resort posters, using poor montages of pin-up photographs and drawings; which the Southern Region seemed to delight in during the 1956-63 period. One doubts whether any additional passengers resulted from these absurdities.

Architecture suffered the worst blight of all in the early postwar period. Destroyed, damaged or just disregarded, the average railway station was not a place to be found in, unless one was perforce catching a train! Filth, neglect and inefficiency were they keynotes of many once-proud Victorian structures (true — the small wayside station could still exhibit signs of pride and respect) and the railway traveller became a hardened and sarcastic personage. This was indeed the age of the music hall joke about rail travel. Fortunately there were better times ahead; but they lie outside the range of our present story. Such ideas as prefabricated unit construction were being expounded in experiment form, but the necessary finance did just not exist nor was it to, until the announcement of the great BR modernisation plan; which also heralded the end of steam.

Although the steam age is the theme of this book a final brief mention should be made of the pioneer attempts to introduce, what were in due course to become the replacement forms of traction — the main line diesels and electrics. Here again, World War II delayed the inevitable and it was not until the eve of Nationalisation that the first main line diesel appeared, built at Derby for the LMSR to the designs of H. G. Ivatt and the English Electric Company. Prior to this some large electric locomotives had been produced by Bulleid on the Southern (in cooperation with H. A. Raworth) and by Gresley on the LNER. There were also two gas turbine locos designed and built for the GWR (but not delivered until after Nationalisation). The subsequent development of these machines lies outside the scope of our present story, but it is not without interest to reflect upon

the fact that they were designed and built under the auspices of some of the final steam locomotive designers of Great Britain — perhaps they could foresee the inevitable.

318 During World War II the liveries of Britain's steam locomotives were reduced to austere black, or in the case of some GWR locomotives unlined green. Cleaning suffered badly and even the largest locos were to be seen in a grime-laden and somewhat run-down state. This striking picture of 'King' class 4-6-0 No 6010 *King Charles* at speed also shows the wartime blackout screens for use between the cab and tender (folded back on cab roof) and the removal of the side window glass.

319 Nationalisation in 1948 brought a new and debased form of heraldry to locomotives and rolling stock, soon to be referred to as 'The Hungry Lion'. This lasted until 1956 when it was replaced by an even worse creation (see photo 322).

320 Postwar return to brighter liveries was a slow affair, and many engines remained black for some years, but a determined effort was made to get the larger engines back to a more presentable state. The LMSR decided on lined black instead of crimson lake; the LNER applied apple green to selected classes, and the GWR restored its brunswick green (later adding full lining out). On the SR Bulleid applied his striking malachite green, with yellow lining for his airsmoothed Pacifics. No 21C164 *Fighter Command* was the 1,000th locomotive built at Brighton (June 1947) and is seen being driven by the Mayor of that town.

318
320

319

321   For publicity and station signs, BR adopted a symbol which also quickly gained a nickname the 'BR Hot Dog'. Colours were varied to identify each Region. In this case the background colour was green, to denote a Southern Region station.

322   The revised version of the BR crest for steam locomotives introduced in June 1956, with the Lion still sadly lacking in anatomy.

323   After some initial experiments, standard BR liveries were provided for locomotives and rolling stock. The mixed traffic category of steam locomotives were finished in a lined black livery, closely based upon the former LNWR practice, as seen here on LMR compound No 41124 photographed leaving Colwyn Bay on a stopping train to Chester. The leading coach is still in LMSR colours but the second is in the standard BR carmine red and cream livery.

324   The Western Region remained faithful to its GWR traditions for locomotive nameplates, even for engines constructed after Nationalisation, and the GWR style of lettering was chosen for BR 2-10-0 No 92220 *Evening Star* (see photo 300), the last steam engine built for BR. Illustrated is the

nameplate of 'Castle' class 4-6-0 No 7007 *Great Western* complete with GWR coat of arms on the splasher.

325   The Eastern Region revived some pre-Grouping heraldry for certain Class A1 Pacifics as seen here on No 60156 *Great Central*.

326   The SR's coat of arms was rarely used, but it did appear on the sides of 'Battle of Britain' 4-6-2 No 34090 *Sir Eustace Missenden Southern Railway*; actually built after Nationalisation.

327   British Railways favoured the Gill Sans tradition of the former LNER for locomotive names, headboards and numbering. For the 1953 Coronation year, the Western Region added some decoration to the headboard of the 'Cornish Riviera', as seen here on a 'King' class 4-6-0 (also displaying the former GWR practice of large reporting numbers, to aid the signalmen).

328   Decorative headboard for the London Midland and Scottish Regions, the 'Caledonian' which departed from standard practice. Seen here on Stanier Pacific No 46244 *King George VI*.

321
323

322

324

326

325

327

328

329

330

331

329 Particularly effective was the headboard for the Southern Region 'Golden Arrow', and the locomotive also carried decorative arrows on the sides. This photograph shows the crew removing the headboard from the last steam-hauled up 'Golden Arrow', at Victoria on 11 June 1961.

330 Standard BR cast metal worksplate, in Gill Sans, seen here on 2-6-0 No 76114, the last steam locomotive to be built at Doncaster.

331 Eyecatching roof level destination boards were for long a familiar feature on Britain's railways, and the BR continued this practice during the final years of steam. Examples of such the one seen here, for a long through-working by a WR carriage, did much to emphasise the services offered.

332 Hand-painted Inn sign, with imitation brickwork below, on the side of one of the Bulleid Tavern cars, introduced in 1949 for the Southern and Eastern Regions.

333 Railway posters, in the early years of Nationalisation, still clung firmly to prewar concepts; so much so in this particular case that only the BR symbol dates this as a postwar design!

334 Montage effect of photography and drawings; SR poster for Kent, 1963.

335 The once-proud Euston portico, submerged beneath layers of soot and grime and lost amidst latter-day buildings. This picture makes a striking comparison with photo 40.

THE QUEEN OF SCOTS

PULLMAN - EACH WEEKDAY

(KINGS CROSS) LONDON and GLASGOW (QUEEN STREET)

calling in each direction at

LEEDS   HARROGATE   DARLINGTON   NEWCASTLE   EDINBURGH

BRITISH RAILWAYS

332

333

334

335

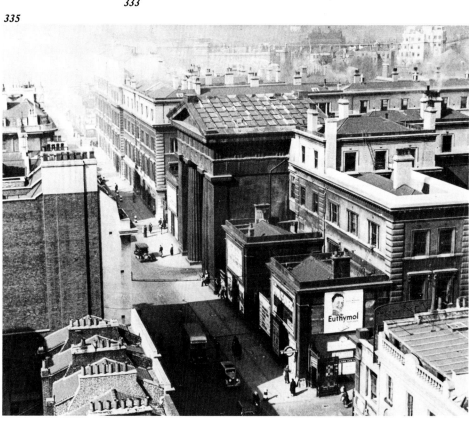

336

337

338

339

340

336 War damage and years of neglect left many of Britain's stations in a very poor condition by the late 1940s, and lack of finance hindered attempts to improve this state of affairs. The LMSR did, however, produce an ambitious plan (never completed) for a range of prefabricated station building units. This prototype, at Queens Park in 1945, was somewhat ironically erected on a platform not normally used by passengers!

337 During the war the first of Bulleid's electric locomotives made its appearance. No CC1, in a grey livery, is seen here on a test run in January 1942. Two further and somewhat modified examples followed later.

338 A prewar design was the Gresley electric Bo-Bo type for the Manchester-Sheffield-Wath electrification. The prewar prototype later ran in Holland for a period, but it was not until BR days that the scheme was completed and the bulk order for locomotives was delivered. No 26010 is seen, when new at Gorton depot in 1956, finished in BR lined black mixed traffic livery.

339 A portent for the future was the first LMSR main line diesel-electric locomotive. No 10000, delivered a few weeks before Nationalisation. A bold livery of black and aluminium was applied by the designer, H. G. Ivatt. No 10000 was photographed near Leicester.

340 Bulleid's main line diesels (actually ordered before the LMSR version) did not appear until after Nationalisation, and then a similar livery to the LMSR idea was applied by BR. The third of the trio, No 10203, was photographed new, at Lewes, en route to Eastbourne for exhibition, towing a new Standard BR Class 4 2-6-4T. Steam was still to enjoy some years of supremacy despite these pioneer diesels.

341 The engine driver's uniform changed but little over the years, and was suitably rugged for the rather dirty tasks involved in the job. In this classic pose of man and machine, Stanier Pacific No 46247 *City of Liverpool* receives the attentions of an oil can whilst on shed.

Credits and Acknowledgements

342

342 **The classic railway oil lamp —
functional symbol of the age of steam.**

For the original work, entitled *Railway
Design Since 1830*, I have already
expressed my warmest thanks to Alec
Swain, J. E. Kite and G. M. Kichenside
for their generous advice and assistance.
For this revised edition I would like to add
the name of A. B. Macleod, of the Ian
Allan Library, whom I have found to be
an erudite and alert source of wisdom. For
assistance in obtaining the illustrations,
the following owners and photographers
are also thanked: the Ian Allan Library
(including the pictures formerly held by
the Locomotive Publishing Company):
page 5, photos: *1, 2, 4, 5, 7, 9, 11, 13,
15, 16, 17, 26, 27, 29, 31, 32, 33, 34, 35,
37, 39, 46, 49, 50, 55, 57, 65, 69, 70, 72,
73, 74, 75, 76, 77, 78, 79, 80, 81, 84, 87,
88, 89, 90, 91, 92, 94, 95, 96, 97, 98, 99,
100, 105, 107, 109, 117, 118, 119, 124,
125, 133, 142, 143, 153, 154, 161, 163,
166, 181, 182, 185, 189, 190, 192, 194,
195, 200, 214, 217, 220, 221, 223, 224,
228, 231, 232, 237, 238, 239, 243, 244,
245, 246, 250, 251, 252, 255, 256, 257,
258, 265, 266, 284, 305, 307, 308, 310,
317, 320, 337* and *342.*

British Rail: *page 4* and photos *8, 12,
14, 18, 19, 21, 22, 23, 24, 30, 36, 38, 40,
42, 43, 45, 47, 48, 51, 52, 53, 56, 59, 60,
61, 62, 63, 64, 66, 68, 71, 82, 101, 103,
104, 106, 108, 110, 111, 112, 113, 114,
115, 116, 120, 121, 123, 128, 129, 130,
136, 137, 138, 139, 140, 144, 145, 146,
151, 155, 157, 158, 160, 162, 164, 167,
168, 170, 171, 175, 176, 177, 179, 180,
183, 187, 206, 211, 216, 218, 219, 225,
227, 229, 230, 234, 236, 240, 241, 242,
248, 249, 253, 254, 259, 260, 261, 262,
263, 268, 285, 288, 301, 302, 303, 309,
311, 312, 314, 315, 316, 322, 325, 326,
327, 328, 329, 330, 332, 333, 334, 335* and
336.

The following individual sources are
gratefully acknowledged:
P. M. Alexander, *273;* John Ashman, *197;*
J. C. Beckett, *58;* C. J. Blay, *289;* W. H.
G. Boot, *83;* C. P. Boocock, *275;*
C. E. Brown, *196;* R. J. Buckley, *292;*
J. R. Carter, *287;* I. S. Carr, *41;*
H. C. Casserley, *141, 222;*
A. C. Cawston, *210;*
C. R. L. Coles, *280, 283;*

E. S. Cox (collection), *210;* A. Dixon, *294;*
M. W. Earley, *122, 184, 274;*
A. Elliot, *235;* T. G. Flinders, *319;*
Greenwich Libraries, *178;*
F. R. Hebron, *191, 193, 207;*
G. F. Heiron, *131, 271;*
T. G. Hepburn, *208;* M. Higson, *169;*
C. C. B. Herbert, *page 6; 212, 277, 286,
304;* P. Hutchinson, *338;*
W. Hubert Foster, *226, 247;*
W. M. J. Jackson, *340;* N. Jones, *132;*
J. H. W. Kent, *295;* Lens of Sutton, *93;*
Tom Lewis, *main title page;*
W. N. Lockett, *282;* G. H. Marsh, *272;*
J. Mills, *323;* S. Oborne, *205;*
Leslie Overend Ltd, *331;*
R. A. Panting, *324;*
Photomatic Ltd, *156, 199, 264;*
D. S. Pollard, *rear endpaper;*
M. Pope, *298;* H. W. Pontin, *233;*
A. R. Prince, *198;* P. Ransome-Wallis,
188, 204, 213, 269, 279; Paul Riley, *297;*
R. C. Riley, *front endpaper, 300;*
B. Sackville, *293;* F. J. Saunders, *126;*
Science Museum, London,
6, 10, 25, 28, 54; M. S. Stokes, *291;*
A. Swain, *148, 172, 173, 174;*
G. N. G. Tingey, *281;*
S. C. Townroe, *149, 186 (collection),
290, 318;* Eric Treacy, *276, 295, 296;*
A. Tyson, *267;*
E. R. Wethersett, *68, 203, 209, 278;*
H. M. Wright, *321;* Alan Whitehead, *215;*
Basil A. Young, *339.*

Every care has been taken to credit the
illustrations used and no responsibility can
be held for error or omission.